D0344958

# The Real College Debt Crisis

# The Real College Debt Crisis

## How Student Borrowing Threatens Financial Well-Being and Erodes the American Dream

William Elliott III with Melinda K. Lewis

*Foreword by Martha J. Kanter*

 PRAEGER™

An Imprint of ABC-CLIO, LLC

Santa Barbara, California • Denver, Colorado

**Library of Congress Cataloging-in-Publication Data**

Elliott, William, III.
    The real college debt crisis : how student borrowing threatens financial well-being and erodes the American dream / William Elliott III, Melinda K. Lewis.
        pages cm
    Includes bibliographical references.
    ISBN 978-1-4408-3646-6 (hardback) — ISBN 978-1-4408-3647-3 (e-book)    1. Student loans—United States.    2. Student loans—Government policy—United States.    3. College graduates—United States—Finance, Personal.    4. Student aid—United States.    5. Debt—United States.
I. Lewis, Melinda K.    II. Title.
    LB2340.2.E47 2015
    378.3'62—dc23        2015008159

ISBN:  978-1-4408-3646-6
EISBN: 978-1-4408-3647-3

19 18 17 16        2 3 4 5

This book is also available on the World Wide Web as an eBook.
Visit www.abc-clio.com for details.

Praeger
An Imprint of ABC-CLIO, LLC

ABC-CLIO, LLC
130 Cremona Drive, P.O. Box 1911
Santa Barbara, California 93116-1911

This book is printed on acid-free paper ∞

Manufactured in the United States of America

# Contents

**PART THREE: Conclusion**

# Foreword

For our nation's students, a quality education offers a critical engine to upward mobility toward achieving the American Dream. Numerous studies have confirmed that college graduates end up happier, more satisfied, more financially secure, and more engaged in their communities compared to students who only attended high school or didn't finish college.[1]

The national conversation about the value and cost of a college or university degree has escalated dramatically over the last decade as Americans weathered a severe economic decline, experiencing high levels of unemployment, the surge of college costs, and an increased dependency on student loans.

From the 1950s through the 1980s, thousands of aspiring Americans were able to attend a college that was affordable. Pell grants covered two-thirds of the cost of a college education in the 1970s. Today, those same grants cover less than a third of costs, and, at too many colleges and universities, less than 15 percent. Interest rates on federal student loans were low and student loans weren't on the front burner in the minds of families when looking at college opportunities.

Back then, we were a nation that helped Americans go to college, with the availability of many federal grants and scholarship programs. College was viewed as a public good, and public policies invested accordingly.

The result? Many graduates who worked hard were able to secure employment, buy a car, and get a mortgage. They took advantage of the assets they had and their assets grew. As their assets grew, they leveraged tax benefits and enjoyed the rewards of a good education leading to a good job, a decent lifestyle, and retirement savings, paving the way for their children to have even greater advantages.

These opportunities opened doors of college attendance to middle-class families and even many with low incomes, albeit inadequately and inequitably. More women, minorities, and veterans walked through those doors as politicians and policymakers made serious bipartisan efforts to enable more people from the middle class to reap the benefits of a college education.

Today, getting a quality education is becoming a pipe dream for too many deserving students, especially those from low-income families. The American Dream that educational opportunities are supposed to shore up is increasingly precarious. When you think about it now, half of our nation's children live in poverty[2] and more than 40 percent of adult Americans are performing at the basic or below basic level of a high school student in language and math.[3] What went wrong? Where did our nation go astray?

Elliott and Lewis have given us an important book that unpacks these questions, asking us to imagine a future built on helping families grow assets that enable college opportunity for the top 100 percent of our nation's students seeking to better their lives, not just those from families of privilege. The authors ask us to take the long view and consider bold alternatives that leverage asset building for all and, most especially, for those families who have not benefited from the privileges afforded to the middle and, especially, upper classes. At the same time, they share their personal stories and offer a sustainable methodology and path forward to curb student debt and the overreliance on student loans, thereby restoring the vision of our founding fathers and the promise to keep higher education within reach of Americans, regardless of income, race, social status, gender, or any additional criterion other than merit.

A more recent reflection underscores the significance of their proposed methodology. Since 2007, when our nation's economic downturn started spiraling out of control, forty-two of our fifty states have taken a scalpel to their higher education budgets. On average, states cut about 20 percent of their higher education budgets; dramatic reductions were seen in New Hampshire (nearly 50%), followed by Arizona, Louisiana, Wisconsin, and Colorado.[4] Since 80 percent of our nation's students are educated in public community colleges and universities, many were turned away because they couldn't get the classes they needed. Even more struggled to keep up with costs that have increasingly shifted to the shoulders of students and their parents. Colleges have admitted more out-of-state and international students to help survive the draconian cuts while unsympathetic politicians and policymakers increasingly view education as a private good, seeking to enable cheaper forms of education with tutors, not teachers, and less contact with faculty, as well as supporting the growth of high-cost, for-profit career schools, which are up to 90 percent federally funded through Pell grants and federal student loans. The for-profit higher education sector grew from 8 percent of total enrollments in 2009 to 13 percent in 2014.[5] Due to increased transparency and federal oversight, the public is coming to understand that this sector houses 31 percent of all student loans and is responsible for nearly half of student loan defaults[6] while reaping large profits from tuition and fees charged, as their students take on exceptionally high amounts of debt.

Since taking office in 2009, President Obama proposed bold initiatives to keep college affordable by increasing Pell grants, scholarships, and other institutional aid; providing tax credits for college persistence and completion; and undertaking multiple reforms to curb the escalation of tuition and fees, stop the loopholes in student loan programs, and streamline federal student aid. But a divided Congress has thwarted many of these efforts.

Given all of these circumstances in our more recent history, we must ask whether a quality education in America is fast becoming a privilege for the few and not the many. Sadly, today the answer is yes. A look at recent data shows that the largest portion of low-income students who do go to college matriculate at a for-profit career school or a community college.[7] Income and education stratification has widened over the decades and we are now more segregated throughout our education pipeline than we were before the Civil Rights Act was passed in 1964. Racial, ethnic, and income stratification has widened and too many families from the lower-income quintiles have larger opportunity hurdles to cross due to college costs. In fact, 82 percent of students from the highest income quartile attain college degrees while only 8 percent of students from the lowest income quartile do.[8]

Whether you look at distribution of Americans by income, race, or ethnicity, we face an enormous challenge ahead: will our nation provide meaningful college opportunities for *all* American children, or only for the rich? And what of the intended and unintended consequences? What of democracy's future? Will the American Dream disappear?

Some policymakers herald "the end of college," but they too suffer from myopic vision. Higher education clearly still matters, for individual students and for the nation's shared future. That is why this book is so important.

Elliott and Lewis have given us the opportunity to reimagine college opportunity as a debt-independent, asset-based paradigm for students who want to go to college and are willing to make the investment of effort, time, and money, according to their financial means. Can we entertain the idea of a nation whose philosophical foundation is set in the concept of asset building? Can we consider our existing federal, state, and institutional funds as revenues to invest in a prosperous future for America because we demonstrate the will to reimagine and redesign our financial strategy and investment that will accrue college savings over time coupled with tax reforms that benefit all families regardless of income, not just the wealthy?

In years past, the open door to higher education drew millions of Americans into college—people from all walks of life who had not had such an opportunity in the first 30 years of the 20th century. As diversity and socioeconomic stratification have dramatically increased since the 1950s, now more than ever is the time to ensure that public and private higher education remains within reach of students who meet college-ready standards and are willing to devote their minds and bodies to the furtherance of their capacities. It is time to build a financial aid system that can actually help students to prepare for educational success and that complements their exertion of effort and ability. We have harnessed too many Americans with college debt that is taking the place of other opportunities to build assets that would serve this and future generations of families. If students cannot enter and complete higher education with affordable debt, they will delay buying a home, a car, or other strategic investments that will offer them tax and employment benefits going forward.

As Elliott and Lewis point out, we can't just tinker on the margins of student aid reforms with the kind of tweaks that have occurred over many decades. Loan consolidation, income-based repayment strategies, interest rate formulas, financial education, and loan counseling have been the starting points for transforming student aid. But Elliott and Lewis take us further. They propose "an asset-empowered financial aid system" in which families can increase their financial education and raise the prospects for their children's future by establishing college savings accounts for all children accompanied by bold education tax reforms, forward funding of Pell grants as an investment, institutional aid and other scholarships to grow the pie, and institutional incentives to keep college affordable for all, irrespective of educational or economic disadvantage.

Redesigning and implementing new systems and incentives to curb the consequences of unbridled student debt, while inspiring student effort, college aspirations, preparation, persistence, and completion could rightly lead us toward increasing the economic, social, and civic well-being of students and families for generations to come.

Elliott and Lewis remind us that economic mobility depends on federal, state, and institutional systems working in concert to achieve the vision of prosperous families in a vibrant society. The downside is ugly. One has only to look around the world to see the results of gross inequities that cause societal devolution. Evidence-based research already tells us that Children's Savings Accounts help families to instill a college-going culture and higher levels of student performance while building assets that grow. The concepts of asset-based financial aid, asset growth, and asset accumulation explored in this book are worthy of further scholarship, policy development, and a national call to action. New directions are sorely needed to solve our longstanding gaps in education achievement, upward mobility, and national prosperity. Elliott and Lewis encourage us to take bold steps forward on a new path to the American Dream. Our future as a democracy may well depend on what we do next—whether we can muster the collective will to move ahead.

Martha J. Kanter

*Martha J. Kanter is a Distinguished Visiting Professor of Higher Education and a Senior Fellow at New York University. She served as the U.S. Under Secretary of Education for President Barack H. Obama from 2009 through 2013.*

## NOTES

1. For example, Taylor, P., et al. (2011). *Is College Worth It?* Washington, DC: Pew Research Center; Walsemann, K.M., Bell, B.A., and Hummer, R.A. (2012). Effects of Timing and Level of Degree Attained on Depressive Symptoms and Self-Rated Health at Midlife. *American Journal of Public Health*, 12 (3), pp. 557–563.
2. See http://neatoday.org/2015/01/16/shameful-milestone-majority-public-school-students-now-live-poverty/.
3. See http://nces.ed.gov/NAAL/kf_demographics.asp.
4. Declining State Support for Higher Education, Illinois State University Center for the Study of Education Policy Grapevine Fiscal Year 2011-12 Data – Updated March 15, 2015.
5. Retrieved from http://www.ed.gov/news/press-releases/obama-administration-takes-action-protect-americans-predatory-poor-performing-career-colleges

6. IBID
7. Institute for Higher Education Policy. (2011). Initial College Attendance of Low-Income Adults. Washington, DC: Author. Retrieved March 18, 2015 from IHEP's website: http://www.ihep.org/sites/default/files/uploads/docs/pubs/portraits-low-income_young_adults_attendance_brief_final_june_2011.pdf.
8. The Pew Charitable Trusts. (July 2012). Pursuing the American Dream: Economic Mobility Across Generations.

# Acknowledgments

## WILLIAM ELLIOTT

I want to thank my wife and kids, Jordan, Michelle, and Michael, for their love and support. I know that my wife has had to change her career goals so that I could have the opportunity to get my PhD and spend the time traveling and studying to get to this point. I would also like to thank Margaret Sherraden for all the time she spent reading and editing my papers as a PhD student. Her dedication and commitment allowed me to become a better writer. Finally, I would like to thank my parents and sister. We lived through a lot of different things together and through it all I always knew that I was loved. You cannot really put a price on that, it has made all the difference in my life.

## MELINDA LEWIS

I am grateful for the scholarship of colleagues, whose work is cited throughout ours and whose contemplation of the policy landscape and its consequences helps to inform my own. And I am inspired by the promise of my own children, committed to making it possible for them to live to this potential, and ever hopeful that we can build structures that will give every child their chance. But it is to those whose significant contributions shaped my life chances, in ways I often failed to appreciate adequately at the time, that I dedicate this work. My grandpa would have chuckled to know I was writing a book, my grandma would have debated our recommendations, and I wish very much that they were still here to see in print the tremendous legacy they left. My parents never doubted that I would do something like this one day, and they organized their time and their finances to make it as likely as possible. This is for them, then, and for a husband who partners with me on all things, today and as we plan our shared future.

# ONE

## Introduction

The central motivation for this book is imagining an alternative to the student loan program that better aligns with Americans' belief that effort and ability should be the deciding factors in determining economic differences. In doing so, we hope to change the conversation around financial aid from one focused almost exclusively on access (i.e., how to pay for college at the point of enrollment) to a consideration about not only financial aid's effects on college access, but also on children's preparation for college, college completion, and postcollege financial well-being. We are concerned with the entire trajectory, then, of what may be thought of as the education path.

The education path is considered by most to be a normative path for achieving economic well-being in America. By expanding the financial aid conversation beyond access, we reveal other criteria by which to judge the instruments used to finance higher education. Here, we particularly focus on student loans and Children's Savings Accounts (CSAs) as interventions with potentially dramatically different outcomes. Seen through this broader lens, financial aid is no longer simply about making sure children have enough money to pay for college, but about improving their chances of moving up the economic ladder by investing in their human capital development. This way of thinking about financial aid is more consistent with higher education being a valuable part of America's economic mobility system. It positions postsecondary education properly as the central lever by which American children can secure for themselves promising futures, and it supports analysis of the extent to which current policy interventions facilitate these mechanisms, or not.

The book is broken into two parts. In part I, we use the framework described above to examine the student loan program as a financial aid instrument. In doing so, we not only chronicle the size and scope of the student debt problem, aggregating others' indicators, but also critically examine the limited nature of financial aid debate today, particularly how conversations about the student debt problem in America have helped to make imagining alternatives to the student loan program hard if not impossible. We recognize how the fear of losing ground—as individual Americans struggling for a toehold on the American Dream, as a field of academics and policy makers concerned about educational outcomes, and as people committed to economic opportunity—has contributed to paralysis, preventing even the imagining of a better approach. And we critique our collective complicity in this thwarted chance to craft better alternatives for our shared future. This narrow scope is not only a matter of academic concern, given our larger view of the financial aid system, but it also has immediate and far-reaching policy implications. Because we have not been able to conjure an alternative to the student loan program, our policy reform efforts have mostly centered on solutions, such as Income-Based Repayment plans, that sustain instead of change the centrality of student borrowing, and may even worsen its negative effects, while also distracting us from the essential reckoning of the real risks we face.

In part II of the book, we explain why moving from a debt-dependent financial aid system toward an asset-based financial aid system is needed to strengthen education's ability to deliver on its promise of economic mobility. We end by imagining an alternative to the student loan program that better aligns with Americans' belief that effort and ability should be the deciding factors in determining economic differences. We outline one such approach that has shown great promise and is more consistent with financial aid acting as a valuable part of America's economic mobility system: Children's Savings Accounts (CSAs).

In the remainder of the introduction we provide a brief outline of each chapter.

## PART I. STUDENT LOANS: A PARADIGM IN CRISIS

Part I of this volume provides evidence of a crisis in the basic paradigm upon which the American financial aid system has been built. It is our contention that, as a result of the growing consensus that such a crisis exists, the field may be on verge of a scientific revolution—a reconsideration of the premises underlying the policy apparatus today and a seismic shift in the approach of the core interventions (Kuhn 1962).

The basic paradigm can be characterized as the assumption that the primary, if not exclusive, goal of financial aid is to help kids pay for college at the point of enrollment. This exclusive focus on paying for college has resulted in researchers and policy makers ignoring significant differences in the functioning and ultimate outcomes of the particular instrument used to help children pay for college, including the potential negative effects on other areas of children's lives. Held accountable only to this very modest standard of aiding in immediate college financing, the student loan program has taken on a growing role in the financial aid system. Overreliance on student loans, however, has created problems related to children's college preparation, college completion, and postcollege financial well-being. These are, of course, not incidental inconveniences, but threats to the foundation of higher education, its role in the U.S. society and economy, and the future of an entire generation. As it has become increasingly clear that the current financial aid paradigm is incapable of solving these problems, we posit that a financial aid revolution is looming.

In his landmark book *The Structure of Scientific Revolutions*, Thomas Kuhn (1962) discusses how periods of normal science are interrupted by periods of revolutionary science. Kuhn identified a cycle of progress that included five phases: (1) preparadigm, (2) normal science, (3) paradigm crisis, (4) scientific revolution, and (5) postrevolution. While it is not our goal to strictly follow Kuhn's model, or to suggest it is the only way progress occurs, we posit that his model—replicated at many points across Western history and seen in the course of most major scientific advancements—can be a useful guide for understanding where we are in what appears to be the dawn of a financial aid revolution.

Phases 2–4 of Kuhn's cycle of progress act as guides for part I of this book. Kuhn suggests that during periods of normal science, phase 2, researchers identify questions to investigate based on the existing knowledge. The insights that spring from these analyses are constrained, then, by the limits of the prevailing paradigm, such that resulting changes tend to mostly comprise tweaks around the margins, rather than fundamental reconsiderations.

We posit that the financial aid model has been functioning in a period of normal science, where the goal of financial aid, as stated above, is to help kids pay for college. According to Kuhn, periods of normal science persist so long as the current paradigm is able to continue solving the problems the field faces, as they are understood. In today's political and economic context, this preoccupation with normal science—and its extension beyond the point when serious cracks in the foundation have been exposed—is likely exacerbated by the pervasive fear that what might come in the wake of a revolutionary shift could signal a retreat from the provision of educational and economic opportunities. When we are busy guarding the status quo, vigilant against perceived threats, we are necessarily less able to reach for more distant—even if far more promising—shores.

Abandoning a familiar, if unsatisfactory, current reality will take a push. In part I of this book, it is our intent to help frame the "crisis" in student loans so that it constitutes such a shove. Then, in part II, we make the step into the unknown less frightening by articulating viable alternatives to debt dependence.

Paradigm crisis, phase 3, arises when the current paradigm is becoming increasingly less able to solve a growing number of the problems the field faces or when external events provoke a clamor for a different vision. This can result in a period of scientific revolution, phase 4, when the underlying assumptions of the field are forced to hold up to new questions that only come to light because people have been freed by the crisis to think about the problems the field faces from a totally different vantage point. Such challenges to the current paradigm, however, are often met with stern resistance because this way of thinking is so engrained into the psyche and routines of most people that departure is almost unfathomable or intolerable.

In part I, then, we seek to walk the reader through the U.S. financial aid system's travels through these tumultuous phases toward a scientific revolution, particularly as the shift to a debt-dependent model solidified a few decades ago.

## Chapter 2. Two Paths, One Dream

In chapter 2, we begin the examination of the effects of the student loan system on higher education's potency as a force for societal equity and economic mobility in the United States by sharing our own stories. In doing so, we trace the institutional pressures and opportunities that shaped our paths. In our own narratives, we find evidence of the fragility of the effort + ability equation that constitutes the core of the American Dream, and we see the imprint of a flawed financial aid paradigm in our own lives. In our histories and in the futures of American children, we see the limitations of what individual exertion can deliver in terms of equitable outcomes without the support of equitably supportive institutions.

Key to influencing American children's trajectories is the role of student loans and their converse—an asset foundation. When one student has to borrow to finance a higher education and one does not, students may realize disparate outcomes prior to, during, and following college, particularly on the dimension of postcollege financial well-being. Our stories suggest that these effects are even strong enough to counter greater educational attainment by indebted graduates and to persist in spite of tremendous innate talent and exerted effort.

We do not share our own stories in search of sympathy or admiration but, instead, as a tangible reminder that real lives are at stake in today's policy debates around student loans and that the imprint of our policies can be vividly felt, when we are honest about our own journeys. These narratives vest the student loan debate with a gravity that has profound implications—for individual students, for striving American households, and for our collective identity as a nation where dreams are supposed to be within reach of all. And our own stories help to explain some of the external events impinging on the financial aid field, provoking recognition of a crisis, multiplied as they are across the personal narratives of millions of American children and families, whose own experiences have sparked questions about whether the system really works anymore.

## Chapter 3. Education Is Still Our Best Hope

While our own narratives reveal the inequities in a higher education system financed largely through student debt, they also emphasize the significance of postsecondary educational attainment as a catalyst for greater financial well-being and a path—albeit a narrow and eroding one—to economic mobility. We begin our analysis of the evidence regarding student loans' effects with a grounding of the policy debate in one of our core animating values as Americans: an abiding belief that one's outcomes should depend primarily on exertion of effort and ability, not on initial position. Our reading of the current political situation and understanding of the force necessary to upend an established knowledge paradigm is that only appealing to these deepest-held ideals has the potential to break through policy gridlock and rebuild institutions that can facilitate a revitalization of the American Dream.

For American children to really believe—with reason—that they can achieve based on their own capabilities, institutions must facilitate their self-efficacy, or the belief in their own agency. We must demand that our institutions work as they are supposed to, rather than consoling ourselves when some extraordinary individuals manage to succeed against the odds. Absent this institutional reform, there is evidence that Americans' belief in the possibility of upward mobility, while still strong in the abstract, is increasingly tenuous in their own case. We are still striving, as a people, as our economic system demands, but with less confidence in our expected outcomes and a growing sense that the deck is stacked against us.

While the labor market perhaps offers an especially vivid example of this institutional failure, particularly postrecession, as the wage/productivity gap widens, it is our contention that higher education is also not functioning well as an arbiter of equity. It is becoming increasingly clear that at least some of the blame for inequality in educational outcomes lies with the student loan system, which evidence suggests influences college preparation, selection, persistence, graduation, and postcollege outcomes in highly unequal ways. Compounding this threat to educational equity are related forces that conspire to reframe education as an individual, not a societal, good, including reductions in state funding, a retreat from need-based aid, and the resulting increase in costs. This is particularly significant because of the outsized role afforded to higher education in the United States as the central feature of our welfare system and, still, most American children's best chance to climb the economic ladder.

## Chapter 4. The Student Loan Program Has an Equity Problem

We build on the analysis that situates higher education as a central intervention in the American welfare state with a discussion of the forces within that educational system that have reduced its effectiveness as a tool for redress of inequity and an agent of economic mobility. Here, we discuss the concept of *wilt*, or the gap between the educational aspirations and the achievement of disadvantaged students, particularly those who are low-income and students of color. This growing chasm clearly reveals that effort and ability are not enough to secure educational attainment. Instead, Americans need access to the institutions that facilitate their realization of these normative expectations if they are to have meaningful opportunities to achieve equitable outcomes.

Higher education is vested with responsibility to serve as such an institution, but it is increasingly incapable of fulfilling this function, largely as a result of policy changes wrought over the past few decades. Among these trends are the increasing "privatization" of public education, or the growing profitability pressures that make wealthy students ever more attractive to even the stalwart institutions that are supposed to serve the larger public interest. The combination of a shift from need-based to merit aid, a reduction in state funding that has seen more costs shift to individuals, and a growing reliance on student debt as financial aid have resulted in a decidedly two-tiered higher education system that is far less capable of leveling the playing field than what disadvantaged children need from their postsecondary options.

While these changes may stem more from pursuit of self-interest than malicious intent to see others fail, the result is that higher education may now perpetuate inequalities as much as mitigate them and protect the preservation of institutions—including student loans—rather than defend the interests of most young Americans. This, in turn, has led to a surreal policy debate that studiously avoids coming to terms with the growing body of evidence regarding student loans' negative effects prior to, during, and following college, preferring instead to suggest pseudoalternatives that would preserve borrowing as the central financial aid mechanism, as though mere *access* was the end of higher education and as though any marginal improvement in children's economic prospects should be acceptable.

Here, again, we do not suggest that the narrow scope of proposed reforms is intentionally shortsighted, but, rather, the expected limits of "normal" scientists (Kuhn 1962), constrained by their operation within a particular way of seeing the world and, in this case, the possible alternatives for financial aid.

## Chapter 5. Evidence of a Paradigm in Crisis

Previously ensconced within "normal" science (Kuhn 1962), the debate around the role of student borrowing in U.S. higher education and financial aid policies has been far too narrow—focusing mostly on delinquency and default as indicators of "distress"—and far too tepid, setting the bar for what we should expect from a financial aid system inexcusably low.

Given the centrality of higher education in the U.S. social welfare and economic mobility systems, Americans should expect far more than mere *access* as the objective of student loans; financial aid interventions should increase education's ability to provide a meaningful path to the American Dream. We push this policy discourse on student loans by first dismantling the straw men that characterize much of the media coverage and even some of the scholarly debate on student loans today. Even if student debt is not the next housing bubble, and even if most students do not owe $100,000 in student loans, there is a significant body of evidence, from a wide complement of inquiries using rigorous methodologies, documenting a real student loan problem. We just have to ask the right questions and know where to look.

In chapter 5, we examine data on the incidence, growth, trends, and demographics of the relatively recent financial aid development of dependence on student borrowing. Then, moving beyond mere access to look at a fuller range of outcomes, we review analysis of student loans' effects on career choices, financial stress, credit constraints (represented by delinquency and default as well as total debt loads), and, in particular, reductions in asset accumulation, including net worth, homeownership, and retirement savings.

This more complete accounting of student loans' effects raises the stakes on the financial aid debate because initial assets may have profound implications for individuals' economic mobility prospects. It is part of the process of raising awareness of the "anomalies" (Kuhn 1962) related to student loans' effects that, particularly when taken in concert, should prompt reconsideration of the premise that student borrowing is a basically sound way to finance postsecondary education.

Galvanized by the recognition of the true nature, scope, and gravity of the student loan problem, then, we must begin to imagine meaningful alternatives and to insist that our financial aid system perform up to the standards of our American values, which hold that only effort expended and innate ability possessed should determine one's relative outcomes. We assert, certainly not uniquely, that it is time for a new paradigm through which to consider our options in financial aid.

## Chapter 6. Delayed Dreams

Higher education in the United States is not about the pursuit of untold riches, but instead a path to an aspiration that is simultaneously more modest—middle-class financial security and increased economic mobility—and more revolutionary, because a college education is designed to put this prosperity within reach of any talented and determined child. Today, though, this link between education and prosperity is threatened. Here, we present evidence of how student debt delays financial well-being by hindering young adults' ability to use income to build assets. Required to divert income flows to debt repayment rather than capital accumulation, these cohorts struggle to fully recover from setbacks experienced in early adulthood. More specifically, we look at the effects that student loans have on asset accumulation by education level.

Findings reveal that, regardless of one's disposable income, outstanding debt is associated with a greater chance of negative net worth for those with associate, bachelor, and graduate degrees. While college may be a particularly poor bet for student borrowers with comparatively low levels of postsecondary education and outstanding debt, given their propensity for negative net worth even with higher disposable income (which affects even those with bachelor degrees), there is a significantly greater net worth return on college without student debt. This has implications for mobility, of course, which often requires some initial level of asset holding and exposes one clear failure of the student loan system.

## Chapter 7. Can't See the Forest for the Trees

There is considerable momentum to do *something* about student debt, but also a real danger that, absent accurate analysis of the true dimensions and causes of the student debt problem, our policy changes will fail to move the needle or, even, take steps in the wrong direction. We cannot arrive at satisfactorily distinct approaches to financial aid without changing the way we think about postsecondary education and how we pay for it. Many of today's financial aid proposals serve to provide more evidence of the need for a paradigm shift. Among the proposals for student debt reform that are concerning are requirements to equip student borrowers with more information about the true costs of their student loans, as though students can somehow cope better, armed with information, absent meaningful alternatives to student borrowing.

Some proposals, including expansion of Income-Based Repayment, Pay-It-Forward, and free study at two-year colleges, could even exacerbate the inequity in the higher education system by funneling disadvantaged students to certain types of institutions, with predictably inferior completion outcomes, and by extending the period of debt repayment such that the associated depression of asset accumulation would be similarly extended. Policy proposals to change the student loan system must be assessed along criteria of increasing equity and catalyzing mobility. Otherwise, we may squander this particular political moment, with significant, negative effects for current and future generations of college debtors.

## PART II. FROM DEBT DEPENDENCE TO ASSET EMPOWERMENT

Part II of this volume moves from chronicling how the financial aid system has been progressing toward a scientific revolution of sorts to discussing an alternative paradigm. In doing so, we document the logic for changing from a debt-dependent financial aid paradigm to an asset-empowered paradigm. This aligns with activities found in phase 5 of Kuhn's (1962) cycle of progress.

## Chapter 8. Assets Provide a Launching Pad for Economic Mobility

Understanding the full implication of our debt-dependent financial aid system on the life chances of American children first requires distinguishing between the concept of economic well-being and standard of living, with the latter recognized as, essentially, one's rung on the economic ladder while the former represents an individual's chance of ascent. A reading of the current economic reality in the United States reveals that wage income is no longer an adequate platform for economic well-being because Americans can seldom work their way up without the support of transfers—in the form of tax-based subsidies for asset accumulation of higher-income households, in particular—and reliance on capital income from accumulated stores.

Significant for our discussion of the inequitable institutions that serve to constrain economic mobility among some in U.S. society, while facilitating the advancement of others, transfer income provided to those in and near poverty is often explicitly asset limiting, which can block upward mobility. To pivot away from these policy traps, including our reliance on a bifurcated approach to financial aid and other welfare provision, we must change the conversation about what is required for an American family to prosper in our postmodern economy. Here, clearly, wage income is not enough. Households need an economic mobility system where labor, transfer, and capital income work to complement each other and support economic well-being, not only for those already advantaged, as we see today, but for all who aspire to the American Dream.

## Chapter 9. Children's Savings Accounts: The Next Evolution in Financial Aid

Essential to realizing this leap away from student debt is the articulation of actual policy options that could provide a real alternative to student loans for the purpose of facilitating access to college while avoiding the negative implications of student debt for educational outcomes, economic mobility, and the equalizing potential of higher education. The shift we believe essential is unlikely without a contest between competing paradigms, and this rhetorical and empirical battle requires a concrete articulation of what an asset-empowered alternative might look like. Toward these ends, Children's Savings Accounts (CSAs) deserve special attention.

CSAs are interventions with the potential to realize improved educational outcomes, greater financial inclusion, and the development of a strong initial asset foundation, in addition to reduction of student borrowing. By providing individuals with opportunities to save and serving as the plumbing for critical asset transfers, CSAs evidence superior outcomes when compared to student debt prior to, during, and following college. CSAs work through the twin mechanisms of asset accumulation and account ownership to foster a college-saver identity and facilitate asset empowerment.

CSAs build on the asset-based approach to combating poverty pioneered by Michael Sherraden in 1991 and subsequently informed by rigorous scholarship and significant field demonstrations, the latter most notably in the Savings for Education, Entrepreneurship, and Downpayment (SEED) demonstrations around the country. Today, CSA approaches are seen in some state 529 college savings plans, particularly in places such as Maine, which automatically opens an account for every child born or adopted in the state and seeds it with an initial deposit. Additionally, some localities and even school districts are applying asset principles to their work, particularly with disadvantaged students; a few, notably San Francisco, California, provide a savings account as part of the educational experience of every kindergartener. The successes sparked by these initiatives are helping to legitimize asset-based financial aid as a viable alternative to reliance on student debt, likely hastening the point of crisis in the financial aid system. The CSA field is still relatively new and we have much to learn, but scholarship has resulted in significant advances in knowledge.

To realize the outcome effects research suggests are possible from CSAs, they should be designed to align with this growing body of evidence outlining asset theory. Accounts should be seeded with an initial deposit or asset transfer, and incentives should encourage regular savings behavior. The account structure should maximize children's identification with their own accounts to foster a sense of ownership and facilitate identity-based motivation. Policy must address savings disincentives currently woven into the financial aid and means-tested welfare systems. And, because these effects are too potent to leave to parental initiative alone, accounts should be opened automatically for every child. To achieve scaled CSAs in line with these principles, those concerned with student debt today and those committed to nudging toward a paradigm shift could look at tax expenditures in higher education (poorly targeted and of relatively little value, then, today), reimagining the Pell Grant as an asset investment earlier in a child's academic career, leveraging community scholarships for greater effect before the point of enrollment, and repurposing the money that the U.S. government currently earns from our corrosive student loan system.

## Chapter 10. Conclusion

The critical question to ask to determine whether reliance on student loans is a defensible and feasible approach to financial aid policy in the United States is not the question most commonly asked in student loan policy debates. Deciding whether we should finance higher education—the core intervention in the American welfare system—through debt should not be confined to questioning whether college graduates are better off than if they had never gone to college but, rather, whether students who have to borrow to finance their college educations are able to attain equitable outcomes compared to those who did not have to borrow for higher education. Through this lens, it becomes clear that debt dependence is fundamentally incompatible with the American values of equality of opportunity and a threat to American insistence that merit—not oligarchical privilege—should determine one's fate. No group in the United States today is more imperiled by our insistence on debt as financial aid than young adults, with evidence suggesting that Millennials and Generation Xers are both, although somewhat differently, harmed by their exposure to and incidence of student borrowing. The damage is not limited to these younger generations, however. Even older adults' asset accumulation and financial security are compromised by student borrowing.

Within the foreboding statistics on student debt and its effects, though, is a real promise that Americans have become so student debt-fatigued that we can harness significant energy to push for new, asset-based alternatives to the college-cost conundrum. Within the smaller population of scholars, policy makers, and others in the financial aid community, multiplying indicators of the negative effects of student loans are prompting similar reconsideration of the premise that borrowing to finance college is always a good bet. With our eyes opened to those facts that do not fit the paradigm under which we have been operating, we are discovering answers to questions that we had not previously considered asking.

This process has led many to consider the role of assets, which are worth investigation not only because they stand as a contrast to student debt for a public increasingly hungry for any change, but also because the evidence suggests superior outcomes from asset empowerment, as opposed to debt dependence, prior to, during, and following college. Assets are understood to exert these effects through the mechanisms of asset accumulation and account ownership; owning educational assets, unlike student borrowing, engages students, cultivates a powerful college-saver identity, and provides a financial platform for later economic security. Through these effects, asset-based approaches to financial aid may offer significant promise for restoring the mobility functions and equalizing power of higher education.

Here, we offer analysis and share commentary designed to contribute to the revolution we believe is sorely needed—and, in ways large and small, already underway—in our most valuable economic mobility lever: higher education and its financing.

# PART ONE

## Student Loans: A Paradigm in Crisis

# TWO

# Two Paths, One Dream

Solving the student-debt problem in the United States today will require that Americans come to terms with what student borrowing means for individual students, for our higher education system, and for the viability of ladders to economic mobility. Wrapped up as they are in a powerful narrative about what this country represents, these concepts can be difficult to translate into concrete terms. We often struggle to even find the language to talk about alternatives.

To begin this conversation, we have chosen to use aspects of our own life stories to set the stage for the remainder of the book. While obviously not representative of every American student's experiences in the two divergent paths to higher education, in some important ways our life stories illustrate two fundamental truths about higher education and financial aid policy today. First, education still plays an equalizing role—albeit a moderated one—in the economy, and second, what we are calling the "debt-dependent" and "asset-empowered" paths produce different outcomes and are differently available to students in predictable ways, influenced by race and class.

Consistent with the American Dream narrative that equates hard work and innate ability with success, both paths are not without challenges, and success in both depends to a considerable extent—but certainly not entirely—on individual characteristics and exertion. This difference underscores the fact that access to resources does not guarantee success any more than facing disadvantages precludes it. Some will still succeed despite disadvantages, in part, because of their innate ability and extraordinary effort, while others will fail because they do not put in the work or have the requisite ability, regardless of the situation into which they are born.

However, these experiences also suggest that providing debt-dependent people with some financial resources, particularly wealth transfers at critical transitional periods in their lives, such as when they enter college or when they begin their financial independence, will not diminish the role of effort and ability in the system nor stunt the desire of those who receive them. Instead, wealth transfers that align with American values facilitate the achievement of those committed to success and make it more likely that it is effort and ability that determine who succeeds and who fails at reaching the American Dream, and not unequal access to financial resources. We start by discussing the debt-dependent path through college, toward the American Dream.

## THE DEBT-DEPENDENT PATH TO THE AMERICAN DREAM

### Dreaming about Football

My name is William Elliott III, or Willie. I grew up in Beaver Falls, a typical small town in western Pennsylvania. Once a thriving steel mill city prior to the 1970s, it became a city in economic decline with few opportunities for escape. Sports, particularly football, provided one of the few rays of hope. It is nearly impossible for people who do not grow up in such an environment to understand how central sports are to the identity of the people in these places, how much of life is shaped by them. Our claim to fame was Joe Namath, the one-time flamboyant quarterback for the New York Jets. Growing up in a place where economic opportunities are almost nonexistent, it is hard to see a world apart from the one you live in, a world of poverty and despair. With few other seemingly viable avenues, it is hard to see how you can make an impact in the world if not through sports.

As a result of the centrality of sports to the community's identity and the understood path to upward mobility, kids, parents, and the larger community invest their hopes in their sports teams and their athletes. You might ask, "How could they?" but I ask, "Why wouldn't they?" It is perfectly reasonable to a kid who only hears stories of success when it relates to people making it out of their local community by excelling at sports, a kid whose everyday experiences reinforce that there is no way his parents will ever be able to pay for college, living in a community where there are no jobs outside of local fast food chains, to believe that sports is one of the best ways out and one of the only ways that will allow him to deliver his family out of poverty. Of course, this dream often only lasts through high school, a pleasant dream when better ones are not available, but ultimately insufficient as a real conduit to mobility for most children.

## Sports, a Type of Opium for Poor Communities

For poor kids, football is not just a dream about moving themselves out of poverty: it is a dream about moving the ones they love out of poverty as well. If you read about the lives of football players or watch their stories on TV, it is rare for them to not talk about getting into the NFL as the only way out of their predicaments; it is the only way they see as being remotely realistic for delivering their families from the despair of poverty. For these talented, but often poor, aspiring athletes, the American Dream is about being able to buy your parents a home and making their lives better. It can be an intoxicating dream when you see the ones you love suffering, when you know how hard they work every day, when you see in some small way that their dreams are tied up in you.

In a football town during the season, people stop you all throughout the week, at the barber shop, at the grocery store, and on the corner, to ask about the upcoming game. Almost everyone in the community knows the names of its star athletes and follows their accomplishments. I can remember one time while in high school that I skipped a day of school. The principal said to me, "If you do this again, you will not be able to play in the game this week." It's hard for a kid not to think of himself as special when such things occur.

My perception of Beaver Falls and communities like it was that wins brought overwhelming joy; after losses, it seemed as though the whole community was down. Young athletes begin to feel responsible not only for the welfare of their immediate families, but for these larger struggling communities as well.

For the longest time, I could not envision a life outside of sports. When I thought of college, I thought mostly of a place where I would go to have a chance at the pros and at the dream of delivering my family. It is not lost on me that, even as a university professor, I cannot relieve my family's poverty the way I always dreamed. With my educational aspirations shaped by my athletic ambitions, I did not even know that graduate school existed until after I was in college for a while. I am not saying sports are bad; I learned so much from being part of them, and they provided me with hope. When no other way out exists, they provide hope for the people.

To this day, I love sports, and my children all participate in some form of sports activities. Thankfully, they don't perceive it as their only chance in life or feel that they need to support their parents. They have a more comprehensive understanding of college and what it can mean for them, and they prepare for higher education differently than the children in my community did. When it comes to influencing college outcomes, these differences may be critical. Providing children in low-income neighborhoods with strategies for paying for college is an important part of making college appear as more than a place where they go to play sports. It is also important that these strategies work to bolster the sense that college is a means of achieving economic mobility that is more tangible and viable than the elusive vision of athletic prowess to which these young people aspire.

## Low-Income People Value Working Hard and Display It in Their Lives

My dad made it through the eighth grade. His parents did not make it as far as the eighth grade, and whatever poverty I lived through as a child, my dad and his family's day-to-day lives were far tougher. My mother fared better and was able to graduate from high school, but because her stepdad believed that college was not for girls, college never seemed possible for her.

I tell this story not to look for sympathy or to suggest that I had it harder than the next person or that we did not make mistakes in life. It is just to illustrate the particular context poverty creates for a child considering his future. And as I reflect today, when one lacks financial resources, mistakes are much more noticeable and painful. There are many people who have had much harder sets of circumstances to endure and overcome than my family had; however, what these experiences did for me is to help me see how the American story that effort plus ability equals success, though an inspiring ideal, falls short in daily reality. Equity is not only about making sure people have equal access to college, but being sure that *how* they access college (e.g., with or without student loans, the type of institution attended, the degree path pursued) does not advantage some and disadvantage others when it comes to the return they receive on their degree.

Despite the disadvantages they confronted, my parents bought into this ideal, that effort and ability should determine one's economic success. With a lot of hard work and determination, more than it would have taken someone who graduated from high school and could already read, my dad eventually became a train engineer for Conrail. My mother helped teach him to read. It was a lifelong dream of my dad's to one day become an engineer and one of his most prized memories. My mother worked in service-oriented jobs when I was growing up, such as waiting tables and working as a janitor at the Pittsburgh International Airport. Her biggest job, however, was holding the family together, which is never an easy task for low-income families.

What strikes me most about my parents, and what has left an enduring mark on who I am today, is their love for me and my sister, that we would fight for each other until the end, and their work ethic. These people worked, often with little reason to believe that their work would change their own lives in any kind of meaningful way. They worked and continued to strive, like many other low-income Americans, because they believed it was what people should do. They worked to provide their children with a chance at a better life, even if it was only a small chance, and even if they had to work much harder for it than those who were born with distinct advantages.

## When Families Are Unable to Pass Down Wealth to Their Children, Their Children Start Their Lives at a Disadvantage

My mother and dad were a biracial couple in a time when it was the norm to condemn such marriages. The story my mother tells is that her parents forbade her to marry my dad and that, under duress, she escaped by night from home to marry him. While this is not a book about race per se, in America, poverty and race are intertwined, and the outcomes experienced by a given child cannot be separated from his or her race. The evidence is clear that Americans of color fare differently in the current systems of higher education and financial aid.

In America, we like to think of race as a thing of the past with no bearing on the present; you know, we have a black president and all. However, my parents grew up in a time when racism was the norm. Through the lens of my experiences, it seems funny when we now debate whether race still matters. You can change the laws that have existed for hundreds of years in a day, but you cannot root out the vestiges of racism in the same way. People do not change as quickly. Many of us were raised by racist parents or parents who suffered under racism. It is hard to imagine that this upbringing has had no effect on us, on me.

I was reminded of this fact in my own life when my children's great-grandfather returned pictures we sent him of them because he did not agree with our interracial marriage; when my wife and I walk up to a house advertised in the newspaper to rent it and an old white man sitting on the porch says, "We don't want your kind here"; or when my children come home from school telling stories of other kids making fun of them because of the color of their skin. Daily, there are reminders that race still matters, and it matters in the pursuit of higher education as well.

Race's role and how my parents started their life together is important in thinking about how children come to the financial aid table. One significant difference is that I had no extended family to rely on. I never knew my mother's parents because they disowned us, and my dad's father was dead. There were no aunts and uncles we could lean on, so there was no one to go to in times of trouble. Extended families play critical roles in how people experience hard times, as pivotal studies of poverty and prosperity have affirmed (Stock, Corlyon, Serrano, and Gieve 2014). How they started their lives together also meant that my parents did not start with money, furniture, or other resources that give so many other families a leg up. There was no bridal shower; they took what they could carry and began their life together. While other families were given money to start their lives, sometimes money for college or a large down payment to buy a house, my parents had to flee and find work on what they had managed to save.

Having a storehouse of money, even if not large, to go into critical transitional periods in one's life (e.g., entering college, starting a family, entering retirement) can make a monumental difference in one's ability to successfully navigate these transitions. While the reasons some start with a nest egg and others do not may differ, and while there are undoubtedly differences between those who receive large inheritances and those whose transfers are more modest, the point here is less about the why or even how much and more about what it means for maintaining the facade that effort and ability are the differentiators in why some achieve a higher return on their college degree than others do. That is, the presence or absence of these well-timed, potentially transformational assets matters if we are to ensure that education is the great equalizer it is meant to be.

## Public Safety Net Not Always Available

Working as a train engineer was a great accomplishment; however, it took some time before my dad got a job at Conrail, and he did not start off as an engineer but as a fireman (they work in the train yard changing signals). Therefore, he lacked seniority, which is a type of protection from protracted layoffs. Even once he became an engineer, because it took him a long time to rise to the level of engineer, he was low man on the totem pole. This meant that he was frequently laid off from work, which made it nearly impossible for my parents to budget or for social assistance programs to determine whether we qualified for assistance and for how much. As a result, the public safety net, which provides only sparse assistance even to those who fit the relatively narrow confines of eligibility, was also rarely of help to us.

Instead, my dad would take work anywhere he could get it. Sometimes he would grab hours at the local junkyard, and the owner would pay him what he wanted, when he wanted. For a time, he started a window cleaning "business" with another man, and they would go out and knock on the doors of local businesses to see whether they needed their windows cleaned. There really wasn't any work he would not take during long stretches of being laid off.

This made a profound and invaluable impression on me—my parents' work ethic, the doggedness by which they attempted to provide for me and my sister. The meager outcomes from this significant outlay of effort also let me know that if anyone makes it in this world, it is not by hard work and effort alone. They had to have had assistance and meaningful opportunities, including access to institutions that make that effort significantly more valuable.

## Poor Children Face Critical Decisions about Whether to Invest Their Energy in School or Survival

Despite their efforts, after the political assault on railroads in the 1980s, we lived more years in financial turmoil than not. We were caught between a month or two of good work and three or four with none, and between making too much money for public assistance and not enough to get by. This financial turmoil made it hard for me in school, and I imagine for my sister, too. People respond to poverty differently; my sister, who was a withdrawn person by nature, only went deeper during periods of hardship, so I never got a sense of how it affected her, as we never discussed it. However, the number of times I would find her just sitting in her room rocking back and forth with her legs crossed, oblivious to the world, let me know it was hard on her. She would have sores on her ankles from rocking back and forth.

Poverty places families under extreme stress that tests their intrafamily psychosocial dynamics. I often wonder, could my wife and I make it if put under such a heavy burden? You don't know whether you can endure such things unless you are thrown into them, and not for a year or two, but for years on end, without any tangible evidence of meaningful hope for future change. Such poverty is a type of war against the family unit that only the really strong families can survive.

With regard to school, I think the hardest period for me was between fourth and seventh grades. Though it also happened before and after these grades, during this period we spent a lot of time moving from one house to another. I am not really sure how many houses we lived in during my childhood, but we moved frequently. Sometimes we lived in a house with no heat, electricity, or water, and other times we slept on a neighbor's floor, on the side of the road, in a park, or in a hotel. Some of my strongest memories are going to the local playground to get our water for the day from a pump.

During this period, I also learned to withdraw, not to my room but into my family, those people who were suffering with me. I started missing a lot of school. It is easy to say poor kids should simply work hard in school and to blame them when they do not, but it is much more difficult to be living in a house with no heat or water or food and to remain fully concerned about school. I did enough to get by, or at least they kept moving me to the next grade. These are times of survival, and though parents would ideally be focused on making sure their kids are in school and doing their homework, they are overwhelmed with figuring out how to eat tonight, how to stay warm, and how to keep their house. This is another way in which the education system fails as an equalizer; success is elusive for those who most need education's transformative effects, for reasons predictably related not to innate ability but to the scarcity of some children's educational environments.

There was also a sense of pride that hindered me during this period. I know poor people are not supposed to have pride, and in many ways are not afforded it, but I did. I did not want my friends to know the depth of our poverty, so hiding the hardship from them became important to me. So when things got bad, I withdrew from friends. To this day, it is very hard for me to let people into my life in meaningful ways. I would disappear from school or out of the lives of my friends and join the fight my family was in by seeking whatever work I could muster: sweeping the floors of local stores, shoveling snow, or whatever job a kid could get, even if it was pumping water for the family. In doing so, I missed out on a lot of fundamental building blocks in school. In some cases, I have never been able to catch up. In other areas, I have had to work twice as hard as the person who learned these concepts during the normal course of school. Even when I ultimately made it to college, these deficits followed me. I entered Geneva College for my bachelor's degree on academic probation and had to take a reduced load my first year and some remedial classes to catch up.

Prior to going to college, at the end of my junior year in high school, I got heavily involved in church and accepted Christ as my savior. During this period, I grew disenchanted with so many different things in my life and decided not to play organized sports anymore. I was told by some community members that I was throwing away my life and the hopes of others. I can remember the principal calling me into his office and saying what a mistake I was making by not playing and being kept after class by some teachers stating similar sentiments. Sometime early in my senior year, it became clear to me that my presence was causing more of a disruption than it was worth, so I left school and eventually got my GED.

Despite this interruption in my schooling, I was able to make it to college and get through it. I attribute much of this success to what I learned from watching my parents all those years. Two things I learned from them have made all the difference for me in my life. One is that you may not be the smartest, you may not have all the resources, others may be against you for reasons you cannot comprehend, but you can always dig just a little deeper and work just a little harder. Really, what else does a debt-dependent person have at his disposal to call upon, apart from God, to compete, to have a chance? So when others slept, I made sure I was studying. To this day, I still live by this. I wonder how I will have to pay for this later in life, having seen the toll on my parents' health. Still, I teach this to my kids now: you always have the choice to outwork your peers.

The second thing I learned from them that helped me make it through school was to hope against all hope. Every day they got up and found a reason to push forward when there really was no reason to believe things were going to change. I could see that work alone would not be enough to change their lot. I am sure they could as well. But, still, they worked.

## Student Debt Shapes the Opportunities We Have

Not only did I enter college behind academically, but my family had few financial resources to help pay for college. This is not a failure on their part. They worked hard and tried but just did not have the funds to pay for the high costs of college. What they had they shared, often to their own detriment—a fact not lost on me. Consequently, I relied heavily on student loans to pay for college.

I had been out of high school for two years, working in a mission I opened in Beaver Falls, and had come to see college as my path to the things I wanted to accomplish in life. I was concerned about borrowing so heavily to finance my degree, but I saw student loans as mostly a positive. That is, I saw them as my only means to attend college. As a result of this reliance on borrowing, by the time I graduated from Geneva College in 1995, I had about $40,000 in student debt.

When I left Geneva, I wanted to be a lawyer and was accepted into Akron University with a generous scholarship. While the scholarship helped with paying for law school, I lived off campus, about an hour and half away, with my parents. I had to quit my job to concentrate on my studies, without realizing how much my job meant to my parents' ability to maintain themselves financially. On top of that, I had this long, costly commute. So while I found law school extremely stimulating and had this great scholarship, by the end of my first year, it had put a big financial strain on my family, and we were evicted from our home. I came to blame myself for that. So at the end of that year, to the chagrin of some of the faculty and administrators who recognized real promise in me, I opted to drop out of law school and enter the military to help my family and pay back my student loans.

This is one of the first times that student loans really negatively affected a decision I made. First, it was decisive with regard to the occupation I chose. I chose the military over trying to find a job because I could get out from under the debt that was mentally weighing me down. Second, going into the military with a bachelor's degree, I had the choice of joining the officer ranks or the enlisted ranks. However, student loans restricted the opportunities available to me, as is too often the case for low-income children. In this case, it was whether I became an officer or an enlisted man. As we will discuss later in this book, student loans also determine such things as the type of college children attend (e.g., two-year or four-year, selective or nonselective)—when effort, ability, and interest should decide—and they can alter career trajectories in other ways as well.

Thus, with the encouragement of my recruiters and the institutional structure of the military's student loan repayment program, I was directed into the enlisted ranks. The way the repayment program was set up, if I wanted the military to help pay off my student loans, I had to join the enlisted ranks. Being an enlisted soldier, in some important ways, offered fewer opportunities than the officer corps, such as far less pay, privilege, and power. This distinction is significant because you have to have a bachelor's degree to be an officer, but the military would pay off my loans only if I entered as an enlisted soldier in an occupation for which they had trouble recruiting people. Thus, I was restricted in whether I was an officer or an enlisted member and by occupation once I became an enlisted soldier, not because of my own abilities or even my educational preparation, but because of the influences exerted by the type of financial aid on which I had depended. I learned a lot from being in the military, and it was an experience I remain proud of. But as a powerful institution in U.S. society, it is an example of how student loan policies reinforce social and economic inequities, rather than equalizing opportunities.

This is just one example of how student loans too often are used to limit the opportunities of low-income children. I say "low-income children" because they are the ones who are forced to make decisions based on having to pay off their student loans, and the children for whom student loans are not one financial aid option among many—used primarily to facilitate specific educational objectives—but, instead, the *only* path to a higher education.

When I was undergoing my physical to enter the military, a nurse told me not to listen to the recruiters who were strongly encouraging me to go enlisted. She said, "You can still easily change now and go in as an officer." A wiser person would have listened to her, but I thought having my student loans paid off would outweigh the rest. Loans totaling $40,000 seemed like a nearly insurmountable burden to overcome at the time; how would I pay them? At the very least, it would take me many years to pay off. Looking at my future through the lens of student loans made for a very bleak picture, and I acted based on that dire prognosis, in ways that were ultimately against some of my long-term interests. In this, I know that I am not alone.

### How We Finance College Helps Determine When We Start to Benefit from College

My time in the military was coming to an end at the same time that the September 11 terrorist attacks occurred in the United States. As a result, my exit from the military was temporarily interrupted due to the stop-loss policy in effect. It so happened that my wife and I had been accepted into a program for exiting military soldiers to teach junior high while taking classes to become principals in the Chicago schools. But because I could not leave the military on time, although my wife got out prior to stop loss being enacted, we lost these positions and ended up going to Ohio where I was on a short list to become a prison inspector. As fate would have it,

Ohio suffered a prison closing as a result of fiscal cutbacks, and before I could start, I was out of a job.

This is relevant because it helps explain the financial condition in which I then enrolled at Washington University in St. Louis. After trying to make ends meet for about one year in Columbus, we were left with two options: head home to live with our parents or head to school and try to retool. And while you might think that my military service would entitle me to assistance with further schooling, one of the drawbacks to entering the student loan repayment program in the military is that it disqualifies one for programs that provide money for future schooling. So once again, I entered school with no resources to speak of and, in fact, still with considerable debt. My only hope to pay for college was again with more student loans, but this time with a wife and a small baby.

Yes, I could have chosen a much less expensive college, but the George Warren Brown School of Social Work at Washington University was one of the top schools in the country for social work and widely considered one of the top universities in the country, period. Unfortunately, it is also one of the worst elite schools for providing financial support to low-income students (Leonhardt 2014). And so, during my time as an MSW and PhD student, but particularly as an MSW student, I incurred still more large student loans, eventually graduating in 2008 with a PhD and more than $100,000 worth of debt. And yes, it was worth the debt, but that does not mean it is an optimal—nor an equitable—system for financing college.

It was worth it to me, in part, because I not only wanted to achieve the American Dream for my family but make it more accessible to others, and I believed that gaining knowledge was imperative, even if it meant taking on huge debt. To a certain extent, though, my assessment of the advantages this education would afford was intuitive; I could not fully understand the benefits that one receives from attending an elite school. I think if the average person could understand the differences among the schools in the top and lower tiers of our higher education system, our understanding of the American Dream as resting on the foundation of a level playing field would be dashed.

Just saying that you attended Washington University in St. Louis comes with a cache that is hard to explain, particularly when entering the job market for the first time. People think about you differently. Furthermore, while you are there, you have the best facilities possible, the best equipment, Nobel Prize winners walking about on campus that you can talk to and access, money for research, money for travel, connections to people I would never have come into contact with otherwise, and just so much more. I was able to work with the preeminent leaders in my field, and these relationships established my career in a way that would be difficult to construct outside of this privileged system. Maybe it was more eye-opening to me because I had never experienced these things than it was to people who always grew up with such privilege—that is, the vast majority of Washington University students.

My journey down the education path toward achieving the American Dream is not over yet, however. I am 44, and though I can now see light at the end of the proverbial tunnel, I have not yet achieved financial well-being for me and my family. I still stay up at nights thinking about how I can begin to pay down this student debt and not hinder my kids' opportunities. It is not because of a lack of effort. I have achieved more than many in my profession, even relatively soon after finishing my PhD. It is not because of ability; I am widely considered a leading expert in my field and have been recognized in many venues for my excellent scholarship and professional leadership. And yes, it is true, I have not made all the right decisions in life. I readily admit this and recognize that there are decisions that I would now make differently if given a second bite at the apple. But, to a large extent, the story of my life has been shaped by forces with roots that were established before I was even born.

Many of my experiences are understood only with a knowledge of where I started in life. In significant ways, the inequities in the U.S. education and economic systems, where privilege compounds privilege and disadvantage multiplies disadvantage, serve to exacerbate initial inequality rather than strengthening the ability of education to act as an equalizer. While the current financial aid system is not the only—or perhaps even the most powerful—inequitable force to which I have been subjected, it is one of the most readily amenable ones. If I did not have student loans, my financial life would look drastically different, as would the lives of many other young adults. I would think differently about what I have accomplished and my future. My own children's futures would be positioned differently, too, even holding everything else in my own past constant. As a frame through which to observe my history and consider my future, student debt looms large.

## THE ASSET-EMPOWERED PATH TO THE AMERICAN DREAM

My name is Melinda Lewis. I grew up Melinda Carden, and I grew up fully expecting that I would go to college. There was never a *moment* of decision about my postsecondary education plans. With two parents who had both graduated from college—my mother had earned her master's degree by the time I was old enough to know that—and an older sister who enrolled in college when I was still in elementary school, my own higher education plans were always questions of where and what, never if.

My extended family members were mostly college graduates, too. Most of my parents' friends had at least attended college, as had several of our neighbors, many of the people at our church, and, certainly, the professionals with whom we regularly interacted. Although my grandparents had very little formal education—my mother's parents, in particular, had grown up very poor and, in my grandma's case, orphaned, and so had not gone to school much—they valued education to the extreme, making schooling a priority for my mom and, as became particularly important later, for us. In powerful ways, their lack of advanced education was wrapped up in the norms around my own educational attainment; ours was a family who had come from little and now had plenty, and education was understood to have played a critical role in facilitating that upward mobility.

Ours was a college-going culture, then. My teachers assumed that I would go to college, my parents made sure that my sisters and I were familiar with college options, and I began to think, from a very young age, about college as an eventuality, instead of just an aspiration. My parents also began saving for my college education when I was young. They did not have enough in savings for my older sister when she enrolled, and I know now that it was a financial hardship for them, made somewhat more feasible by my mom's reentry into the workforce a few years earlier. By the time I was in high school, though, my dad told me that he had reached his savings goal and comfortably had enough to pay for at least four years of public university for me—an education that cost far less than it does now, but one that was, nonetheless, still costly enough to require an infusion of additional resources.

Because college had always been presented as a certain part of my future, I don't remember feeling any real relief in learning that my dad's budget projections had worked out. My family had, in ways both subtle and explicit, always conveyed the sense that they would pay for me to go to college or that we'd find a way to make it happen. In sharp contrast to the high hurdles that so many disadvantaged American children must surmount to continue their educations, then, I didn't so much *choose* to go to college as walk into a path already laid out for me. Going to college was part of the role I was expected to play, and my subsequent success in performing it is owed to individual initiative, yes, but also and, importantly, to powerful institutional forces.

## Purchasing Educational Advantages

At the time, and especially in retrospect, there were elements of my educational environment, particularly prior to college, that I found less than satisfactory. I went to good suburban public schools and participated in enriched programs for gifted students most of my academic career, but I remember that some of the experiences seemed mediocre. My parents must have perceived some of these limitations as well, and they compensated by surrounding me with enrichment from an early age. Most of these investments were relatively inexpensive, but they helped to shape my learning in very significant ways. Critically, they also required an infusion of parental "bandwidth" (Mullainathan and Shafir 2014), intellectual and emotional resources that my parents had at their disposal because they were not overly preoccupied with our economic survival. When I thought I wanted to be a photojournalist, my dad bought me a completely manual camera and a book about apertures and F-stops. I took a dozen photos of a sewage treatment pond, I remember, but he was proud of my light exposure.

My parents were not the hovering, uber-involved types, but I had opportunities that less-advantaged children may not even know exist. I took theater classes, piano lessons, and advanced academic courses, the latter of which required that my dad drive me to a different school at 7:00 a.m. five days a week. When my dad wasn't working weekends at his managerial job or managing his inventory of rental properties, we would take family field trips, and my parents indulged my educational interests from an early age. My dad took me to see Mikhail Gorbachev speak, even taking the day off work to accompany me. When I was into Laura Ingalls Wilder, he took me to historic sites with living history volunteers and even helped me cook over an open fire. When I was assigned a class project on Germany, he found a man I could interview who had smuggled Bibles into East Berlin and took me to his apartment so that I could talk with him. When I wanted to be a genetic counselor, he found a Saturday genetics program at a nearby research institute and convinced them to let me attend.

Our vacations included quizzes that required us to learn to use a compass, read a map, and choose activities from printed guidebooks. Our receipt of limited spending money was usually predicated on completion of the math problems required to determine how much we would have and how far we could stretch it. We visited colleges on our vacations and went to national parks instead of amusement parks. I gave a slideshow in third grade about the St. Patrick's Day traditions in Chicago after our spring break trip that year. My parents read to me extensively, and I had access to a top-quality public library with a nearly unlimited catalog. My parents and the privileges they leveraged on my behalf are evident in every aspect of my early upbringing, from the vocabulary I learned to the confidence I displayed to the options I perceived as realistically available for my future.

I had teachers who were captivated by my interests and aptitudes and who, encouraged by my parents, provided me with extra academic input. The district provided me with a bus so that I could return to my school after the accelerated math class and also participate in a gifted education program that was offered only in certain elementary schools in the district. My parents were comfortable advocating for these services, particularly my mom, who was herself a highly awarded public school teacher.

In high school, I had the opportunity to earn advanced college credit through a partnership with the local community college. I don't know whether students could qualify for financial aid for these courses, but I know that my parents just wrote a check when it was time to pay the tuition, and I know that some of my classmates took the same courses and didn't receive college credit because they didn't—or couldn't—pay for it. I graduated high school with more than a year's worth of college credit and finished my undergraduate degree in three years, a leg up that I never could have achieved if my parents hadn't had the disposable income to absorb the extra few hundred dollars per course when I was still in high school.

All of these "choices," and the imprint they left on me, were facilitated by our family's economic privilege, even though many times as a child I felt deprived in comparison to my peers. As kids, we feel the slights far more acutely than we perceive the cushions that protect us. I vividly remember the wire that poked out of the backseat of our station wagon, and how we had to keep driving it until it fell apart anyway. I know that on those vacations we got to eat in a restaurant only once each trip, usually at Pizza Hut. The rest of the meals were cooked on a hot plate at the campsite or in the motel room. I will never forget the one and only summer we had cable television, when my mom was participating in a market-research project. Certainly compared with my own children's financial standing and material comforts, my family was only "comfortable," not ensconced in luxury. Still, I sailed through my childhood, buoyed by my parents' strategic use of our more than adequate resources and as the beneficiary of their investments in my human capital. I was smart, and I worked hard. Both of those attributes mattered far more than they otherwise would have, if not for the supportive context in which I could exert them.

## Intergenerational Transfers as a Safety Net

The story of my family's finances and the advantages I enjoyed does not begin with my parents, however. From a very young age, I knew that my maternal grandparents, who lived far more frugally than we did (I still remember when my grandma refused my now-husband a second glass of milk at dinner because "milk is expensive"), were providing critical financial support to my family. In many ways, these transfers served as a sort of safety net, keeping my family from hardship when circumstances could have meant otherwise. When my older sister's college expenses exceeded my parents' savings, when extreme weather sent our utility bills skyrocketing, when a car accident necessitated an unexpected purchase, when my younger sister needed braces, or when my dad needed a loan so that he could invest in some rental property, they had ready access to these resources. Ours was not a multimillion-dollar inheritance. I never felt like a "trust fund kid," and I didn't directly see any of my grandparents' money until I was far older, but there was still a security that came from knowing that our family's well-being depended not just on the considerable effort of my own parents, but also on the legacy built by the previous generation.

My grandpa never went to high school; he dropped out in, I believe, the eighth grade, because his sister needed shoes, so he had to go to work, as the family lore recites. He left the farm, served in the Merchant Marines, and then took a job at Phillips 66, a company for which he would work his entire career. He worked hard, long, and irregular shifts at manual labor undoubtedly made additionally onerous since an early farm accident—and lack of money to pay a doctor—had taken most of the fingers on one hand. But he always had a job. In a display of corporate largesse rare today, Phillips 66 provided $2,000 scholarships for my mom and her sister, making college an affordable reality even on their limited incomes.

My grandmother supplemented the family's income by taking in sewing, cutting hair, and trimming costs however she could. She was the family's money manager, zealous in her thrift and smart with her investments. By the time I was old enough to understand money, my grandparents had enough in savings to bequeath more than $200,000 to each of their five grandchildren, even after years of plugging holes in my family's budget and paying thousands of dollars in medical expenses for my late aunt's illness. In ways that I didn't comprehend then, this money is a relic of an economy that no longer exists, the product of jobs that are no longer available, and the result of an "effort + ability + long-term planning" equation that no longer computes.

I am conscious every day of the fact that, despite putting in long hours for my family and my career, I never come close to working as hard as my grandparents did. They were exceptionally dedicated to climbing out of poverty, and nothing pleased my grandpa more in his old age than driving around town to point out the banks where he had money saved (up to the FDIC-insured limit), except perhaps showing off his granddaughters. They worked harder than I can really imagine, and they delayed their own gratification all the way to subsequent generations. But still, two high school dropouts with poor families would be very unlikely to attain their heights in today's global economy.

## Privilege Goes to College

As a reward for my intellectual abilities, bolstered by the supportive context in which I was raised and reinforced by my parents' considerable investments in my learning, I was named a National Merit Scholar my senior year in high school. Although I likely could have gained admission to a selective institution, I enrolled in the same public university my parents, sister, and many friends attended. To some, this could look like "undermatching." Certainly, my best friend, whose ACT and PSAT scores were the same as mine, went to Harvard University instead. But my choice of a relatively affordable although considerably less prestigious school was strategic, stemming not from inadequate information, stunted aspirations, or scarce financial resources, as is so often the case for less-advantaged students, but from an intentional plan. My parents' assistance in navigating these options was extremely influential. Their ability to do so with confidence was likely facilitated by their prior financial preparation and their own educational credentials.

My dad and I met the university chancellor during an honors student visit day my senior year. My dad told him that I was seriously considering several selective institutions, including Northwestern, Princeton, and Stanford. The chancellor offered his admittedly self-interested but also, I think in hindsight, wise counsel that I could attend the University of Kansas for free with the merit scholarships I would be awarded, building a quality education from the university's honors offerings, and then use the money that my parents had saved for me to finance a graduate degree, once I was certain of my specific career choice. My dad was sold, and while I was always encouraged to apply to any institution that interested me, I know that he was pleased when I chose the path he and the chancellor had envisioned.

Once at the university, my academic choices and interactions were continuously shaped by my upbringing, in ways that are only now apparent. I chose social work as a major because I wanted to help people and was fascinated by the blending of direct service and macro policy change, with almost no regard to how much I would likely earn, an oblivion afforded by my lack of any student debt and confidence in my parents' willingness and ability to help me transition to economic independence. I studied abroad every summer, a luxury my middle-class family otherwise could not have financed, because my parents allowed me to divert some of the savings I had not needed for my undergraduate studies. Fresh from a successful secondary school career, I felt comfortable asking my professors to serve as mentors or challenging my classmates on points of theory.

I did not have to work full-time while in school, so I built an impressive volunteer resume, including founding a new on-campus organization, spending every week serving breakfast to people experiencing homelessness, and starting a history discussion group at an assisted-living facility. I had a computer of my own before most of my peers, purchased with one semester's research award, because my parents were helping me pay my living expenses already. I could focus on college, unencumbered by financial concerns, employment responsibilities, or worries about my family's finances.

I certainly worked hard; my story intersects with Willie's in this respect. I was active in community service and extracurricular activities, earned straight A's in those honors courses, worked part-time on campus, and regularly took on additional projects and studies. And I was relatively thrifty, giving up my car so that I could pay for one study-abroad course with the savings in car insurance and seldom ordering pizza or going to the movies. I was far more profligate than my mother, whose own mother forbid her as an undergraduate to ever spend a dime on the campus bus, even in the snow, but I felt an imperative to spend responsibly.

I took the opportunity of a college education very seriously, although this, too, was I think more the product of my pro-education upbringing than my innate virtue. I remember my college graduation very clearly. I had already been named a Truman Scholar and selected Washington University for that promised (and now paid for) prestigious graduate degree. I still have the photos taken in front of the student union with my parents, both alumni, and my grandparents, whose sacrifices over a lifetime provided my family with the financial security that, in turn, became the platform on which I constructed my dreams.

### Intergenerational Transfers as a Launching Pad

Intergenerational transfers of wealth ensured that my parents' upward climb stayed on track, even when financial insecurity threatened. My grandparents' support made my parents' lives more secure and mine more comfortable. As I grew, their financial contributions facilitated my educational attainment, both directly and indirectly. What was a source of financial security for my parents became the foundation of economic mobility for me. The first transfer directly to me—and not to an educational institution—that I can remember came from my dad. He opened an individual retirement account in my name while I was still in college and deposited some of the money left over from my college savings account as a retirement starter. He felt confident to do so once I received the Truman Scholarship, which, combined with an institutional merit award from Washington University, covered all of my graduate studies.

When I started at Washington University, my grandparents gave me money directly—I think $10,000—to match what they had given my older sister to help her pay for her PhD program. They were very deliberately equal in their transfers, so even though I didn't need the money for graduate school, I still got it. I used some of the money for a summer study in Guatemala, and the rest was still in that account when I got married.

Here, my parents' guidance—especially my dad's—was instrumental in ensuring that these funds were used productively. Importantly, this wasn't a one-time lesson in money management. My father had been teaching me how to handle money, in the routine ways that people comfortable with and around money can, since I was small. I remember much of his teaching very well: "It's always better to choose between A and B instead of yes or no on A"; "Save the money automatically, so you're never tempted to spend it"; "When you get a windfall, remember that you weren't expecting that money, so you don't need it"; and "Never loan money that you can't afford not to get back."

Growing up, we were expected to work for our expenses. I paid for my first car with the money I earned working at a retirement home, often rising at 4:00 a.m. to serve breakfast in the dining room at 5:00. But the teachings that had the greatest impact on me were those that I absorbed from watching the financial decisions my parents made, decisions they could make because they had money with which to make them, and decisions that they made informed by their priorities and by the lessons they, in turn, had learned from their own parents.

After finishing my Master of Social Work degree, I took a job back in Kansas City and got married shortly thereafter. The job I started just three days after graduating and held for the next six years didn't emerge from family connections; my family was well-off enough to move comfortably through the economy but certainly was not part of the civic or economic elite. In part, then, I was fortunate to be graduating in May 2001, when the economy was still mostly strong and many nonprofit organizations were still hiring.

Even this success, though, is not devoid of context. I convinced the CEO to create a position for me largely on the strength of my accumulated experiences—internships, study-abroad courses, volunteer leadership, academic and community service awards—that I would not have been able to accomplish if forced to finance my own education. I could afford to take a relatively low-paying first job where my salary would nearly double within two years because I had no pressing student loan repayments to face. I could live at home before I got married because my parents had a house large enough to accommodate me, and my salary those first few months went straight to savings. Even once I had completed my formal schooling, my asset-empowered path to higher education and the financial security of my family of origin continued to influence my trajectory.

Even more significantly, the intergenerational transfers that had greased my way so far continued to facilitate the realization of my goals. My grandparents gave us another $10,000 as a wedding present, and that went mostly into a savings account, too. As newlyweds, then, while I can still remember walking to the grocery store to look for something inexpensive to serve as an appetizer for our housewarming party, we were quite financially secure. We both had jobs, I had no student loans, and my parents paid for most of our relatively modest wedding. We opened 401(k) accounts immediately upon securing our first jobs, and both of our employers contributed as well. A few months after we got married, we pulled from our savings account (really, an "economic mobility account" that held my grandparents' transfers, as it had little of our own savings in it at that point) to pay off my husband's small student loan. We then set to saving from our respective incomes to pay for our first house.

Despite this long history of financial support, I am embarrassed to admit that it was only when we were house searching that the full import of my family's intergenerational transfers became apparent. My parents advised us that my grandparents would give us $50,000 for the down payment, as they had done for my sister and my cousins. We were able to not only purchase a home in a nicer neighborhood than we might have otherwise, but also could avoid mortgage insurance and unfavorable credit terms as a result of the sizeable initial investment. We would have been able to purchase a house eventually, certainly, but their financial support put us on a much faster track to homeownership than our peers, even those who were also college graduates. My husband was even able to quit his job and return to earn a graduate degree shortly after we moved in, using some of our savings to avoid having to take out any student loans. My grandparents were proud to help finance his education, too, in addition to mine. We took another photo in front of the student union.

We maintained our 401(k) and IRA investments during this period, even when living off one income, in large part because our debt obligations were so minimal. We were more financially secure at a much younger age than my parents. Even well into our financial independence, my grandparents continued to cushion us from many of the economic shocks that would otherwise accompany life events. When we unexpectedly found out we were having twins, my grandpa gave us $10,000 to buy a minivan, before we had even fully come to terms with how expensive it would be to have two babies at once. This support relieved our anxieties, prevented costly financial decisions such as pulling from our retirement accounts, and positioned my immediate family for a level of financial security at a young age that my grandparents could not have fathomed and even my parents could not attain. The intergenerational transfers we received at critical points in our lives—when I started college, when I was going to graduate school, when we got married, when we bought a house—served to launch us to a higher standard of living, a fact not lost on my father, who still can't believe that my own family eats out nearly every meal when we go on vacation.

## Economic Mobility, Multiplied

Because we started building home equity before we turned 25, had access to retirement savings vehicles through our employers, and had no outstanding student debt with which to contend, my husband and I were well-positioned for a head start on college savings for our children. We have four, close in age, but we are on track to have their college paid for before they finish high school. Certainly, again, our own effort and ability come into play here; my husband and I both have good jobs, live beneath our means, and prioritize saving. We still don't have cable television, and my children are just as appalled as I was as a child. Our friends cannot believe how much we set aside each year for college, and we visit a financial planner annually to stay on track.

But to attribute our net worth to any individual characteristics is to completely obscure the significant—and ongoing—influence of intergenerational transfers and of inequitable public policy in facilitating our success.

We have the careers we do because of our educational attainment, start-ing with our relatively advantaged school district (we met in high school) and continuing to our completion of graduate degrees. We were able to pay for those educations without resorting to sizable student debt because we both finished our undergraduate degrees before the sharper climb in tuition prices that began with the 2001 recession (Quinterno and Orozco 2012). And we built on the significant financial support transferred from previous generations to construct a sound foundation for our children's futures. Before they died, my grandparents gave each of our first three children $20,000 in college savings, and my parents started 529 college savings plans with $10,000 per child, as well. As the exclamation point to this process of wealth transmission, my husband and I put nearly all of the final inheritance we received after my grandparents died—more than an additional $60,000—into college savings for our children.

As a result, when the talk at school parties or neighborhood gatherings inevitably turns to nervous chatter about the high cost of college, we get quiet. Our financial realities are far different from many of our friends', due largely to factors other than our own initiative. Our children will always know, too, that college is part of their future. They have visited not only the university where I work and the one from which my in laws graduated, but also Harvard University, the Massachusetts Institute of Technology, Brown University, and others in the places we visit on vacation. Nearly every adult they know, including of course all four of their grandparents, went to college.

Our children are exposed to degree choices and career options that didn't even exist when I was growing up, and they will have affordable access to the institutions that can prepare them for these paths. They may even have financial help to purchase their own homes or launch their own adult-hoods, depending on the support their grandparents and we will be able to provide. While they would still say that they are deprived because they don't have a game system or their own rooms, they have more books than we can keep track of, after-school science classes, summer theater camps, and a home robotics kit. We live in a neighborhood that places them in one of the highest-performing schools in the region. They have excellent public libraries and parks within walking distance. They have visited the city's art museums, science centers, and historical monuments multiple times and have banners hanging in the basement with all of their National Park Junior Ranger badges. They have parents with the disposable income, educational preparation, and mental bandwidth to invest in their intellec-tual development. We energetically outsource some of the routine tasks of household management—I have someone clean the house twice a month, for example, which my mom always wanted—so that we can spend more time answering their questions and asking challenging ones of our own.

In so many significant ways, they have advantages that took root long before they were born and that surpass even the facilitative environment that carried me to success. From high school dropouts to college graduates to graduate-degree holders to children positioned to succeed even in today's constrained environment, ours is an American success story, proof that the Dream still lives.

But it's a story that, below the surface, reveals a reality far more complex than just "effort + ability = achievement." Instead, ours is a story that affirms that assets matter, that degrees financed without student loans pay a better return, and that early expectations give children an advantage. My grandparents' contributions were largely invisible to the outside world, but they mattered dearly, and still do, and still will, far into my descendants' futures.

Collectively, Americans look at stories like mine and conclude that we achieved because we worked hard, or were bright, or perhaps because we were in the right places at the right times. What we should see, instead, is that context makes a difference and that policy interventions that mimic the "natural" supports on which I stand, could work for disadvantaged children, too.

## CONCLUSION

Although we both attended the same graduate school and work in the same profession, our paths to these degrees diverged sharply, and the resulting outcomes stand in sharp contrast, too. Even with additional schooling—I, Willie, went on to receive my PhD while Melinda stopped with her Master of Social Work—I have not been able to achieve the same level of financial success as quickly. Clearly, other factors must explain these disparities. Again, while we do not pretend that our experiences are universally generalizable, the fact that the differences in our journeys cannot be explained by differences in ability or effort suggests that these stories might offer some important lessons and reveal the critical failings in the institutions that are supposed to facilitate equitable access to the American Dream.

In this book, after providing more rigorous evidence from policy analyses and empirical analysis, we suggest that it is not good enough that a low-income child is better off from having taken out student loans and gone to college than if he or she never continued his or her education. That's not the only counterfactual that must be considered, and it sets the bar for financial aid policy far too low. From the policies that finance our most valuable economic mobility intervention, we should expect more than just "does little harm." The United States and, most importantly, our children deserve a financial aid system worthy of our aspirations and consistent with our collective narrative. If student loans prevent children from attaining the American Dream or delay them from reaching it for increasingly longer periods of time, while others who put in the same amount of effort and have the same amount of ability are able to achieve the American Dream much more quickly, this approach to financing higher education may be not only unwise, unsustainable, and inefficient, but, indeed, un-American.

# THREE

## Education Is Still Our Best Hope

The term *American Dream* was popularized in James Truslow Adams's 1931 book, *The Epic of America*. This dream of working hard to build a better life—a central driver in the history of our nation—is associated with the constitutional right of all citizens to the "pursuit of happiness." It is fueled by the idea that if people put forth enough effort and have sufficient ability, they will be able to obtain desired outcomes through normative behaviors such as attending college. This idea grew out of the rich and plentiful land of America and the institutions that were established early in the nation's history. This combination supported the belief that anyone could access the resources needed to achieve desired outcomes. Deeply rooted in the fabric of American culture, the American Dream resonates in the belief structures of Americans of all socioeconomic classes (Hochschild 1995; Rank 2004; Wilson 1987). The American Dream has been a central ideology of Americans for decades, if not centuries (Hochschild 1995), shaping not just our collective identity but the lens through which we see social policy interventions as well.

### UNDERSTANDING THE IMPORTANCE OF IDEOLOGY AND SOCIAL VALUES

Paradigms, or what might be thought of as social values, such as the American Dream, provide part of the context for conducting and interpreting research. From the beginning of inquiry, researchers are influenced by their values, even when their goal is objectivity. The questions we ask and the interpretations we draw are shaped by the way we see the world. For instance, when we began to think about the student debt problem, we realized that researchers almost exclusively asked, "Are students better off if they take out student loans and go to college than if they do not go to college at all, all other things being equal?" This question frames research that compares poor students who attend college to poor students who do not attend college to find out whether the return on college is worth it. This aligns well with the long-held belief that college is an important path for achieving the American Dream, and that differences in financial aid mechanisms matter relatively little for determining college outcomes and the return on a degree.

In some cases, this narrow, and we would argue misguided, focus of analysis stems from an incomplete understanding of the effects of student loans; in others, scholars' authentic inquiry may be stunted by political or pragmatic considerations. In our private talks with some of the leading scholars studying student debt's effects, for example, we found that a reason they focused on this question was because they feared that challenging the student loan program would provide grounds for discontinuing it, without a viable alternative replacement, a policy move that could further limit college access for low-income students and exacerbate the achievement gap.

To determine the extent to which student loans align with or undermine the totality of the dream of economic mobility, we must ask different questions and examine different metrics. The American Dream, as we understand it, not only holds that additional education will provide some payoff; it also conveys the message that people who work equally hard and have roughly equal ability should, in the end, achieve roughly the same financial outcomes. Our belief in this basic tenet of the American Dream, speaking not just to opportunity but also to equity, freed us to ask, "Are children who have to pay for college with student loans able to achieve the same outcomes as children who do not have to pay for college with student loans when effort and ability are the same?" As a result, we end up telling a very different story about the effectiveness of student loans as a way to finance college than researchers who only ask whether students who finance college using student loans are better off than if they had not gone to college at all.

Thus for some researchers, their belief that college is an important—indeed, perhaps the only viable—path for achieving the American Dream, when couched in the context of seemingly hopeless gridlock in the U.S. Congress, precludes asking the more damning question about equity. Being afraid that something worse could follow in its wake can blind us from seeing the failures of what we have, or, at least, prevent us from fostering the necessary conversation about the dangers of the status quo. Maybe Sandy Baum of the Urban Institute's Income and Benefits Policy Center states this sense of hopelessness best when she says, "And from the perspective of students planning on taking out loans to continue their education, what is the alternative?" (Woluchem and George 2014, paragraph 6).

Furthermore, it is important to acknowledge that how people, whether researchers or the general public, interpret research findings is also influenced by social values. The political Right has recognized and embraced this fact for years, while the political Left is skeptical of any foray into what appears like ideology, fearing acknowledgment of the power of social values as a slippery slope and a sign of intellectual inferiority. One extreme example, relevant here, of how researchers with different social values interpret results differently is a pair of articles by Lawrence Mead (2001) and Mark Rank and Thomas Hirschl (2001).

Rank and Hirschl conducted a study examining the likelihood that Americans will experience either poverty or affluence between ages 25 to 75. They found that about 30 percent of Americans experience at least one year of affluence with no risk of poverty during this period of their lives. This group of Americans is mostly white with 12 years of schooling or more. Another group of about 30 percent of Americans experiences at least one year of poverty with no prospect of experiencing affluence. Rank and Hirschl interpret this as evidence that some people start in a more vulnerable position than others, making them more likely to fail in the first place, while Mead, in sharp contrast, interprets this as evidence that "the affluent typically work *much* harder than the poor" (672, emphasis in original).

## SOCIAL VALUES IN THE CONTEXT OF THE FINANCIAL AID CONVERSATION

Our social values and the lens they construct are at work in the context of financial aid as well. Here, people accommodate support for the student loan program within their framework of the American Dream because it seems consistent with their idea of working hard for one's own success. Significantly, this support has remarkable endurance, even as dissatisfaction with the outcomes associated with reliance on student borrowing increases. Our collective perception of congruence with our most cherished values provides a sort of insulation for new student loan policies that expand their use, which has proven very difficult to penetrate. In marked contrast, advocates have not been able to similarly muster strong support for transfers to help finance college because transfers seem incompatible with this effort + ability = outcomes equation.

This perceived clash with the rhetoric of the American Dream blocks momentum for alternative interventions even when they may be more likely to realize results that align with the American Dream. In this narrative, student loan programs and merit-based aid are articulated as requiring an investment of personal resources—financial or intellectual—by individuals, while need-based aid is framed as a "handout." This handout designation dooms transfers to the political margins, as U.S. political rhetoric has largely framed handouts as rewarding the lazy, while student loans and merit aid flourish in part due to their alignment with the belief that college—and rewards that make it more affordable—should be made available to those who are willing to work.

Clearly, then, people's beliefs about appropriate ways to finance college are not founded only on objective facts but are at least shaped in part by our social values. Social values (or our ideologies) are not necessarily bad; they can provide core consistency to our disparate beliefs, animate our collective identity, and motivate prosocial behaviors. However, they can be illogical and intransigent, even at times blinding us from being able to see the truth, which may make policy reform more difficult, as it requires first untangling our mental maps before productive policy change can happen.

Thus, if we want the student loan research presented in this book to matter, we contend that it is not enough to have good findings or to simply state our own theories of how the world works. Individuals seldom discard their own worldviews in light of even the most methodologically sound evidence, and a paradigm is not easily abandoned without a contest over a new way of thinking. Instead, people are likely to mentally discount or even reject data to cling to their assumptions and understandings. They may not even be able to see the collisions between facts and their theories, with their vision constrained to the field as they have defined it.

To break through those blockades, we must show how our findings align with the core beliefs of the general public on different parts of the political spectrum while simultaneously knitting together the anomalies that demand a new financial aid paradigm. This requires first precisely analyzing what those beliefs are and what they will accommodate. It seems to us, with regard to financial aid, that what the general public is against is not wealth transfers per se, but the watering down of one of the very things they think matters and defines America, the axiom that effort and ability should determine people's outcomes.

Page, Bartels, and Seawright's (2013) findings provide an example of how the general public supports wealth transfers with regard to college. They find that 78 percent of the general public favors the federal government providing resources to make sure that everyone who wants to go to college can do so. In today's divisive political context, this is near unanimity. But all too often, the general public does not vote that interest because they have not received a message that allows them to reconcile the idea of a wealth transfer with their belief that people should work for what they get. This suggests that, even as recognition of the failings of the student loan system grows, individuals will be unlikely to reject student loans wholesale unless and until they can point to an alternative that they view as consistent with their core ideas about how the world should work.

## DEMANDING EXCEPTIONALISM OF INDIVIDUALS BUT NOT OUR INSTITUTIONS LEAVES THE AMERICAN DREAM HOLLOW FOR MANY

Institutions provide the economic conditions that make it possible for hard work and ability to determine an individual's success or failure. However, it is easy to blind the general public to the important function of institutions in determining success because of the American people's strong desire to feel as though they control their own destinies. This ideal that those who work hard succeed is woven into many of our cultural artifacts, inculcated in children through literature and storytelling and romanticized in motion pictures for decades through the acting careers of such movie stars as John Wayne and Clint Eastwood. We not only tell this story to ourselves but, indeed, have exported it throughout the world as a core part of the American mystique, even as its power to truly explain the workings of the American economy has eroded.

### SELF-EFFICACY: PEOPLE'S I-CAN-DO BELIEFS

Self-efficacy helps explain how the American Dream has been so central in making America what it is today, by facilitating striving and encouraging Americans to ascribe their failures to internal deficits rather than adverse external forces. Bandura (1994) defines self-efficacy as "people's beliefs about their capabilities to produce designated levels of performance that exercise influence over events that affect their lives" (71). A self-efficacy assessment sounds like this: "I can put forth the designated level of effort, and I have the ability to perform the task; therefore, I can conclude with confidence that I will achieve a desired outcome by investing my individual resources." If this is true, then we can assume that if the person fails, he or she will attribute that failure to a lack of effort or ability—or both—and is then more likely to seek strategies that increase either effort or ability, or both, rather than looking externally for contributors to the failure. We could also expect that this individual is likely to display the characteristics of persistence, increased effort, and coping skills (Bandura 1977, 1986, 1997).

I saw this American spirit in the lives of my parents, and it inspired me, a kind of doggedness that has defined America in times of war and great calamity and in the everyday lives of its poor. This spirit is evident in the black-and-white photograph that hangs on the wall in Melinda's living room of her grandmother as a child, sorting fabric scraps on the floor underneath the counter of the butcher shop Melinda's great-grandfather opened when he arrived in the United States from Denmark, and where he worked seven days a week until he died before he turned 40. As a result of self-efficacy's emphasis on individual resources, the individual is seen as having the capability to change his life circumstances, sometimes referred to as "personal causality" (Franzblau and Moore 2001, 85; Scheier and Carver 1987). Self-efficacy reflects that part of the American Dream that conservative academics emphasize, that owners of capital need reinforced, that psychologists need to instill in their clients because it is the part of the equation that their clients can control. It is seen in the perennial news stories about people who climb out of poverty against all odds and is part of every commencement speech across this country every spring.

Similarly, when I talk to my kids about their academic outcomes, I talk to them about what they can control—the level of effort they put into a given task. Like many other parents, I don't want to hear about what the teacher is doing or not doing, but instead, what my children are doing to control their own outcomes. This ethos resonates with people. It is core to the stories we tell ourselves about why we succeed and why we fail. As a result, it is easy to create an imbalance between individuals' contributions toward their own success and what institutions contribute, even when evidence clearly reveals the extent to which institutions influence outcomes. As a result, we end up demanding exceptionalism of people while we demand something far less of institutions. The outcome, as we will contend throughout this book, is patterns that make hollow the American Dream.

## Individual Effort without Acknowledgment of Institutional Facilitation Produces a Fascination with the Exceptional

When people have confidence in their personal capabilities (effort and ability) and when institutions are responsive to their effort and ability, the individual is unlikely to even notice the role that institutions are playing. When institutional arrangements function properly, they can be taken for granted. Melinda's early life was a classic example of this, surrounded by quality schools, adequate infrastructure, available jobs, fair financial institutions, accessible health care, and safe neighborhoods. Her parents did not have to spend much energy navigating those systems to secure what the family needed, nor did they have to grapple with the insecurities confronted when these institutions are unresponsive, unavailable, or ill equipped. So Melinda was able to focus her energy on performing tasks.

When institutions nearly invisibly facilitate individual success, they fade to the background, and arriving at success can easily look like the "natural" result of this exerted effort and ability. This skews our collective attribution of causation and then obscures significant differences in the contexts experienced by different individuals and their effects. Institutions are like breathing—they are taken for granted. However, if breathing stops, or is interrupted, the individual is forced to think about the essential nature of oxygen to survival. Similarly, the facilitating role of institutions may not be noticed unless it is interrupted or disappears. People in everyday life should not have to think about whether institutions will be responsive to their use of effort, just like they should not have to think about breathing. Children, in particular, should be secure in the availability of these institutional supports.

The problem is that, in America, institutions are not functioning properly for many people, particularly disadvantaged children. Critically, they are failing in systematic ways, not randomly. Low-income and minority children, in particular, are routinely failed by the very institutions that are supposed to facilitate their achievement. Every day, these Americans are forced to think about how institutions will respond to their investment of effort when performing normative behaviors. They may have to compensate for institutions that are absent or destructive. Too often, then, they can only succeed when they are exceptional—compensating for institutions that have failed—and are blamed when they fail to rise to this unjustly higher hurdle.

## SELF-EFFICACY THEORY AND INSTITUTIONS

While much of this theory downplays the significance of institutions, Bandura (1997) does discuss the influence of inequitable institutional structures in people's perceptions about their capabilities. According to Bandura (1984), when people make a self-efficacy judgment, they not only judge their personal capability to perform a task; they also judge the role that institutions play in their performance:

> Self-appraisal of efficacy is, therefore, a judgmental process in which the relative contribution of ability and nonability factors to performance success and failure must be weighed. The extent that people will alter their self-percepts of efficacy from performance experiences will depend upon such factors as the difficulty of the task, the amount of effort they had to expend . . . *the amount of external aid they receive, the situational circumstance under which they perform, the quality of the apparatus.* (243, emphasis added)

He uses the following example to distinguish between the two types of control: "Piece-rate workers may control their incomes by how hard they work but exercise no control over the unit pay rate the system sets" (Bandura 1997, 21). Their individual effort can influence their outcomes, but only up to a ceiling, conscribed by the rate set by the institution and the natural limit of the number of hours in a day. Conversely, an institutional intervention—here, increasing the rate of pay—could exert an unlimited influence over the wages earned. Similarly, technology that increases the worker's productivity could also increase pay, holding the pay rate constant, such that an individual with access to this superior technology would have an inherent advantage.

Bandura further distinguishes between the role of personal and institutional factors in the following passage:

> There are two aspects to exercise of control. The first concerns the level and strength of personal efficacy to produce changes by perseverant effort and creative use of capabilities and resources. The second aspect concerns the modifiability of the environment. This facet represents the constraints and opportunities provided by the environment to exercise personal efficacy. (Bandura 1993, 125)

Despite recognition of the role of institutions, the application of Bandura's theory of self-efficacy, much like in the case of the American Dream, tends to focus on the former (role of the individual) more than on the latter (role of institutions). So, too, in U.S. political discourse, we often give superficial recognition to the relevance of institutional factors in shaping individual outcomes, while our policies and shared values continue to emphasize the centrality of individual effort and ability.

## IMPLICATIONS OF BANDURA'S THEORY OF INSTITUTIONS FOR DISADVANTAGED STUDENTS

According to Bandura (1997), two criteria should be met for self-efficacy to be an accurate predictor of choice of behavior: (1) individuals must have access to sufficient levels of resources, and (2) the resources must have utility for influencing events that matter to the person. The same can be said of the American Dream. When a person's efforts and ability have little effect on outcomes, "I can do" beliefs have little explanatory power: "Efficacy beliefs account for only part of the variation in expected outcomes when outcomes are not completely controlled by quality of performance" (Bandura 1997, 24). In explaining why self-efficacy does not appear to influence earnings, for example, Duncan and Morgan (1981) suggest that self-efficacy, as currently used, applies best to privileged groups:

> A possible reason for weak attitudinal effects is that we are taking a theory that applies to a small group of people at the margin with real choices and opportunities and testing it on a whole group, many of whom may be totally constrained by environment and circumstances. (655)

Similarly, Rosenbaum, Reynolds, and Deluca (2002) claim that self-efficacy underemphasizes institutional factors that shape individual behavior. They find that people "learn whether they have efficacy by whether environments reward or punish their actions" (Rosenbaum, Reynolds, and Deluca, 81). My parents' fervent belief in and exercise of hard work were not sufficient to deliver my family from poverty. Similarly, the ardent aspirations of a talented child will be inadequate to catalyze educational attainment and upward economic mobility without institutions that translate those hopes into meaningful opportunities.

Consequently, when effort and ability are not perceived as the deciding factors, outcome expectations that are related to people's perceptions about institutions are a more accurate predictor of an individual's behavior than efficacy beliefs. Much like the American Dream, self-efficacy theory is based primarily on the assumption that a "normal contingency" exists

(Scheier and Carver 1987, 198), a level playing field on which performance is the primary predictor of outcomes. By ignoring the importance of institutions in determining success, we imperil people's belief in the connection between effort and ability and their own success. This may already be occurring. For example, Hochschild (1995) finds that black Americans "believe in the American Dream—but only sort of" (174). Surrounded by institutions that fail them, the assurance that they can control their own destinies becomes increasingly hollow. Disadvantaged groups learn to doubt, through experience, that their performance is the primary explanation for the outcomes they experience.

## AMERICANS ARE STILL STRIVING

There is no evidence that Americans today are less capable or less committed than in previous generations, in the aggregate, even though they evidence poorer outcomes in terms of economic mobility or even financial security. As an example of how people are exerting similar levels of effort but achieving less financial security, research conducted by the Pew Research Center indicates that in 1971 the middle-income group made up about 61 percent of all Americans, but by 2011 it had shrunk to about 51 percent (Taylor 2012). Moreover, income among the middle-income group fell by 5 percent in the decade of the 2000s, while wealth among this group declined by 28 percent. These losses have resulted in 85 percent of middle-class adults reporting that it is more difficult now than it was a decade ago to maintain their standard of living (Taylor 2012).

These changes do not simply reflect the Great Recession of 2007–2010. The economy expanded in the early 2000s, yet real median household income fell and inequality increased (Mishel, Bernstein, and Allegretto 2006). As Harrison and Bluestone (1988) put it, American families are on a treadmill: they must run faster now to maintain the same standard of living they enjoyed in the early 1970s.

Noting these trends emphasizes the ubiquity of economic concerns in today's America. It is not only the children and families struggling to claw up from the bottom who have reason to doubt the viability of the American Dream, but also those who, having made it to the middle class, confront anxieties and erosion of their quality of life. These concerns extend even to the college-educated. Although during the recent recession workers with a college degree fared slightly better than workers with only a high school diploma, they have also experienced declining wage growth over the past several years. For example, between 2000 and 2011, their wages grew a modest 0.2 percent; between 2002 and 2011, they declined by −2.2 percent; and between 2003 and 2011, they declined by −1.9 percent, on average (Mishel, Bivens, Gould, and Shierholz 2013).

Particularly in today's highly specialized and technology-driven global world, the upward mobility that animates the American Dream is possible only if effort and ability are combined with facilitative institutions. To help explain the facilitative nature of institutions, Elliott and Sherraden (2013) introduced the concept of institutional efficacy. Institutional efficacy takes into account systemic differences in how institutions respond to different groups of people in society (see, e.g., Shapiro, Meschede, and Osoro 2013). Institutional facilitation is the process by which institutional efficacy (a person's perceptions of the extent to which institutions facilitate his or her achievements) promotes healthy self-efficacy beliefs (a positive perception of one's ability to accomplish goals) and the development of positive future identities. If an institution is consistently unresponsive—does not provide people with the power over required resources they need to perform a task successfully—they develop low institutional efficacy.

Post–Great Recession, Americans are surrounded by examples of unsupportive institutions and the crumbling aspirations of those whose effort and ability have failed to yield advancement or, in some cases, even security. An example of an unsupportive institution is the labor market, specifically the productivity/wage gap discussed in more detail in chapter 8. Americans' realization of these factors and their influence on their own likelihood of attaining the American Dream has been slow to develop, hindered again by the nearly invisible workings of institutions. Thus, there has been significant attention given to receiving welfare payments as a disincentive to working (work is an outward manifestation of one's effort) but little attention to the growing gap between productivity and wages (an outward manifestation of institutions' response to effort) as a disincentive to attaining a college degree.

Questioning the labor market's functioning and the value of advanced education as an economic tool requires at least partial rejection of the powerful myth of the American Dream, a pivot away from our dominant paradigm that has, to this point, obscured recognition of the ways in which reality conflicts with our understanding of how the world is supposed to work. This high hurdle makes more noteworthy recent findings that Americans are, indeed, coming to these realizations. Fifty-six percent of workers believe that it is unlikely they will receive a significant pay raise from their current job, and the same percent believe that they will not be able to find a new job that pays more in the next five years (*Washington Post*-Miller Center 2013), even while 68 percent of Americans believe that being rewarded for hard work is very much in line with what they understand the American Dream to mean (*Washington Post*-Miller Center 2013). This lack of connection between wages and productivity may be why the same poll finds that 53 percent of Americans in the middle class perceive that they will either remain there or slip backward in the next few years. As many as half of Americans, then, may have concluded that the American Dream has little relevance in their own lives, at least in the near term.

Not surprisingly, college graduates express similar concerns and face similar challenges; their higher education does not inoculate them from the erosion of the effort + ability equation as a driver of success. For example, Abel, Deitz, and Su (2014) examined the quality of jobs held by underemployed college graduates (i.e., college graduates who are working in jobs that do not require a degree). They find that the segment of recent college graduates in low-wage jobs (an average wage of around $45,000 per year in 2012) rose from nearly 15 percent in 1990 to over 20 percent in 2009. Moreover, the segment of recent college graduates working part-time rose from about 15 percent in 2000 to 23 percent by 2011. Importantly, the U.S. economy is still largely dependent on individuals' willingness to expend significant effort in pursuit of elusive economic gain. Therefore, what is being suggested is that not just having a job but being rewarded according to the level of effort and ability a person puts into that job is also important in motivating an individual to pursue a college degree and to work at a high level, which is important individually and for the macroeconomy. When these outcomes are increasingly out of many Americans' reach, the social underpinnings of the U.S. economy begin to unravel.

So even while people cling to the calculus of the American Dream in the abstract, they question the explanatory power of effort and ability in their own lives (e.g., Hochschild 1995). Adverse conditions are not just a factor in constraining financial progress. Relatively poor outcomes for many Americans today—even those with college educations—are not just a practical concern for those struggling to pay off student loans or for parents eager to see their adult children financially independent. Aggregated across the population and seemingly resistant to the policy tweaks proposed to ameliorate them, these forces and the conclusions they compel imperil the foundation of even this robust American Dream. Unmoored from the paradigms that have governed their understanding of their world and their future, many seek new tools for making sense of what is happening to them and their children.

Today, a majority of Americans (63 percent) no longer believe American institutions are able to facilitate children being better off than their parents (Luhby 2014). Instead of aspiring to the economic mobility they fear will elude them, many now hope just for financial security—not dreaming of getting ahead but striving not to fall behind. In this sense, belief in the American Dream as it relates to one's own life is more malleable for the normal person than the vague ideal one might hold for the country; it can and does readily change depending on the economic context in which one finds oneself.

This diminished hope suggests that people see the American Dream as more or less achievable in their own lives based largely on how institutions such as the education system, labor market, and economic markets are functioning for them (Hochschild and Scovronick 2003), even if they persist in clinging to the American Dream as viable and vibrant in the larger society. Multiplied across the many Americans whose own experiences belie the American Dream, this calculus may be in serious danger.

## EQUAL OPPORTUNITY, NOT EQUAL OUTCOMES

It is common to read about how Americans do not value equal outcomes but instead value equal opportunity. Mead (2001) states it this way: "Social research also focuses on questions of economic inequality when, according to opinion studies, the public is much more interested in equal opportunity. Average Americans care little about whether the Lockean race ends equally, but they insist that everyone have a fair chance to get ahead" (672). What this means is that Americans do not require of their institutions that they be designed with the goal of ensuring that everyone has, for example, a middle-class lifestyle. The mere presentation of evidence showing the magnitude of inequality does not indicate to many Americans that the system is broken, if they still believe that equality is *possible*.

And it does not help, after presenting the evidence of inequality, to explain the liberal theory of structural inequality. The message conveyed when Americans say they want equality of opportunity, not equality of outcomes, is that they aren't interested so much in *how many* people are poor; what they care about is *how* they became poor and what chance they have to leave poverty. If they became poor because they are perceived as not working hard or they don't have the requisite ability, their poor outcomes are quite compatible with the American Dream and not at all indicative of a system that needs to be fixed. Similarly, if they could exit poverty by working harder or making better choices, we can console ourselves that their poverty, while perhaps a tragedy, is not a political crisis.

For example, Gilens (1999) contends that Americans oppose welfare because they perceive welfare to be a program that predominantly serves lazy blacks. In support of his contention, Gilens (1999) reports,

> In 1990 and again in 1994, the General Social Survey asked whether blacks tend to be hardworking or tend to be lazy, allowing respondents to choose any point along a seven-point scale. Forty-four percent of respondents placed blacks on the "lazy" half of this scale, while only 20 percent chose the "hardworking" half. (68)

The perception of blacks as lazy—and the rhetorical linkage between this belief and the policy of income assistance—has had the practical implication of leading to a shift toward decreasing welfare caseloads by quickly returning individuals to work and placing time limits on how long people can receive benefits. When many of these poor black Americans were unable to exit poverty, the worldview that judged them as "lazy" placed causality for this continued poverty squarely on the shoulders of their presumed inadequate effort. Their vision obscured by the constraints of a narrow understanding of poverty's causes, most Americans did not even look elsewhere.

## FOR CAPITALISM TO THRIVE, PEOPLE MUST BE CONDITIONED TO STRIVE FOR EXCELLENCE

What is important for a capitalist system like ours is that everyone has the opportunity to succeed. Capitalism thrives when its institutions create a competitive environment in which people are incentivized to work harder than their neighbor to achieve financial success (i.e., to strive for success). It is in the process of striving, pushing oneself to limits not thought possible, that innovation occurs. This is likely why many Americans are drawn to sports and heroes. It explains American invention and the considerable sacrifice of many in our own families and throughout our shared history.

Sports is a very visual example of striving, not only at the moment of competition but in all that leads up to it in the gym, on the track, and at the table. We can see the results of this striving in the athletes' sculpted bodies or the superhuman feats they perform. It is also why so many of us are drawn to the stories of poor people fighting against all odds to overcome poverty and to one day become well off. It is woven into the origin stories of some of our most successful companies and held out to our children as though it was an axiom rather than an extraordinary case. We treasure these stories as affirmations of the American Dream and inspiration for our own struggles.

At the same time, because we value striving, the idea of giving some-one a wealth transfer can create a very negative emotional reaction from Americans. We don't want our own stories to be ones of being given a hand up. We want to tell others and for them to believe that it was through our own hard work that we—against all odds—achieved success. Similarly, we don't want to see others receive a handout that we fear may give them an advantage, if we view that we are solely responsible for our own outcomes.

What we are suggesting is that Americans favor individualism and have a tendency toward diminishing the role that institutions play in who suc-ceeds. Therefore, we should not be stunned that in the public discourse, at different times in our history, the role of institutions in people's success has taken a backseat to the role of the individual. In some ways, we want individuals to take center stage, but a problem arises when institutions are allowed to ignore their own roles in success and failure. Since at least the 1970s, the political Right (or maybe more specifically the wealthy; see Page, Bartels, and Seawright 2013) has capitalized on this tendency of the American people to favor individualism. That is, they have been very adept at framing the discussion of who succeeds as a question of institu-tions versus individual behavior. This framing was helped by the fact that we had just waged the War on Poverty, which emphasized the role of insti-tutions, and so the pendulum was perhaps poised to swing back. Framed as favoring individual agency over the idea that we are at the mercy of external forces, it is no surprise that Americans choose to believe and side with the Right even when the policy interventions that spring from this worldview do not favor them, and even when their own experiences give reason to doubt this accounting.

The Right has been able to frame the discussion of success in this man-ner, in part, because the Left has been unwilling to acknowledge the role of individuals in determining their success both in public discourse and also in the theories they have put forth about economic inequality. By largely excising individual agency from explanations of outcomes, they have cre-ated a vacuum that has allowed others' articulation of the role of individu-als to prevail. They often view individual-level explanations as "victim blaming," though they could be viewed as emphasizing the importance of human agency. Consequently, a false argument has dominated our time, one that pits institutions against individual behavior rather than correctly understanding their interplay and interdependence.

The structural failure versus individualism debate is one that the Left is doomed to lose in the minds of the American public, in the lived experi-ences of individuals in most of the U.S. economy, and in the annals of history. In our system of capitalism, programs and ideas that are portrayed as diminishing the need for striving are seen as counterproductive, even ill-advised. And because liberal researchers have been seemingly either too high-minded or too myopic to talk to the general public about how their findings about structural failures align with American individualism and how institutions work best when utilized by individuals also leveraging their own contributions, their research has had little effect on policy in the last 40 years. They have largely talked to each other about how structural failings are paramount in understanding poverty. They focus on method-ological rigor, not pragmatic application, and as a result, they have ensured near irrelevance in policy and general public discourse. At the same time, Right-leaning researchers have taken their message that individual behav-ior is paramount for explaining poverty to the general public. They have gone so far as to create their own research institutes and think tanks where their researchers can be rewarded for their efforts. They present a unified message, and that message has largely carried the day.

Certainly we are painting with broad brush strokes; not all Left-leaning academics disregard the public, and certainly some ideas advocated by the Right have been quickly discarded as out of touch with reality. Moreover, it should be clear that it is not as though the Left does not have ideologi-cal grounds on which to build a case to the general public; they have just largely failed to do so. Many Americans would readily embrace the idea that individual effort must be complemented by supportive institutions and are, in fact, primed to concede the importance of external factors in shap-ing their own success and that of others, to a degree.

For instance, Page, Bartels, and Seawright (2013) found that while only a minority (40 percent) of the wealthy believe that the minimum wage should be high enough to prevent full-time workers from living in poverty, the vast majority (78 percent) of the rest of America believes it should. These findings represent a lost opportunity to make a case for institutional interventions that can be readily accommodated within the rhetorical foot-print of the American Dream. What is needed is a conceptual framework that incorporates how individuals maximize human agency while recog-nizing the meaning of institutional constraints on the ability of the poor, in particular, to achieve successful outcomes.

## THE PRESENCE OF EXCEPTIONS COMFORTS US INTO BELIEVING THAT THERE IS EQUALITY OF OPPORTUNITY

What has been lost in the public discussion of structural failures is a dialogue that roots wealth transfers as not only acceptable within but even essential to American social values. As we stated earlier, to challenge the dominant ideology, it is not enough to say that inequality exists; inequality itself is no threat to the American political system. People need to know that *why* it exists is because not everyone's use of effort and ability is treated equally. Without providing the debt-dependent person with a wealth transfer—in fact, through an asset investment or, in kind, by the free provision of human capital, or both—he can never match the success of the person born into the asset-empowered family by using the same amount of effort and ability. Even outpacing the more advantaged person's investments of skill and labor may fail to yield commensurate outcomes.

For example, farmers can no longer compete in the modern world unless they have access to a tractor, no matter how hard they work or how well they plan. Few teachers could succeed without projectors and computers, regardless of their talents. In this highly capital-dependent and technology-driven world, failing to provide people born into debt-dependent families with more than the minimum required to survive ensures that only the exceptional among them—and, likely, not even all of those—can possibly succeed. On the converse, for those born into the asset-empowered family, even inferior expenditure of effort and ability may result in considerable success. Surrounded by supportive institutions and the technological advantages their resources purchase, they can put in less effort and have less ability and achieve higher heights; they do not have as steep a hill to climb, and their individual capacities are augmented, not thwarted, as a result of the resources to which they have access.

The workings of these institutions—for and against individuals' return on effort and ability in predictably inequitable ways—are obscured by the relative invisibility of these institutional forces, hidden as they are by the powerful narrative of the American Dream, which predisposes people to see their success and failure as deriving primarily from individuals' own characteristics and behaviors. This flawed causation not only skews attribution at the individual level, magnified across society, but this frame has potent political effects as well.

As a result of inadequate articulation of the role that resources play in augmenting people's use of effort and ability, when it comes time to vote, people often vote against wealth transfers and redistribution policies, even when those policies would support their own success. This has led to a welfare system—of which education is a central part—that is focused on ensuring that those who "deserve to be poor" remain poor unless they can display exceptionalism. Predictably, then, it is a welfare system that fails the majority of those who participate in it. That is, our institutions demand exceptionalism of the poor, and consigns them to remain in poverty unless they can sufficiently exceed expectations. Exceptionalism is demonstrated when the debt-dependent are able to achieve success similar to the asset-empowered without the same advantages. This narrow needle through which an individual can expect to thread one's hopes for the future does little, of course, to affirm the reality and vitality of the American Dream in the lives of most people, even as we collectively cling to these extraordinary stories as "evidence" of the world as we want to believe it to be.

The average person requires grounds for believing that achieving the American Dream is possible; these grounds come from having experiences with facilitative institutions augmenting their use of effort and ability that leads to higher levels of success. It is not very compelling to identify people born into debt-dependent families who have beaten the odds through abnormally high levels of effort or ability, as we are wont to do as a society, and say, "See, opportunities exist for the poor; they just don't work hard." These people are exceptional in their ability to hope against all hope, if not being downright delusional on some level. Moreover, if we look at their lives long enough and hard enough, we will likely find that they may be exceptions also in that they received help at important times in their lives that allowed them to turn their effort into success. They may have a story of one teacher who went to extraordinary lengths to assist them, or someone giving them a place to stay when they had none, or of being discovered while singing in a bar.

These exceptions are poetic and certainly personally meaningful, but they do not constitute evidence of the viability of the assumptions within the American Dream. Nor do these stories answer the counterfactual of what those individuals could have achieved, similarly endowed but supported, instead of challenged, by the institutions surrounding them. Instead, as befitting a welfare system that relies too heavily on philanthropy, our system does not help all the poor equally. It helps sporadically and usually only those who in some way stand out from the rest; it is only our desperate search for shreds with which to affirm our view of how the world works that convinces us that these are anything but rare and noble cases of beating incredible odds.

## REWARDING BASED ON EXCEPTIONALISM AMONG THE POOR BREEDS INEQUALITY

As our own stories illustrate, the person born into a debt-dependent family will have to expend additional effort to achieve financial well-being, often long after the person born into a resource-rich family with similar attributes does. And these disparate outcomes are not just damaging to the disadvantaged individuals. The existence of such inequity undermines the validity of the institutions that are supposed to facilitate equitable chances of success and thus weakens our social contract. When the same amount of effort results in a debt-dependent individual being less likely to achieve financial well-being than the asset-empowered individual, and when the effort and ability required for one who starts from a disadvantage to reach success are far greater than for one who begins ahead, these inequities expose failings in the American economic system and threaten our ideals. This is inequity in the American context, when people begin to recognize that effort and ability are no longer decisive in who succeeds and who fails. Those who are advantaged in the current system and those who are not should all be concerned about growing inequity, given the dangers it poses to the social order as we know it.

Particularly in education, long considered an important institution for leveling the playing field, the clash between what we tell ourselves about our American institutions and what those institutions actually deliver is glaring. This collision between narrative and reality is not just rhetorically significant; history suggests that if people are consistently confronted with inequitable institutional structures, they attempt to alter those structures. As Bandura (1997) writes, "Conditions combining high personal efficacy and environmental unresponsiveness generate resentment, protest, and collective efforts to change existing institutional practices" (21). If they fail, these people remain confident in their abilities but seek alternative avenues to obtain what they want. These behaviors are not deviant, then, but rather are understandable conclusions drawn in the face of consistently unsupportive institutions.

This suggests that, in some cases, poor children confronted by low-quality schools and only distant prospects for return on their educational investments, for example, may be making a rational decision if they disengage from academic pursuits in favor of other alternatives, such as sports or even crime. Even casual observers of the U.S. political system can note signs that we may be approaching this magical tipping point. As more people—including those who believe that they have acted as the system has taught them—conclude that it is time to attempt to alter existing institutional structures because of a lack of responsiveness to their investment of effort and ability, the strains on the status quo will increase. Tinkering around the edges of these institutions—by reducing the interest rates on student loans or modestly limiting increases in tuition—is unlikely to forestall revolution born of existential crisis. We see this in incidents around the country, such as in the Ferguson protests, the fast-food restaurant strikes, the Occupy Wall Street movement, and others. Increasingly aware that their own efforts are not yielding promised returns, Americans—particularly young people—are examining the institutions that surround them with a more critical eye.

## EDUCATION AS AN EQUALIZER AND KEY PATH TO THE AMERICAN DREAM

The significance of the U.S. education system in sustaining the American Dream cannot be overstated. Americans' understanding of "effort and ability" prominently features educational attainment, particularly the higher education widely understood to correlate with superior employment and earnings prospects and then upward mobility. Education—particularly beyond high school—is the primary medium through which Americans believe the U.S. economy works to realize individual dreams. Here, too, however, the aspirations of a generation of young people are colliding with the economic realities they confront, contributing to the shaky foundation on which the American Dream stands today.

Cumulatively, these anomalies are provoking a crisis in our financial aid paradigm, leading to growing calls for a different way of structuring this critical institution. As in questions about financial aid more narrowly, assessing the failings of education as an equalizing institution requires asking the right questions and carefully examining the right indicators. Understanding the limits of "education as equalizer" demands more than just satisfying ourselves that those who go to college are mostly better off than those who don't. Instead, it should demand that individuals' exertion of their efforts in pursuing a degree and their abilities—primarily intellectually—yield commensurate outcomes. Instead, while it is clear that it does pay to get an education, there is plenty of evidence to suggest that it pays off unevenly.

First, economically disadvantaged students carry their inferior academic preparation—forged in inferior primary and secondary schools and exacerbated by familial differences in educational investments—into postsecondary education, where it contributes to lower completion rates (Bailey and Dynarski 2011) and longer paths to a degree because of the need to take remedial classes (Engle and Tinto 2008). Second, even highly qualified students do not achieve equitably in college, as the economics of higher education strongly influence institutional selection to steer even high-achieving low-income students or students of color to less selective schools that spend less per student on instruction, have lower graduation rates, and yield poorer labor market returns than more competitive institutions (Carnevale and Strohl 2013).

Indeed, analysis of this 'undermatching' (Hoxby and Avery 2012) suggests the existence of two tiers of higher education and powerful forces that track students into one or the other, based more on socioeconomic status than innate ability. Higher education cannot be an equalizing force if it delivers an unequal product with highly disparate outcomes. As evidence of the gap between different types of institutions, more than half of community college students fail to complete a degree, receive a certificate, or transfer to a four-year institution within six years (NCES 2011), considerably poorer interim outcomes than students at more selective four-year institutions.

Even college completion does not erase the legacy of inequity. Despite the fact that education nearly always "pays" compared with failure to pursue postsecondary studies, research suggests that the precise level of economic advantage afforded by a higher education depends on school selectivity, major, and chosen occupation. Specifically, the rate of return on a bachelor's degree from a noncompetitive four-year private institution is under 6 percent, whereas the rate of return on a bachelor's degree at the most competitive public institutions is over 12 percent (Owen and Sawhill 2013). Although there is certainly an economic need for diverse majors and a case to be made for the nonfinancial benefits of postsecondary education, the extent to which career choice may be influenced by the student's socioeconomic background also warrants examination because the lifetime difference in earnings between, for example, a student who majored in engineering and a student who studied arts or humanities can be well over $1 million (Schneider 2013).

Finally, even when two students earn the exact same degree from the exact same institution, the real value of that credential may vary depending on how they financed it, as student loan debt may erode asset accumulation for years following degree completion, thus increasing the real cost of the degree (e.g., Hiltonsmith 2013). And, of course, the accumulated advantages that some privileged students carry throughout their lives—connections, social mores, and cultural norms, in particular—can facilitate superior labor-market outcomes, particularly in the upper echelons of the economy.

All of these disparities assume a core equity in the likelihood of making it to the point of higher education decision making when, in reality, the structure and context of higher education today work in many ways—some explicit, and some nearly imperceptible—to affect the calculus with which differently situated children and families contemplate their futures. Today, high college costs, due in part to diminishing state funding and declining availability of nonrepayable financial aid, as well as poorer labor-market outcomes, may raise doubts in the minds of parents and children about whether the return on college is too risky to justify the investment of required financial and personal resources. These questions, of course, are far more common and far more salient for low-income and otherwise debt-dependent students than for those with slack in their family finances and a history of seeing institutions mostly facilitate their success.

The population raising these doubts has grown significantly, however, as the universe experiencing efficacy-building success has successively shrunk. In the lives of individual students and in the aggregate for this generation, education—one of the most critical institutions shaping opportunity in today's America—may be seen as less capable of facilitating a path to the American Dream. In the absence of substitute institutions capable of playing this role, Americans are well justified in worrying that this dream is slipping beyond their grasp.

## Education's Welfare Function in America

Since the beginning of the 20th century, education has become a locus for the American emphasis on opportunity through expanded support for public schools, colleges, and universities and eventually through provision of government subsidies to facilitate individual access to higher education. In 1976, discussing the function of education in the American welfare system, Janowitz wrote,

> Perhaps the most significant difference between the institutional bases of the welfare state in Great Britain and the United States was the emphasis placed on public education—especially for lower income groups—in the United States. Massive support for the expansion of public education, including higher education, in the United States must be seen as a central component of the American notion of welfare— the idea that through public education both personal betterment and national social and economic development would take place. (34–35)

Although now an accepted part of our approach to fostering upward mobility, placing education in this central role was not a foregone conclusion but instead an explicit and intentional decision about how our nation, specifically, would build policy structures to complement individual effort and ability. While European nations have relied on the "direct redistributive role of the welfare state to reconcile citizenship and markets," the United States has chosen to use education as a lever for ensuring equitable outcomes (Carnevale and Strohl 2010, 83). This distinctly American conviction—that economic disparity can be narrowed through individual effort in school, the pursuit of higher education, and calculated public investments in educational opportunities—runs deep.

In the past few decades, however, while Americans individually still mostly see education as a gateway to opportunity, there has nonetheless been a repositioning and repurposing of education policies within a shifting frame of "welfare." Education has been increasingly viewed as a primarily individual, rather than societal, good, with the accompanying retrenchment paralleled by cuts in other areas of welfare policy as well. These changes have had the cumulative effect of reshaping the social contract such that accessing this key conduit to the American Dream becomes an increasingly individual obligation. Occurring in tandem with changes in the labor-market outcomes realized through these educational investments, this "risk shift" (Hacker 2006, 1) has further escalated Americans' sense of the elusive nature of their own ladders to upward mobility.

## CHANGE IN THE COMMON PARLANCE

In the higher education domain, this shift can be clearly traced by examining political pronouncements about financial aid since the 1965 enactment of the Higher Education Act. In talking about the Higher Education Act Reauthorization of 1968, President Lyndon B. Johnson (November 8, 1965) said, "So to thousands of young people education will be available. And it is a truism that education is no longer a luxury. Education in this day and age is a necessity." During this period, the federal government's role was understood as making education available to all. This represented a focus on opportunity for all low-income children as a critical part of maintaining the American way of life. An example of this is when, speaking of the Higher Education Act Reauthorization of 1980, President Jimmy Carter (October 3, 1980) said, "We've brought college within reach of every student in the nation who's qualified for higher education. The idea that lack of money should be no barrier to a college education is no longer a dream—it is a reality."

In education as in labor arrangements, income supports, and other policies that touch family finances, a shift occurred in the mid-1980s in how we discuss education and in what that rhetoric says about what we prioritize and how we see the world. Instead of education being framed as a subject in which the federal government had a large stake, the burden of paying for college shifted to the individual. For instance, President Ronald Reagan (August 16, 1983) explicitly articulated this shift: "The cost of education is primarily the responsibility of the family. The Federal Government has a role to play in helping needy students get a chance to receive a college education." Clearly, then, as with other welfare policies, one's view of education is based on values—assumptions about how systems are to work and which goods are to be maximized—which then drive the metrics emphasized and the outcomes considered acceptable.

With this shift toward individual responsibility for paying for college came a shift toward financial aid policies that defined opportunity as opportunity for the exceptional few: those so economically constrained that they should be given some remedial assistance and those so demonstrably talented that they should be explicitly rewarded. In essence, then, the American education system and the "welfare" it secures has come to be defined more by outcomes (i.e., you have to first achieve exceptional outcomes, which ignores the fact that achieving exceptional outcomes is, in part, about having the opportunity to do so) than by opportunity, in sharp contrast to how we traditionally think about what policy is supposed to secure.

This is ironic because the American system is not supposed to be focused on outcomes, but on the process, the opportunity, the "how." In this frame, we tell ourselves that all that matters is that two students can both end up in college, as though it doesn't matter how much one has to borrow to get there. We pretend that it's fair if two students both end up in the same elite school, even though they didn't have the same opportunities for achieving this outcome or, then, have to expend the same effort and ability to realize it. When their similar educational paths lead to different states of financial well-being, we tell ourselves that these disparate outcomes are inconsequential because even the disadvantaged student is better off than he would have been without that education.

But of course the *how*—the process, the opportunity—does matter. It's at the center of the story we tell ourselves about how the American economy—and education system—is supposed to work. The *how* matters for charting viable upward paths for disadvantaged students, and it matters for maintaining the legitimacy of the education system as the great equalizer in society.

## RISING COLLEGE COSTS THREATEN EDUCATION'S WELFARE FUNCTION

It is well documented that high college costs make the education path to economic mobility more difficult for low- to moderate-income youth. As these costs have risen precipitously, so, too, has Americans' sense that this path is narrower. The College Board (2012), which produces an annual report tracking college costs, estimates that the average total cost of college attendance and room and board at an in-state, public four-year college for the 2012–13 school year was $8,655, an increase of 4.8 percent from the prior school year and a continuation of trends of nearly uninterrupted cost increases over the past several years. The average total cost of a private four-year college also rose by 4.2 percent in 2012–13 to $29,056 (College Board 2012).

When it comes to determining children's educational outcomes, these costs are significant. College choice researchers consistently find that rising college costs have a negative effect on college enrollment decisions (Heller 1997; Leslie and Brinkman 1988; McPherson and Schapiro 1998). For example, McPherson and Schapiro (1998) estimated that a $150 net cost increase (in 1993–94 dollars) resulted in a 1.6 percentage point reduction in enrollment among low-income students.

Even after financial aid, family contribution, work study, and loans are considered, youths still face significant unmet need. According to the 2002 Advisory Committee on Student Financial Assistance (ACSFA), a group charged by Congress with enhancing access to postsecondary education for low-income youths, unmet need is "the portion of college expense not covered by the expected family contribution and student aid, including work-study and loans" (5). Oliver and Shapiro (2006) suggest that high unmet need for college is largely the result of low asset accumulation, which, of course, manifests predictable patterns according to race and income class. According to ACSFA (2002), low-income youths on average face an unmet need of $3,800 per year at four-year public colleges and $6,200 at four-year private colleges. They estimate that financial barriers prevent 48 percent of college-qualified, low-income youths from enrolling in postsecondary institutions.

## EROSION OF STATE FUNDING

Increased college tuition has not happened in a vacuum, nor is this cost increase solely the responsibility of educational institutions. Rather, rising college costs are driven in part by decreased state funding for colleges and universities and exacerbated by financial aid that has failed to keep pace (Long 2010), both factors largely out of the control of institutions of higher education. Nationwide, states spent 28 percent less on higher education in 2013 than in 2008, cuts that are directly correlated with increases in tuition and other fees and reductions in educational quality (Oliff et al. 2013). Rising college tuition prices have consequently taken the place of taxpayer-funded state support (Geiger and Heller 2011) in balancing the books at institutions of higher education—prices that are increasingly untenable for their consumers. According to Geiger and Heller (2011), in 1980, student tuition accounted for about 20 percent of major universities' operating funds, but by 2006, this share had more than doubled, to 43 percent.

These trends have resulted in a de facto privatization of higher education, even at public institutions. This accounting, seemingly inconsistent with our purported priority on education and its central role as the welfare intervention that is supposed to fuel upward mobility, compels a reexamination of the policies that animate our higher education system. There is urgency around this cause because the evidence clearly suggests an immediate cost to those disadvantaged young people who are dissuaded from continuing their studies by a reluctance to assume all of these costs themselves.

## COLLEGE IS STILL OUR BEST HOPE

The belief in the potential of education to act as an equalizer is supported by research, which consistently shows that a person who attains a four-year college degree earns more than a person who does not attain a four-year degree. A four-year college graduate's median earnings in 2008 were $55,700 compared with $21,900 for a high school graduate (College Board 2010). Even for those who do not graduate, having some college appears to pay off. Adults with some college have median after-tax earnings that are 16 percent higher than those with only a high school diploma. Carnevale, Rose, and Cheah (2011) found that, over his or her lifetime, an adult with a high school diploma earns an average of $1,547,000, while an adult with a four-year college degree earns $2,268,000.

Similarly to the processes leading up to college graduation, this college wage premium does not function equitably, however. Not surprisingly, women and racial minorities earn less than white men at all levels of educational attainment. For example, a woman with a four-year degree earns about 25 percent less on average than a man with a four-year degree over the course of their working years. The type of degree also matters, particularly in today's increasingly specialized economy. An adult with a master's degree earns about $2,671,000, while an adult with a doctoral degree earns about $3,252,000 over the course of his or her working years (Carnevale et al. 2011).

Despite unequal distribution of the gains, attaining a college degree continues to be one of the few remaining paths out of poverty in America. For instance, Urahn, Currier, Elliott, Wechsler, Wilson, and Colbert (2012) found that 47 percent of children born in the bottom family-income quintile remain in the bottom quintile as adults if they do not earn a college degree. In contrast, only 10 percent of those children born in the bottom family-income quintile with a college degree remain there as adults. Children who are born into the bottom family-income quintile and attain a college degree are as adults three times more likely to make it to the top family-income quintile and four times more likely to move from the bottom family-wealth quintile to the top when compared with those poor children who do not earn college degrees. In an era of declining economic mobility, a college degree appears to be the surest way to climb the ladder of opportunity, an affirmation that only serves, of course, to further raise the stakes in the quest to make higher education attainable.

In today's economy, a college degree is a prerequisite for most so-called good jobs that provide a living wage. A recent report by Carnevale, Smith et al. (2011) found that only 36 percent of high school graduates without any college education earn at least $35,000 a year (which the authors consider to be a living-wage cutoff, nearly 150 percent of the poverty level for a family of four). In contrast, 46 percent of those with some college and 69 percent of college degree holders earn above this living-wage cutoff. In addition, the number of living-wage jobs accessible to those without any college education is declining (Carnevale, Smith et al. 2011), which suggests that postsecondary education will become even more important for access to living-wage jobs in the future.

Research also suggests that bachelor's degree attainment begins to equalize opportunity by parental class and income (Hout 1984, 1988; Torche 2011). However, while poor students who make it through college today may enjoy more equitable opportunities than they would otherwise, the unequal chances of completing a degree—which is itself heavily influenced by parental resources (Bowen, Chingos, and McPherson 2009)— make college graduation an important factor in the intergenerational transmission of inequality (e.g., Carnevale and Strohl 2010; Haskins,

Isaacs, and Sawhill 2008). Essentially, then, higher education itself still evidences strong potential to deliver low-income children out of poverty, but the prospects for and conditions surrounding completion of that college education serve to mute these equalizing effects. These are the policy levers to which we must direct our attention, beginning with an accurate assessment of the threats posed by our overreliance on student debt and the real risks to the American Dream.

We raise these questions about the viability of the higher education path to economic mobility—and the equity of the benefits it offers—not because we doubt the importance of education as a catalyst for financial well-being in the United States economy today, but precisely because we believe that the human capital children can accumulate in our educational institutions is so valuable that its elusive and inequitable nature imperils the very foundations of our shared sense of what it means to be an American, and to have a real chance. We examine the student loan system with critical eyes, not because we want to poke holes in the status quo for the sake of inquiry or intellectual sport, but because we believe that an unquestioning allegiance to this approach of financing higher education is alarming in light of the evidence of its corrosive effects and because our reading of history suggests that only drawing attention to these problems can prompt the revolution we believe imperative. We share the analysis and narrative here, not because we think they are the definitive answer on issues of higher education reform for greater equality, but because we desperately want to spark debate about the most important questions that should guide our policy making. We start from this discussion of the values that color Americans' consideration of these issues not only because beginning from this shared foundation increases the likelihood that we can place proposed interventions firmly within the rhetorical landscape of our American Dream, but also because that's what it feels like to have this debate—about student loans, economic mobility, and the future of American higher education policy—in the United States of America.

# FOUR

# The Student Loan Program Has an Equity Problem

Prior to the Servicemen's Readjustment Act of 1944, commonly known as the GI Bill, college students were predominately male, white, and wealthy (Rudolph 1990). There was very little competition from other groups for selection into higher education, especially into the most selective universities. The GI Bill signaled the severing of this tight linkage between economic standing and college enrollment, but it did so unequally, extending greater opportunities to those of relatively lesser means, but still unjustly restricting benefits based on gender and, in particular, color (Herbold 1994–95). Historically black colleges and universities (HBCUs) were not able to accommodate the increased enrollment demand, and most other universities had segregationist policies and practices that made it almost impossible for returning black veterans to be admitted.

During the 1946–47 school year, HBCUs turned away an estimated 20,000 black veterans because of lack of capacity (Herbold 1994–95). With few other institutions to which to turn, just over 1 percent of blacks completed college (Herbold 1994–95). They sometimes faced higher admission requirements than their white counterparts and discrimination in GI Bill lending, along with the accumulated disadvantages of their inferior primary and secondary school preparation. These barriers for black Americans were the result of some white Americans strategically acting to constrain the expectations of blacks with regard to the responsiveness of the education system to their use of effort and ability, even as relatively privileged American veterans. And while these events occurred in another era, we will see later in this chapter how these dynamics continue to persist today, if only in a different form.

What this illustrates is that disadvantaged individuals often hold normative expectations, such as attending college, but are compelled to adopt less desirable patterns of behavior and values (subcultures) to support these behaviors because they lack access to institutional capabilities necessary for achieving these normative expectations (Gans 1968; Gould 1999; Rodman 1963). In the end, the GI Bill, one of the biggest wealth transfers of the 20th century, further augmented the effort and ability of white Americans, thus exacerbating in many cases the disparity faced by black Americans who were further disadvantaged in comparison. Critically, it also may have resulted in black Americans forming beliefs about their own efficacy, as they failed to achieve academically even when nominally afforded access to institutional support for that success. The legacy of this self-doubt may ripple, then, through black Americans' interactions with other powerful institutions as well.

## HIGHER EDUCATION ACT OF 1965

The racist norms and economic self-interest of powerful white interests have proved, of course, remarkably resilient over the course of American history. Shifting political alliances and pressing economic needs slowly opened doors, however. In particular, the growing need for skilled workers and the evolving social climate in the 1960s led to the federal government enacting the Higher Education Act of 1965, which made basic education opportunity grants and a number of other financial aid programs available to minorities as well as to poor white students.

During this period, the goal of financial aid was to keep tuition prices down and increase financial aid to the poor and minorities, those least represented in colleges and universities. It is important to highlight here that, in America, financial aid has been thought of exclusively as a tool for influencing access (access, with respect to the tenets of the American Dream, really has to do with opportunity).

During the 1960s and 1970s, need-based aid was the dominant form of financial aid. Need-based aid is determined based on the assets and income of the prospective student and his or her family, with the financial assistance serving to bridge the gap between a household's own resources and the net price of college access. Factors such as test scores have no bearing on the aid decision, largely in recognition of the effects of relative disadvantage on later academic performance and the importance of providing educational opportunities for all college-committed students, irrespective of their prior academic achievement.

## PRIVATIZATION FAVORED THE WEALTHY

In 1972, changes to the Higher Education Act of 1965 opened the door for the privatization as well as the marketization of higher education (Mendoza 2012). Never understood as a basic right for all children but instead as a benefit to which there was also a significant social utility, higher education was less and less thought of as an integral part of the American welfare system (i.e., as a way out of poverty for low-income students) and increasingly as a commodity to be bought and sold. This came about, at least in part, because the 1972 amendments also facilitated giving aid directly to students instead of to institutions. While seemingly more responsive to the unique financial circumstances of individual students, this shift of resources toward the individual as the unit of intervention set the stage for cost shifts. Over time, individuals and families have been increasingly expected to take on the lion's share of the burden of paying for college, and as a result, colleges have been thrust into competition with one another for students' tuition and financial aid dollars (Burd 2013).

Both of these policy changes, toward privatization and individual aid, favored the wealthy, who were in a better position to take on increased responsibility for paying for college and then were more attractive to universities, particularly the more costly, selective ones. Understanding these market forces and their influence on the higher education system is critical. Through this lens, it is not that wealthy students and their families acted to create laws that favored them; instead, because of their wealth advantage, they were able to benefit more from the changes that occurred and then to angle for perpetuation of a system they found to their satisfaction. In a society that claims effort and ability are the determining factors for success, shifts toward privatization have inherent appeal and easily gain support. However, low-income families and minorities are disadvantaged. Without the resources to successfully compete with wealthy students, they cannot similarly work the rules of privatization to their advantage. Instead of financial aid redressing the disparities these students confront in higher education, it serves to multiply them.

In the 1960s and 1970s, low-income students and their families could rely more heavily on grants to make up for a lack of income and savings, but the shift in the 1980s from need-based to merit-based aid led to a financial aid program that largely subsidizes middle- to upper-income white students to attend college (Baum and Schwartz 1988; Woo and Choy 2011). In the case of merit-based aid, of which scholarships are the most common form, a student with little financial need is just as entitled to aid as students with high levels of financial need, eroding the aid's equalizing power.

Indeed, because of the strong correlations between economic advantage and academic performance, merit-based aid can serve to further intensify inequity (Kiley 2013). Test scores are often the key factor for determining eligibility for merit aid, and privileged students enjoy advantages that may translate into higher scores. Woo and Choy (2011) found that the proportion of undergraduates receiving merit aid rose from 6 percent in the academic year 1995–96 to 14 percent in academic year 2007–08. Between 1982 and 2000, spending on need-based scholarships for undergraduates by the states increased 7.4 percent annually, while spending on merit programs increased 13.6 percent annually. The proportion of state grants awarded based on merit rose from 9 percent to 22 percent during this period (Heller 2002; National Association of State Student Grant and Aid Programs 2001). As of 2001, the 13 states with broad-based merit scholarship programs planned to distribute a combined $709 million in merit awards annually, more than twice the $325 million provided in need-based aid by those states in 1998–99 (Selingo 2001).

Underscoring the importance of narrative and collective ideology in explaining policy preferences, this shift was facilitated by the fact that need-based aid was perceived to be more like a handout, rewarding those who did not put in the effort needed to be successful and who did not have the requisite ability, whereas, in contrast, merit-based aid fit the message that we should reward those who display the most effort and who have the most ability. Critically, this is a message that poor and rich could agree on, even when they fared very disparately as a result of these different policy approaches.

In sum, colleges and universities increasingly are incentivized to act like publicly traded companies whose objective is to drive up the price of stock, in this case, by providing the best facilities, rewards, and amenities to attract students with the most money, which allows them to continue to raise prices. This market also incentivizes having the brightest students because it costs less than offering remedial courses for youths who come from low-income communities and because these students are well-positioned to accrue the accolades that can, in turn, attract additional resources to the institution. Perhaps even more destructive is the fact that this accounting also creates an incentive for universities to bring in the wealthiest students to maximize their profits (Burd 2013), which is increasingly important in an environment of ever-decreasing state support (Hiltonsmith 2013). In general, these financial imperatives make it more appealing for universities to act in ways contrary to their mission of promoting equitable educational opportunity.

Increasingly alarmed at these closing doors of opportunities, some are quick to blame colleges and universities. However, these institutions are, to a certain extent, acting like organizations are supposed to act as part of the market. Through this lens, it is federal and state policies of privatization and marketization of higher education that have created the imperatives to which institutions respond. As a result, rather than serving the very important role in society of being an equalizer for a capitalist system that requires forces outside of the market to ensure that equality of opportunity exists, higher education increasingly works to perpetuate inequalities. Higher education is, then, at best a very weak intervention in our capitalist economy; more frequently, it operates as part of that system.

## CLASS WARFARE IN HIGHER EDUCATION

Elliott and Sherraden (2013) define role expectations as socially shared expectations about how a person, as a member of a group, can be expected to act. As such, they specify a role that a person is expected to play in society. Role expectations are based on the historical and contemporary experiences of a particular social group with institutions and institutional resources for achieving desired ends. Role expectations result from a struggle between individuals over the distributional advantage that institutions provide. Not surprisingly, in an economic system like ours, based on capital, those with wealth are often able to structure role expectations such that they constrain the actions of disempowered groups, as in the case of the implementation of the GI Bill.

Knight (1992) suggests that strategic actors (actors motivated by a desire to maximize their own goals) make choices to achieve desired outcomes. People are strategic in the sense that they make choices based on their expectations about the choices of others (Knight 1992). According to Knight (1992), institutions affect the decision-making process of an individual by providing that individual with information about the choices of others and some form of sanction when an individual does not behave as expected. He describes the struggle between strategic actors in this way:

In any single social interaction the task of a strategic actor is to establish those expectations that will produce his desired distributional outcome, to constrain those with whom he interacts in such a way as to compel them by the force of their expectations to choose that strategy that will lead to the outcome he prefers. (49)

Americans do not want to discuss the reality that there is an ongoing class war over who has the opportunity to attend America's higher education institutions. Whether it is explicit (intentional/planned) or implicit (unintentional/unplanned), it exists, and we need to call it what it is: a battle over the distributional resources higher education provides. It has constrained the opportunities of American students for at least the last generation, and it parallels similar battles in other policy realms, including within the labor market and the social safety net.

One reason for this war is the simple fact that the self-interest of the wealthy and the self-interest of the rest of the population are often at odds. In addition to the chasm in support for raising the minimum wage, described earlier, only 19 percent of the wealthy want the federal government to see that everyone who wants to work can find a job, compared with 68 percent of all Americans (Page et al. 2013). Because the wealthy are largely the ones who invest the most in U.S. enterprises, they stand to lose the most and gain the least from an increase in the minimum wage, and providing everyone with a job is a waste of money from their perspective because they don't need jobs and, in fact, make very little of their money from wages (Elliott and Lewis 2014). They may even view such economic intervention as counterproductive, viewing excess labor supply as a release valve that prevents upward pressure on wages.

The fact that these divergent policy preferences can be ascribed more to rational calculation of self-interest than malevolent machinations underscores the disconnected economic lives of the wealthy and the rest of America; their fates are literally divergent, and this assessment inevitably leads to very different preferred outcomes. Charitable inclinations have never been a good enough reason for most people to deny what is in their own best interest. This clash between the interests of wealthy Americans and the rest of the populace is not our invention. Fox News, the leading conservative news station, frames the opposition between the wealthy and the rest as opposition between "the Makers and the Takers" (see Boguhn 2014).

Regardless of the nefarious or comparatively innocuous origins of these disparate policy priorities, they are maintained in effect through the deliberate and systematic intervention in the U.S. political system.

Our economy, including the education system and the rest of the welfare apparatus, serves to produce the outcomes desired by the wealthiest Americans in no small part due to the influence that money (e.g., campaign funding and lobbying) has on political power today (see e.g., Ferguson 1995). Page et al. (2013) found that about two-thirds of wealthy Americans contributed money to political campaigns or organizations, far more than the general public, giving them more political influence and ensuring that policy decisions will continue to serve their narrow interests, even if they collide with the aspirations and even the needs of the majority of Americans.

These individual exertions of political influence are in addition, of course, to the civic and corporate institutions whose respective power is also leveraged on behalf of these same elites. For instance, the U.S. Chamber of Commerce is a lobby group representing companies, business associations, and state and local chambers. This group, which strongly opposes raising the minimum wage, spent $36.1 million on election activities in 2012 (Callahan and Cha 2013). In *Affluence and Influence: Economic Inequality and Political Power in America*, Gilens (2012) writes,

> The American government does respond to the public's preferences, but that responsiveness is strongly tilted toward the most affluent citizens. Indeed, under most circumstances, the preferences of the vast majority of Americans appear to have essentially no impact on which policies the government does or doesn't adopt. (1)

This power matters because institutions (formal and informal) govern the bargaining situation and provide sanctions when expectations are violated (Knight 1992; North 1990). Because people with assets have power over institutions, they also have the upper hand in changing social expectations (i.e., informal institutions) into rights (i.e., formal institutions) that are enforced by government sanctions and compel poorer households to act in ways that reinforce the interests of the wealthy.

To maintain a system that gives them a distributional advantage, the wealthy, through their control of the political system, favor rules such as merit-based aid that reward their particular characteristics and multiply their inherent advantages. Some colleges, such as Washington University in St. Louis, which Melinda and I attended, have been able to leverage the shift toward merit aid to help them move up in the university rankings to become an elite private school. However, they have openly done so at the expense of low-income students (Burd 2013). For example, as of 2008–09, the year I graduated from their PhD program, the school's low-income students faced a hefty net price of more than $18,000 a year, despite being one of the richest schools in the country (Burd 2013, 11). Largely to answer criticism that alleges that Washington University, as a particular example of a much broader trend, has abdicated its public mission in pursuit of revenue maximization, in more recent years, the university has begun covering the full costs of its neediest students, although the composition of the student body still tilts decidedly toward the economically privileged. This seems to acknowledge that the staggering debt that many of their low-income students accumulated prior to this policy change was not fully the fault of the student but, *in part*, the fault of the policies of the university. In the interest of equity, one must then question whether these students are owed at least a partial bailout from the university, from society.

The shift toward merit aid has allowed many schools to leverage their financial aid budgets to bring in not only the brightest students, which would appear to align with American values that exalt ability, but also the wealthiest students who can afford to attend without help to maximize the institutions' revenue (Burd 2013). Here the true distortion of the ideal of the American Dream is revealed. The goal of strategic actors is not only to compel *individuals* to act in ways that benefit them or to operate within the existing structure in ways that produce their desired outcomes, but also to compel *institutions* to act in ways that benefit them as well.

As in the case of the GI Bill and black veterans, research suggests that universities are being compelled to manipulate requirements for who is eligible to receive merit aid so that the requirements favor the wealthy:

> The competition for the wealthy is so strong that 10 percent of college admissions directors at four-year colleges (and nearly 20 percent of those at private liberal arts colleges) reported that they give affluent students a significant leg up in the admissions process—meaning that they are admitting full-pay students with lower grades and test scores than other applicants. (Burd 2013, 4)

At the same time, some colleges and universities are deliberately offering low-income students financial aid packages that are underfunded to establish expectations that will discourage them from enrolling (Burd 2013, 4). This has implications for "wilt," a topic that will be discussed at the end of this chapter, and it is another example of how the very institutions that are supposed to foster the educational attainment of bright but poor students instead thwart their achievement. Aggregated across many individual examples, these actions have the tendency to reshape groups' expectations about educational opportunities, charting new patterns of achievement.

Particularly inexcusably, our current political discourse blames these students when they are unable to successfully navigate this paucity of options: failing to transition to college, leaving without a degree, or ending up with unsustainable debt. But, as with supportive institutions, these mechanisms are rendered nearly invisible. By turning a blind eye to the ways in which these institutions are failing low-income students, we can prevent even the students themselves from observing these forces' impact on their lives.

## FIGHTING TO MAINTAIN THE STUDENT LOAN PROGRAM

When the Higher Education Act of 1965 was enacted, student loans were not meant to be the primary instrument for financing college. In fact, student borrowing did not become the primary financial aid approach until about the mid-1980s. Instead, grants were primarily intended for lower-income students, with loans, a compromise of sorts between Democrats' and Republicans' different ideas about how to expand educational opportunities, meant to help middle-income families confront the short-term cash crunch associated with the cost of college. During this period, student loans were made by private lenders. However, to get private lenders to be willing to offer loans to students who for the most part had no credit history, the banks had to be given a guarantee that they could recoup their losses if a student defaulted. The concessions that resulted took student loans down a path that has resulted in a fairly unique debt instrument, one with an outsized significance in U.S. policy and, today, Americans' balance sheets. Unlike when a person takes out a loan for a car or house, students as well as universities and lenders cannot accurately estimate what monthly payments will be, how much will be owed, or how long it will take to pay back. This is because students often take out loans annually causing them to progressively increase their debts, financial aid changes from year to year, there are origination fees on student loans which increase initial balances, borrowers do not have to start paying back loans while they are in school or sometimes they do not have to start repayment until three years after leaving school if their loans qualify for forbearance all the time they are in school or in forbearance interest is building on their loans (Delisle and Holt 2014). As a result, it is not surprising that many students report being surprised by the amount of their monthly payment. Given the number of unpredictable variables associated with student loan debt, Del-isle and Holt (2014) point out that it would be nearly impossible to develop a policy that could accurately estimate what a student's future loan payment would be let alone expect students themselves to be able to figure this out regardless of the information school and universities provide them.

Private loans made up $150 billion of the $1.1 trillion student loan market in 2012 (Hartman 2013). Sallie Mae, the nation's largest private student loan lender, reported making $939 million in net profit for 2012 (Hartman 2013). One of the unintended consequences of student loan policy is that it created incentives for banks to act to protect the student loan program from any potential threats to its survival. As Mettler (2014) explains, "Then in turn, the profitability of the enterprise led the banks to engage in rent-seeking behavior, mobilizing to protect the student loan system and to make its terms all the more favorable to them" (54).

Essentially, the market has determined that the payoff from helping students finance a college degree is high enough, certain enough, and profitable enough that lending money to pay for college comes at an acceptable risk. At the same time, this tool has been carefully crafted so that taxpayers and financial institutions are largely protected against the risk of default by rules that forbid students from discharging their student loans through bankruptcy and that allow repayment to be collected through such means as garnishing tax refunds or wages. Furthermore, financial institutions or the federal government make the investment in student loans as they do with most loans, with the expectation that they will be paid back with interest, though at very favorable terms compared to private loans. In fact, the Congressional Budget Office (CBO) reported that the federal government stood to make a profit of $50 billion from student loans in 2013 (Jesse 2013). And the lucrative externalities of student loans extend beyond the lenders themselves. The U.S. Department of Education, for example, spent $1.4 billion to pay collection agencies to track down borrowers who were delinquent or in default in 2011 (Martin 2012).

Therefore, it can be said that keeping students indebted serves a functional purpose in society. This substantial profit creates an incentive structure for some actors, such as the U.S. Department of Education, the U.S. Department of the Treasury, commercial banks such as Sallie Mae, servicing companies, and politicians, to act to maintain the current system of financing college and even expand it when possible.

Understanding student loans as profit making provides insight into how the marketization of higher education takes place. This profit also provides an incentive for maintaining student loans and increasing access to student loans as the primary way of financing college. In this sense, the federal government and private companies that have the potential to benefit from the college loan market are likely to act in ways that maximize their goal to maintain or, if possible, increase the number and amount of student loans available, particularly if they can do so in a way that appears to be an altruistic effort to assist low- and moderate-income aspiring college students.

However, the federal government and private companies are not the only actors who have a stake in maintaining the existing financial aid model. Others have bought into the rhetoric of individual responsibility for financing higher education to such an extent that they see nothing within the student loan system that is incompatible with their understanding of how education is supposed to work. Unable to imagine an alternative that would bring better outcomes and better alignment with American ideals, these individuals and institutions—including some who champion access to higher education as a pathway out of poverty—end up providing political and moral cover for those who profit at the expense of children's futures, even as they collectively constrain our ability to imagine another path.

## IS STUDENT DEBT HELPING TO JEOPARDIZE EDUCATION'S ROLE AS AN EQUALIZER?

While many of the problems associated with our reliance on student debt as a financial aid mechanism fly largely under the political radar, one element of today's financial aid landscape that has received significant—even outsized—attention is the "epidemic" of loan delinquency and default. Here, again, placing the individual at the center of the analysis leads to blaming the wrong players for student loan default. Rather than assuming that those who default are in some way morally deficient, we should understand student loan default as a result of the inherent difficulty in accurately predicting the return on college and accommodating high tuition prices within a normative expectation of educational attainment. Through this lens, we see the request for rules that preference lenders, though practical from the perspective of financial institutions, as creating a kind of perverse outcome where the goal becomes more to protect the *financial institutions* than the *recipients*.

This skewed system would be disturbing in a niche financial aid instrument; given the subsequent trajectory of student loans, where borrowing has become a primary mechanism of college access for most prospective students, this positioning of financial aid within the larger credit market should have perhaps raised more alarm. Again, here it is important to recognize education—and public support for it—not as mere academic instruction, but as a sort of "American welfare," vastly preferred to the alternative—direct payments, and fundamental to our system of helping individuals to better their lives. Therefore, these regulations and the actions they permit, which some have deemed predatory (Steiger 2012), are concerning not just as a violation of sound consumer finance principles but as a threat to the central way that poor Americans, in particular, are to secure a stronger economic future for themselves.

It is in this role of education, then, that we find greatest concern over this protection of institutions instead of individuals. Here, for our particular emphasis on the educational attainment and equitable outcomes of low-income and otherwise disadvantaged students for whom education functions more explicitly as a form of welfare than for high-income students, student borrowing may be especially ill-suited. These are the students least able to protect themselves from untenable loan balances and least likely to use loans strategically. Yet, the reality of college financing, including rising college costs and a retreat from progressive, need-based aid, forces precisely these students to depend disproportionately on this inappropriate mechanism. Prior to, during, and following college, they pay a high price in compromised educational outcomes, thwarted aspirations, and an increasingly fragile hold on the ladder of economic mobility.

To show how the student loan program is hindering the ability of education to fulfill its role as an equalizer, Elliott and Lewis (2013) pull together a growing body of research that suggests student loans, large and small, can have negative effects on far too many potential students' college preparation, the decision to enroll in college, which career to pursue, which college to select, whether to stay and complete college, which job to take after college, whether and when to marry, when to have children, the amount of overall financial stress experienced, whether to buy a home, and whether, when, and how much to save for retirement. Reviewing the growing body of research makes a compelling case that the student loan program exacerbates uneven returns on a college degree and consequently erodes some of the equalizing potential of our higher education system. Indeed, as we will contend throughout this book, there is emerging evidence that the student loan program is magnifying already existing inequality in the education system.

Although we believe that no one study can completely tell the story of the effect of student borrowing on our education system and the outcomes it is supposed to deliver, we acknowledge the importance of constructing a sound case to shift the public's thinking to such a significant extent.

This accumulation of the evidence of anomalies in the paradigm of today's debt-dependent financial aid system should catalyze recognition of the crisis that, then, prompts the need for a different way of seeing this world. We are certainly not the first to discover or document these facts, but we hope to make a significant contribution by exposing and highlighting them and by suggesting the gravity of their relative weight.

Even when research and analysis can expose the true costs of student borrowing, some may view these adverse student loan effects as small costs to pay for the right to receive an education. Indeed, some Americans may choose to delay buying a home or getting married, and generational differences may lead some to make different life choices altogether (Nielsen 2014). It is not our place to make the value judgment as to how expensive is "too much" to expect students to pay or what opportunity costs are unreasonable or unwise for a given student, but instead to point out the reality that there are significant costs associated with student borrowing and that these effects extend beyond higher education itself, often stretching years beyond college exit. Our intention is to point out the unacceptable inequity of a system that asks some but not all students to pay these costs, and frames such inequity as an inevitable price of higher education access, without questioning the injustice that such an accounting weaves into an institution so critical to our nation's current identity and shared future.

We believe that the American Dream requires that personal preferences and life goals must determine individuals' paths, not the constraints leveled by the way in which they financed the higher education they pursued on their journey. This leads us to different conclusions about the seriousness of student loan effects and the urgency of constructing alternatives, as compared with other prominent voices in the student debt debate, who we view as being relatively more bound by the current paradigm. For example, Rose (2013) states, "A sizable number of people are certainly *inconvenienced* for their first 10 years after graduation and face a long period of repayments, but a relatively small percentage confront default" (30, emphasis added). We would and have agreed with Dr. Rose that it still pays to attend college, even if you have to take out student loans. However, this certainly does not mitigate the harsh reality that college pays *more* for those who do not have to take out loans. It is that inequity that is problematic, for individual students and for the nation. And the disparity in outcomes is often quite consequential.

The average time that it takes to repay student loans grew from about 7 years in 1992 to a little more than 13 years in 2010 (Akers and Chingos

2014), and this is likely to continue to grow as Income-Based Repayment plans gain popularity (Akers and Chingos 2014), touted as a way for over-burdened students to cope with the strain of their debt burdens. These programs, which have doubled in use over the last two years—itself a sign that there is a student-debt problem in America because entrance into a IBR is usually triggered by a student's assessment of the unsustainability of his or her loan repayment terms—extend normal repayment plans from 10 years to up to 25 years.

Again, correctly viewing higher education as a conduit to greater economic prosperity and financial aid, then, as the instrument designed to facilitate these ultimate outcomes exposes the counterproductive nature of these "reforms." In light of evidence of the long-term financial implications of diverting income to debt repayment instead of asset accumulation (Hiltonsmith 2013), payment schedules that extend the period of indebtedness may only exacerbate the divides between those who must borrow and those whose financial foundations avoid it. Even if the advantage realized by a student who does not have to borrow for higher education is small, and even if the student who had to take out loans is better off than he or she would be without a college education, these gaps are still at odds with the goal of education being an equalizer in society. Even more fundamentally, this landscape is incompatible with the spirit of the American Dream that promises that effort and ability will determine who succeeds and who fails.

Reflecting the degree to which we have failed to reckon with these fundamental problems with our policies, it is particularly disturbing that the proposed "solutions" to the growing public angst about student loans' effects on the economic mobility and financial security of young Americans so utterly fail to address the underlying causes of their distress. Clearly, this is not a time for normal science (Kuhn 1962) that would tinker around the edges of the financial education puzzle but, instead, for a reckoning of the extent to which the current paradigm is failing.

## STUDENT DEBT IS CREATING A TWO-TIER HIGHER EDUCATIONAL SYSTEM IN AMERICA

Although these postcollege effects compromise education's equalizing effects and constrain individuals' ability to realize significant gains on their college degrees, student loans' gravest threats begin far earlier in students' careers, as they insidiously erode children's hopes. Particularly out of sync with the stated and understood purpose of student loans to facilitate greater access to higher education are the ways in which borrowing influences students' decisions prior to college entrance, again in highly unequal ways. The looming prospect of significant indebtedness does little to instill in disadvantaged students a confidence in education as an institution capable of and willing to facilitate their exertion of effort and ability. Apart from the fact that the mere thought of having to finance college through the student loan program is associated with some students opting not to attend college—debt aversion—the student loan program helps to institutionalize separate educational paths for those who have money for college and those who do not.

For instance, field evidence suggests that students facing the prospect of considerable debt may be steered toward two-year colleges as opposed to a four-year colleges by high school personnel such as teachers and counselors, even when they are academically qualified to attend more selective institutions (Elliott 2013a). One high school counselor put it this way:

> Being able to see it made a big difference because I had students that were accepted into 4-year colleges around the state but once we looked at the aid packages, they realized, OK, it doesn't make sense for me to go down to [4-year college] and take out some loans when I can get money back if I start at [2-year college] and just get my associate's and then transfer so that, they have to see it, they have to be able to touch it. And I'm the same way, like you can talk to me all day but until I see the numbers, it's not really going to click with me. (Elliott 2013a, 19)

The idea that students who cannot afford to pay for college or are not comfortable taking out large loans should attend two-year colleges even when qualified to attend more selective colleges creates the expectation that there are different paths for students with and without money to pay for college. It further pretends that these distortions are somehow compatible with our understanding of equal opportunity or, at least, inconsequential for students' ultimate outcomes. It creates the rhetorical space for policies that further legitimize these disparate paths, as in states that are proposing free college education, but only at certain types of institutions (Perez-Pena 2014), usually with demonstrably poorer outcomes.

Despite the obvious contradictions, today's conversation about higher education and, specifically, about financial aid is dominated by this thinking. In justifying the student loan program as not diminishing the return on college, some researchers have expressed a similar rationale as the counselor. For example, one said,

> Nonetheless, for many borrowers even modest student debt crowds out other spending. But our postsecondary system is huge and provides many options. Students can minimize debt by going to a less-expensive public 4-year college or by starting at a community college and then transferring to a state 4-year school. (Rose 2013, 30)

Again, these ideas are then codified in state and national policy. For instance, the Tennessee Promise offers last-dollar scholarships to ensure free two-year degrees or certificates from the state's 13 community colleges and 27 technical schools. Proposals in Michigan, Oregon, and elsewhere to provide two free years of community college to high school graduates attracted considerable attention in recent years. Although we recognize the good intentions in these policy prescriptions, serving as they do to attempt to preserve routes to college completion for students facing significant cost burdens, this approach runs counter to education acting as an equalizer, particularly given evidence of unequal outcomes and returns on degree at different types of institutions and the reality that wealthy students have far more options from which to choose.

This is not to deny that a two-year college is the best option for some students. The value of these institutions in the U.S. higher education system is clear, but student debt should not be part of why students have to decide to attend a two-year college or a four-year college, nor should financial aid options determine how educators advise students. This is an artifact of the overreliance on student loans, a symptom of the shift in cost burden from society to individuals, and a distortion of how Americans believe higher education works.

Importantly, we do not ask this of students who have the financial resources to attend college. Potential students from upper-income families are much more likely to walk into a pattern of higher education, such that they may never consciously and intentionally "decide" to attend college, as discussed in one of the narratives in the opening chapter. For them, higher education still largely serves as an institution that supports the realization of their American Dream, which makes it even more imperative that we find policy levers capable of strengthening this same promise for less-advantaged children.

Higher education cannot be an equalizing force if it delivers an unequal product with highly disparate outcomes, and this is where pinning some of the "blame" on institutions of higher education may be well founded; surely all colleges and universities should be accountable for providing students with valuable degrees. As evidence of the gap between different types of institutions, more than half of community college students fail to complete a degree, receive a certificate, or transfer to a four-year institution within six years (NCES 2011), considerably poorer interim outcomes than students at more selective four-year institutions. Notwithstanding the responsibility borne by these institutions, it is of course the case that some will struggle disproportionately to demonstrate positive outcomes as long as policy and economic realities serve to channel certain students— systematically disadvantaged and less well prepared—to specific types of institutions. While precisely parsing these causes is beyond the scope of our treatment here, it is certainly true that these inequities in outcomes are both reflective of and contributing to disparities in the education system.

It is because of the role that education has been given as part of our welfare system that education has become America's largest investment in ensuring equitable outcomes for all Americans. The stakes are high for properly financing and administering higher education, given its outsized function in our economy and our collective identity. Therefore, financial aid is not just a matter of providing students with the money they need to pay for college, even if the current paradigm largely confines the debate as such. We must assess whether these finances align with education's role as an important facilitator of the American Dream. We must expect more of our financial aid system than just not worsening students' individual situations, and then we must muster the political will to build a financial aid system up to this task.

## WILT: WHEN EFFORT AND ABILITY ARE NOT ENOUGH

As a result of current financial aid policies and the incentives they have created to pit the wealthy against the poor, a sizable number of minority and low-income children work hard at school and have the ability to attend college, but they fail to transition to college after high school graduation or to succeed once enrolled—what we call "wilt." This is simply anti-American in the truest sense because it is such a complete break from the belief that effort and ability should drive outcomes.

For example, about 52 percent of low-income and 82 percent of high-income youths enrolled in a two-year or four-year colleges immediately upon graduating high school in 2010 (Aud et al. 2012). Another more telling way of looking at this disparity is to compare students with similar achievement levels but different incomes. For example, the lowest-achieving children from high-income families attend college at a much higher rate than the lowest-achieving children from low-income families (65 percent versus 33 percent, respectively). Similarly, 88 percent of the highest-achieving children from high-income families attend college while only 69 percent (a similar percentage to the lowest-achieving, high-income children) of the highest-achieving children from low-income families attend college (ACSFA 2010).

Even bigger gaps exist when considering college graduation rates. Mettler (2014) found that 74 percent of the highest-achieving children from the highest income group graduate college by age 24. In sharp contrast, only 30 percent of the highest-achieving students from the lowest income group graduated college by the same age. Maybe even more troubling is that 29 percent of the lowest-achieving high-income children graduate college, a percentage similar to the highest-achieving children from the lowest-income group. These students are carried to superior, or at least equal, outcomes despite their inferior exertion of effort and ability, sustained and supported by the institutions that facilitate their success and may even compensate for their deficiencies. At the same time, poorer students are likely to have to expend far greater levels of effort and ability to reach the same outcomes, a relatively narrow needle through which only the most talented thread their aspirations. That a relative few manage to do so should be taken as evidence of the system's overall soundness is not only an injustice; it defies the parameters of logical argument.

The expectation-attainment difference among college-qualified children may provide one of the more vivid illustrations of the failure of the education path to act as the great equalizer in today's society. It suggests that addressing the educational challenges facing disadvantaged children today will require innovations that can create greater equality of opportunity so that their innate talents and academic effort can translate into meaningful access to college. In a report to Congress, the Advisory Committee on Student Financial Assistance, or ACSFA, (2001) suggested that poor children's pattern of educational decision making is not the result of choice or academic preparation: "Make no mistake, the pattern of educational decision making typical of low-income students today, which diminishes the likelihood of ever completing a bachelor's degree, is not the result of free choice. Nor can it be blamed on academic preparation" (ACSFA 2001, 18). This suggests that an uneven playing field exists, so effort and ability may no longer be the determining factors in who succeeds in the education system.

In a national survey of college-qualified, low-income students, Hahn and Price (2008) found that over 80 percent of non-college-goers identified financial aid as "extremely" or "very" important in their decision not to enroll in college. These concerns appear to lead to inaction. The authors found that among college-qualified, low-income students who did not enroll in college, only 15 percent applied to any college, 12 percent applied for financial aid, 10 percent took the SAT, and 7 percent took the ACT. These college-qualified non-goers were disproportionately minority (52 percent) and low and moderate income (38 percent). In a 2006 report, the ACSFA found that during the 1990s, between 1 and 1.6 million college-qualified high school graduates did not earn a bachelor's degree, and they estimated that between 1.4 and 2.4 million would-be college graduates will be lost in this decade. The estimates exclude those college-qualified, low- and moderate-income students who do not graduate high school, although certainly the same forces implicated here are at work earlier in children's school careers as well.

One way to capture the effect of financial constraints on actual college attendance is to identify children who expect to graduate college but do not attend college soon after graduation, what Elliott and Beverly (2011) have coined "wilt." For example, using a sample of high school seniors who expected to earn a college degree after leaving high school, Hanson (1994) examined whether talent loss is stratified by gender, race, or socioeconomic status. One way she defined talent loss is when children expect to graduate from college while in high school but fail to attend college six years after leaving high school. She found that socioeconomic status was a stronger predictor of talent loss than either gender or race.

In a similar study published in 1999, Trusty and Harris (1999) restricted their sample to eighth-grade children who had above-median scores in reading and math. They built on Hanson's (1994) research by including material resources in the home (i.e., availability of printed educational materials and computers). In addition, they define socioeconomic status as the parents' educational levels, income, and occupational prestige. They also found that low socioeconomic status was the strongest predictor of lost talent. Critically, this lost talent is lost not just to the individual, whose life chances will be diminished unless institutions intervene to restore the efficacy needed to realize equitable outcomes; it is lost as well to the nation, which faces an acute need for a well-educated workforce to catalyze continued economic growth (Alter 2012).

We contend that there is a battle raging among strategic actors, in this case the wealthy and the poor, to establish expectations that will produce one's desired distributional outcomes. We further conclude that, in the case of college attendance and completion and the superior economic outcomes this advanced education can secure, it is clear that the wealthy are winning. At this point, the analysis of the battle points to several factors that tip it in favor of the wealthy: they control the political apparatus, which is in control of enforcement; divisions among the classes adversely affected by shifts in education policy prevent their coalescence as a political force; relatively few actors have emerged who can assert a compelling vision of alternatives to the status quo; and many of those who would otherwise champion the interests of the poor have ceded considerable ground, clinging to a defensive posture rather than challenging the underlying assumptions that legitimize student borrowing.

The primary reason for the serious defeats suffered so far by the interests of those economically disadvantaged, however, is our collective failure to recognize just what is being lost as education moves out of reach and fewer children grow up counting on college as a pathway out of poverty. We are trapped in a paradigm that not only fails to serve our intellectual demands but, of greater immediate significance, also fails a majority of American families today. It is only when we correctly claim education as a particularly American conduit to combating poverty and facilitating opportunity that we will demand a financial aid system that can deliver those outcomes. It is only when we insist on such a system that we have a chance of countering the interests that today hold us back and hold our children down.

# FIVE

# Evidence of a Paradigm in Crisis

The conversation about student debt in the United States isn't just too narrow—largely ignoring evidence that student loans erode equity and compromise outcomes—it also sets the bar too low, often pretending that there is no problem unless college debt rises to the level of creating a national financial crisis or assuming that all's well that ends well when it comes to student debt and college completion. Part of our contention is that we must raise our expectations if we are to pivot away from student loans in time to avoid widespread harm to individuals, to institutions, and to the path of upward mobility. We aim, then, to connect the dots on the data points that should serve to spark recognition of a crisis before too much is lost to create space for an alternative financial aid paradigm.

A financial aid program that in the 2011–12 school year cost Americans $70.8 billion (College Board 2012), from which the federal government earned $41.3 billion in 2013 (Jesse 2013), and from which Sallie Mae (the nation's largest private student loan lender) made $939 million in net profit for 2012 (Hartman 2013), should be held to a higher standard than "most students will eventually recover" or "not yet a national economic catastrophe." Such a financial aid arrangement, as the vehicle through which many Americans access the core intervention of our welfare system—education—should actually have to be shown to be an equalizing force with regard to educational attainment and financial well-being.

It is not just our financial investment that makes this so important, although the individual and societal opportunity costs are substantial. We have also invested considerable regulatory and legislative legitimacy in student borrowing, imbuing these loans with tremendous significance in our policy structure—including preventing discharge in bankruptcy and deploying collection agencies to recoup debts—in ways that leak into other policy dimensions. We allow our consideration of the *possible* in financial aid to be largely confined to the margins left in the vacuum *around* student loans, rather than imagining what we could build in the space that would be left. Our continued tolerance of student debt also sends an important message to children about the institutions that will—and will not—be available to them as they seek to advance economically. Despite these high stakes, there is little evidence that we are holding student loans to an appropriately high standard. Instead, we are largely limping along, putting up with a level of mediocrity that would be inconceivable in other arenas.

And while this book is about student debt and its effects on American children throughout the college pipeline, what we contend is that a successful financial aid system is not solely or even most importantly about providing children with mere *access* to college. The true measure of a financial aid system is its ability to strengthen the capacity of education to serve as a path to the American Dream, or social and financial well-being after college. Here access is inextricably tied to social and financial well-being both prior to college, when the kind of financial aid available depends in part on students' financial position as children, and after college, when outstanding student debt may hinder social and financial well-being, even for college graduates. Therefore, we contend the kind of aid children receive matters for their ability to achieve social and financial well-being in a timely fashion upon leaving college—in other words, on their "return on degree."

Our own narratives give evidence to this, and our reading of the literature and our own data analysis suggest that we are far from alone. By exacerbating the inequities already present in this system, student debt further intensifies the divide among relatively privileged and disadvantaged children. Given the large investment—financially, politically, and ideologically—in the student loan program, this just should not be the case. To counteract these corrosive effects, the United States must fight for financial aid interventions that align with how we want the U.S. economy to work for children.

## BATTLING STRAW MEN

We talk about the student-debt discussion in America as one that all too often has fabricated straw men, which are then used to lower the bar for suggesting there is no student debt problem in America. The straw man fallacy occurs when one researcher, for example, says that student debt is a serious problem in America, as we do in this book, and another researcher sensationalizes the problem of student debt (e.g., student debt is the next housing bubble, or students owe hundreds of thousands of dollars) and then suggests that there is no student debt problem because it doesn't rise to this invented, sensationalized level (e.g., the student debt problem does not rise to the level of the housing crisis; therefore, we do not have a student debt problem).

Our national policy discourse and, in particular, the young adults whose lives are deeply affected by the status quo deserve more intellectual honesty than these fallacies of logic afford. To raise the quality of the debate and create a foundation for productive consideration of policy alternatives, we present some common straw men fallacies permeating the student-debt conversation in America. Exposed in their frailty, we believe that this collection gives further evidence of the last gasps of the failed paradigm of student debt as financial aid.

## The Next Housing Bubble

With student debt rising to over $1 trillion dollars and total student debt now higher than credit card debt in America, some have compared the student-debt problem with the next housing bubble. For example, the Federal Advisory Council, made up of 12 bankers who meet quarterly to advise the central bank, warned that growth in student loan debt parallels the housing crisis (Foley 2013). This appears to be an attempt to sound an alarm to draw greater attention to the problem. It is debatable whether these actors actually meant that it would *be* the next housing bubble or only that it has some characteristics that are similar to it. However, a simple Google search confirms that other voices picked up this line, similarly hyperbolizing student loan debt as an imminent threat to U.S. financial markets.

To understand how dangerous these inflated arguments are, consider that the U.S. housing bubble is seen as one of the primary causes of the Great Recession in America from 2007–09, one of the biggest recessions in U.S. history (Financial Crisis Inquiry Commission 2011). The housing bubble occurred, in part, because of the growth in subprime lending (i.e., loans made with unfavorable terms to people who have low credit ratings). In 2000, the top 25 nonprime lenders originated $105 billion in these high-cost loans. In 2002, the figure had jumped to $188 billion; in 2003, $310 billion; in 2004, $730 billion; and by 2005, the total value of nonprime loans topped $1 trillion (Financial Crisis Inquiry Commission 2011). The influx of subprime housing loans increased the demand for housing, which in turn artificially increased housing prices. This was followed by a sharp crash, as these loans imploded and financial institutions retreated from these practices. In 2010, housing prices had dropped 35 percent from their peak in 2006 (Urahn, Currier, Wechsler, Wilson, and Colbert 2012). The recession hit low- and middle-income households the hardest, as many homeowners ended up with negative equity (mortgage debt higher than the value of the property). For homeowners with income of less than $70,000, home equity is estimated to have declined by 54 percent between 2006 and 2010 (Urahn et al. 2012).

This sensationalized debate has then become a distraction within the academic and policy discourses, with serious attention diverted to discussion of whether, in fact, the student debt problem rises to the level of the housing bubble before the Great Recession. This, of course, obscures many of the real issues within the student loan system; comparing the student loan problem with the housing bubble has created a situation where all that researchers have to do to discredit the argument about student loans' dangers is to raise doubt about whether the current student-debt problem actually rises to the level of that bubble. Set against the backdrop of this dire recession, when average household wealth declined 15 percent between 2007 and 2010 and has only recovered 45 percent of its value (Boshara and Emmons 2013), even serious problems with student loans could look relatively mild.

Most reasonable people would probably agree that a lot of things are harmful to individuals and to the macroeconomy long before they reach the catastrophic level seen in the Great Recession. For millions of American households, the Great Recession produced an economic devastation almost unimaginable; because wealth is so unevenly distributed, median declines were even more dramatic, with a median household wealth drop of 39 percent (Emmons 2012). Three-fifths or more of families across all income groups reported a decline in wealth between 2007 and 2009 (Bricker, Kennickell, Moore, and Sabelhaus 2012), and the typical household lost nearly one-fifth of its wealth. Certainly, if this becomes the new standard for what is "problematic," the United States is in for an extended period of surreal economic debates, when even disastrous conditions would be judged fairly innocuous. As such, it seems somewhat disingenuous to suggest that we do not have a student-debt problem in America simply because it might not be the next housing bubble. But this is what it means to battle a straw man.

## $100,000 Loans

This confusion—intentional and unintentional—about what constitutes a student debt *crisis* unfolds on the individual as well as the societal level. Today, largely as a result of media depiction, problematic debt has been roughly defined as $100,000 or more per student borrower. This inaccurate definition moves the goalposts, allowing some analysts, policy makers, and pundits to divert attention from the negative effects associated with student debt by merely demonstrating that average student debt is far less (latest estimates are $29,400; Miller 2014) than $100,000 (see also Sanchez 2012; Edmiston, Brooks, and Shepelwich 2012).

Significantly, this accounting seemingly arrived at this figure devoid of any empirical basis, ignoring compelling research that shows that amounts much smaller than $100,000 (and even smaller than the median amounts owed today) can create financial hardship (Akers 2014; McCann 2014). For example, Akers (2014) finds that "high-debt borrowers face financial hardship at only slightly higher rates than comparable households with less debt" (4). What this suggests is that high debt does not necessarily lead to hardship because people with high debt often have higher earnings; equally importantly, however, it also means that low debt does not necessarily mean absence of hardship. Additionally, this simplistic accounting glosses over the significance of variables such as how people come to borrow and why, factors that may matter more than how much they borrow, particularly when it comes to disadvantaged students who borrow as their only option versus wealthier students whose loans complement other financial aid or facilitate the achievement of specific educational goals and who likely have resources with which to confront debt obligations postgraduation.

The fact that debt of any size may bring about financial hardship raises the question of whether making student loans the centerpiece of the U.S. financial aid system is an inherently flawed idea. It also points to the potential futility of policy reforms that merely seek to tweak the student loan system to mitigate its worst effects and the circular futility, then, of the period of normal science with which the financial aid community is currently occupied. As we understand student borrowing today, the factors that influence whether student debt will be harmful for a given student include not only the amount of debt but other, more complex considerations, including the kind of postsecondary institution attended, the major pursued, the kind of job students secure after graduation, what the economy will be like, and the options they have before, during, and after higher education.

Beyond the fact that answering these questions accurately is nearly impossible for a supercomputer, let alone a high school graduate, even if answered correctly (i.e., college will pay off), the need for this calculus may itself weaken the ability for the education path to act as an equalizer. In fact, getting more information about how harmful student debt is may just further depress postsecondary education participation, particularly among low-income and minority students who are more likely to be loan averse, unless an alternative way to pay is provided. To the extent to which pursuing the elusive American Dream requires, today, a level of suspension of disbelief, more information may only serve to dampen individuals' unrealistic but powerful optimism.

## CONFRONTING REAL GIANTS: AMERICA'S STUDENT-DEBT PROBLEM

Immersed in a particular paradigm, it can become difficult to remember the preceding period, when there was far less certainty about particular "truths" and, often, greater disagreement about the correct way to see the world. In fact, a debt-dependent financial aid system was far from a foregone conclusion and is, instead, a rather recent development. Geiger and Heller (2011) found that federal, state, and private grants were the largest form of financial aid until 1982, when loans began to outpace grants. During most years, this has only escalated. For example, in 2000, student loans made up 38 percent of net tuition, fees, room, and board; by 2013, they made up 50 percent (Greenstone, Looney, Patashnik, and Yu 2013). This policy shift coincided with the solidifying expectation that students— not states or institutions—would bear most of the burden of college costs (Hiltonsmith 2014). This shift fell particularly hard on disadvantaged students, who were least likely to have a cushion of parental support to sustain them (Elliott and Friedline 2013) or the support of well-positioned K–12 institutions that could help them navigate the nonloan aid (Dynarski 2002; Marin 2002).

## THE SIZE OF THE PROBLEM

As other forms of financial aid, particularly means-tested grant assistance, have eroded in value while college costs have risen, students have not only become more likely to borrow, they are borrowing more. These cost shifts accelerated following the Great Recession, as many states slashed budgets for higher education with relatively few having restored this public support to pre-2008 figures, even today (Mitchell, Palacios, and Leachman 2014). The amount borrowed by the average student increased only marginally between 2003–04 and 2007–08; however, debt loads increased by $4,700 (19 percent) between 2007–08 and 2011–2012 for bachelor's degree recipients and by $3,100 (23 percent) for associate degree holders (Miller 2014). Total borrowing for college hit $113.4 billion for the 2011–12 school year, up 24 percent from five years earlier (College Board 2012).

As a result, households are faced with ever-growing debt, and this heavy borrowing threatens the financial security of more than just young college students. According to the Federal Reserve Bank of New York, about 2.2 million Americans 60 years of age or older were liable for repayment of $43 billion in federal and private student loans in 2012, up $15 billion from 2007 (Greene 2012).

## Student Loan Use by Type of Degree

In an effort to further quantify and better understand the dynamics associated with student loan usage, we present descriptive findings from the 2012 Educational Longitudinal Survey (ELS) that indicate that regardless of degree type, student loans are heavily used (Elliott, Lewis, and Johnson 2014; see the appendix in this volume for description of data and methods). Among young adults with an associate degree or some college, 50 percent report having outstanding loans. For young adults with a bachelor's degree, it is 66 percent, and 78 percent for young adults with a graduate degree (Elliott, Lewis, et al. 2014).

Not only do a higher percentage of graduate students report having debt, they have more debt as well. On average, students with an associate degree or some college have $8,148 of outstanding debt, bachelor's degree holders have $21,433, and graduate degree holders have $55,716. While the advanced education their borrowing purchased is inarguably valuable, this outstanding debt comes at a price. All young adults with outstanding student debt have average monthly payments of $62.77, bachelor's students $188, and graduate students $367 (Elliott, Lewis, et al. 2014). These payments have to come from somewhere. This is where we see a constrained ability to translate labor income into capital accumulation, given the need to divert wages to debt management.

These effects may be magnified given the comparatively advanced age at which many students complete their graduate studies, which means fewer years in which to recover financially before the negative effects of constrained asset development are felt. Equally important and harder to quantify may be the psychic toll having such payments can have on young people's beliefs about such things as their ability to start a family, buy a home, and save for retirement, especially if they perceive that they are unable to match their parents' achievements at their age or even those of their less-educated peers (Pew Charitable Trusts 2014).

## Student Loan Use by Race and Ethnicity

Reflecting unequal resources with which to confront college costs, blacks and Hispanics are more likely than whites to have student loans, at all education levels. For example, Elliott, Lewis, et al. (2014) found that 82 percent of blacks and 77 percent of Hispanics with bachelor's degrees have loans, compared with 64 percent of whites and 59 percent of Asians. Most students depend on student loans to complete a graduate degree, regardless of race or ethnicity, but there is little evidence that students of color have any other alternatives to borrowing if they are to complete advanced degrees. Almost 90 percent of black graduate degree holders in one sample have student loans (Elliott, Lewis, et al. 2014).

Additionally, there is evidence that the increasing shift to merit aid (see Levitz and Thurm 2012) may not greatly reduce the need to borrow among high-performing high school students. At the baccalaureate level, 65 percent of students with a high school GPA at 3.0 or above have student loans, compared with 72 percent of those with lower grades (Elliott, Lewis, et al. 2014). This may reflect the institutional practices referenced above, where colleges and universities use merit aid to incentivize the attendance of desirable, wealthy students, with distributions that fail to eliminate unmet need for low-income, high-performing students. As would be expected, given prevailing trends in pricing and financial aid, students at private for-profit colleges are most likely to use loans, at least for associate and bachelor's degrees, where 76 percent and 84 percent of completers, respectively, have student loans (Elliott, Lewis, et al. 2014).

This certainly aligns with growing public concern with the performance and costs of these for-profit institutions and their increasing prominence in the U.S. higher education landscape (Liu 2011). This is not to suggest that less-expensive colleges are always the best bet, however; 57 percent of those attending public universities finish with less than a bachelor's degree, a disturbingly low completion rate that must prompt reconsideration of the current policy innovations to reduce loan debt for students who begin at the least-expensive state schools (Perez-Pena 2014), some of which may result in a delayed or interrupted path to a degree.

## Student Loan Use by Socioeconomic Status

Particularly for bachelor's degrees, family economic status seems to be the strongest protective factor against student loan reliance; 76 percent of low-income and only 53 percent of high-income individuals with bachelor's degrees have student loans (Elliott, Lewis, et al. 2014). These figures also reveal an important nuance in interpreting population statistics on student loan usage because, while middle-income families are most heavily represented among student borrowers, given their prominence in the population, low-income students are most likely to borrow, as described above, at least among bachelor's degree holders.

The distinction among bachelor's degree holders is important because evidence indicates that low-income and minority students, in particular black and Hispanic, are more likely to be loan averse (Callendar and Jackson 2005). Thus, student loans can prevent some low-income and minority students from attending college, while those who do attend are much more susceptible to having to rely on loans to pay for college once there, which leads to more risk of dropping out (Kim 2007) and then diminished financial health after leaving college (Elliott and Lewis 2014). As higher education is a particularly critical intervention for these disadvantaged populations, evidence that suggests that student loans may be particularly ill-suited to charting a path to mobility for them should be cause for significant concern.

No one set of data can definitively quantify the extent and depth of the student loan problem in the United States. The descriptive data depicted here are but another representation of the characteristics of student loan usage in the U.S. higher education system today: prevalent, but more essential for low-income than high-income students; rising in average amount and therefore more likely to persist throughout Americans' economic lives; and not necessarily controllable by manipulating the conditions one would expect to drive indebtedness, including institutional choice and academic achievement.

However, as other analysts have cautioned (Akers 2014), the mere incidence of student-debt assumption does not provide evidence of its problematic nature. Instead, understanding and accounting for the consequences of student borrowing requires first changing the metrics by which we gauge these effects and then turning to data about the ways student debt compromises achievement of the end goal of higher education: economic mobility and greater societal equity, in keeping with the American Dream.

## Enrollment Growth Cannot Fully Explain the Student-Debt Problem

Despite descriptive evidence of a sizable student-debt problem in America, some research correctly notes that about 20 percent of the growth in student debt since 1989 can be explained by an increase in the number of people attending postsecondary education (Akers and Chingos 2014), a core objective of the student loan program as it is framed in the policy debate and arguably a societal good. But while 20 percent is meaningful, that still leaves 80 percent unexplained by growth in attendance, revealing growth to be an inadequate explanation for the sharp upward trajectory of student borrowing.

Some of these same researchers also correctly point out that growth in the number of people continuing their educations into postgraduate study has played an important role in the rise of student debt by extending the educational path and therefore increasing the total cost of higher education (Akers and Chingos 2014; Delisle 2014a). As Akers and Chingos (2014) indicate, student-debt levels among graduate degree holders quadrupled ($10,000 to $40,000) between 1992 and 2010; however, during the same period, the amount of student debt among bachelor's degree holders almost tripled ($6,000 to $16,000), again pointing to the inadequacy of this supposed explanation for increasing debt. Certainly, looking at amount of borrowing as an indicator of the scope of the problem, just because bachelor's degree debt *only* tripled does not mean that it does not warrant serious concern.

## NOT JUST A QUESTION OF ACCESS

As stated elsewhere in this book, the focus of current financial aid paradigm has been, rather narrowly, on its effectiveness at helping children enroll in college. However, even on this metric, college loans seem to be underwhelming. For example, after conducting an extensive review of the research, Heller (2008) concludes that existing research indicates that educational loans have little or even a negative impact on college enrollment. Research on student loans' effects on college completion are equally uninspiring. While there are some studies that find that student loans have no effect, or even a positive effect, on educational outcomes (e.g., Bowen, Chingos, and McPherson 2009; Cuccaro-Alamin and Choy 1998; Lam 1999; U.S. General Accounting Office 1995), the preponderance of evidence indicates that as student debt load rises so too do dropout rates, particularly for poor and minority students (Institute for Higher Education Policy and Education Resources Institute 1995; Institute for Higher Education Policy 1999; Cofer and Somers 1999, 2000; Ishitani 2006; Kim 2007; Knight and Arbold 2000; St. Johns, Andrieu, Oescher, and Starkey 1994; Zhan 2012, 2013). But because the effects of student loans on college enrollment and completion have been previously reviewed (see Heller 2008; Elliott and Lewis 2013), our focus here is on student debt's postcollege effects.

The prevailing paradigm through which we view financial aid serves to confine analysis to the dimensions considered most salient, here in ways that obscure some of student loans' most pernicious effects. If the counterfactual of interest in assessing student loans' effects is "Are students who finance their college educations better off than if they had not gone to college at all?" an assessment of postgraduation disparities in financial well-being will be largely ignored. Because the real purpose of higher education is not just access, however, or even completion, but facilitation of individual and societal well-being, these outcomes are central to the true policy debate. Here, evidence is clear that college completers from all groups are better off than noncompleters.

However, just as clear is the incomplete nature of this evaluation, which frames the discussion as though student loans were the only financial aid strategy available. Instead, we should imagine a college degree obtained through other mechanisms, such as savings, with complementary structures to support college success and avoid the pitfalls of a debt-dependent financial aid system. Therefore, we should judge whether students who could depend on these alternative mechanisms would realize greater return on their educational investment than they would if saddled with student debt.

## Career and Social Choices

Survey data from American Student Assistance (2013) reveals that 30 percent of respondents say that student loan debt played a role in their career choice. In line with the survey data, Rothstein and Rouse (2011) found evidence that student loan debt drives graduates away from low-paying and public-sector jobs (also see Minicozzi 2005). Similarly, Field (2009) found that the rate of placements in public-interest law were roughly a third higher when law students were given tuition waivers instead of loan repayment assistance. Taken together, what these findings suggest is that borrowers may see their career opportunities differently than nonborrowers and in ways that distort their postcollege planning. Given the widespread reliance on student loans across this cohort of college students, these selection pressures may have significant repercussions in the broader economy.

Beyond career decisions, student loans also appear to provide people with the message that they should wait to start their social lives. This is perhaps exacerbated by meta-messages that reinforce higher education's role in facilitating economic independence and a foundation for a higher standard of living, likely perceived as requisite for launch on a variety of dimensions. Gicheva (2011) found that students with outstanding student debt have a lower probability of marriage than students without outstanding debt among people younger than 37 (also see Baum and O'Malley 2003). If they marry, graduates with student debt express less satisfaction with their marriage than students with no debt (Dew 2008). Moreover, when asked, survey data indicate that 43 percent of student loan borrowers say they have delayed having children (American Student Assistance 2013; also see Baum and O'Malley 2003).

## Psychological Functioning

While there is some evidence that suggests student loans can have a positive psychological effect (e.g., improved mastery and self-esteem), particularly for low-income students while they are in college (Dwyer, McCloud, and Hodson 2011), these effects appear to disappear once students leave college (Dwyer et al. 2011; Fry 2014; Walesmann, Gee, and Gentile 2014). For example, Walsemann, Gee, and Gentile (2014) find evidence of a negative association between student loans and young adults' mental health among young adults aged 25 to 31. Fry (2014) discovered that 18- to 39-year-olds with two- or four-year degrees who had outstanding student debt were less satisfied overall with their financial situations than similarly situated young adults without outstanding student debt (70 percent versus 84 percent, respectively). Further, he found that 18- to 39-year-olds with two- or four-year degrees who had outstanding student debt were less likely to perceive an immediate payoff from having gone to college than similarly situated young adults without outstanding student debt (63 percent versus 81 percent, respectively).

The shift from a positive to a negative association with young adults' psychological functioning may occur because at the same time that debt is accumulating, students are also learning more about their career opportunities and potential future earnings, which may make college seem like a bad investment given the amount of debt they are accumulating (Dwyer et al. 2011; Kamenetz 2006). Compounding the problem of financial stress associated with repaying student loans postgraduation may be the evidence of abusive debt-collection practices and the lack of consequences collection agencies face for these excesses (Burd 2014). Student borrowers face large penalties if they are late with payments or fail to finish paying back their debt on time, and they may be frustrated in their efforts to better manage their debts by onerous restrictions, many of which are peculiar to this type of consumer borrowing (CFPB 2013). This distress is real, and it escalates as students get closer to college exit. So while media attention and cohort effects may increase the perception of distress among student borrowers, it must be emphasized that the strains felt by many student borrowers today are, indeed, grounded in the economic realities they face.

### Delinquency and Default

Considerable popular attention and significant financial resources have been dedicated to the problem of student loan delinquency and default. Student loans become delinquent when payment is 60 to 120 days late. In 2011, the U.S. Department of Education spent $1.4 billion to pay collection agencies to track down students whose loans were delinquent or in default (Martin 2012). While all types of consumer debt have some experiences of repayment difficulty, there is evidence that something about the student loan product, or the context in which it is situated, makes it particularly difficult to service successfully. According to Brown, Haughwout, Lee, Scally, and van der Klaauw (2014), the measured student debt delinquency rate is currently the highest of any consumer-debt product. Cunningham and Kienzl (2011) found that 26 percent of borrowers who began repayment in 2005 were delinquent on their loans at some point but did not default. Brown, et al. (2014) reported that by 2012 just over 30 percent of borrowers who began repayment were delinquent at some point.

And some of the practices utilized by borrowers and lenders to cope with repayment difficulties may have the perverse effects of deepening loans' negative implications for student borrowers. About 21 percent of borrowers avoid delinquency by using deferment (temporary suspension of loan payments) or forbearance (temporary postponement or reduction of payments for a period of time because of financial difficulty) to temporarily alleviate the problem (Cunningham and Kienzl 2011). While this strategy may allow borrowers to stay out of official trouble with their loans by stretching out the period of total indebtedness, these practices may further retard capital development. In total, Cunningham and Kienzl (2011) found that nearly 41 percent of borrowers have been delinquent or defaulted on their loans. Again, these trends have effects far beyond the cohort of young adults most plagued by student loan difficulties. Accompanying the increase in student loan indebtedness, delinquency is also a growing problem among older adults. Among student loans held by Americans aged 60 or older, 9.5 percent were at least 90 days delinquent, up about 7.4 percent from 2007 (Greene 2012).

Defaults are also on the rise. According to the U.S. Department of Education (2012), the national two-year student loan default rate was 9.1 percent in 2010 and the three-year default rate was 13.4 percent. Not surprisingly, defaults occur unevenly. Students from low-income households are more likely to default (Woo 2002), along with students of color (Herr and Burt 2005). With fewer familial resources to cushion the repayment strain and greater likelihood of inadequate income upon leaving college (Woo 2002; Lochner and Monge-Naranjo 2004), these borrowers may have to confront the failed economics of student loans very shortly after exiting higher education. A recent report from the Federal Reserve Bank of New York highlights the fact that a staggering percentage of Americans are unable to pay their student debt, no matter how big or small it is. Their analysis reveals that 34% of students with just $5,000 of outstanding debt—hardly "high"—default on their student loans (Brown, Haughwout, Lee, Scally, and van der Klaauw 2015).

Given the rising rates of delinquency and default regardless of the size of the debt, some researchers have suggested making loan eligibility determinations on an individual basis, taking into consideration all of the circumstances faced as well as the outlook for future ability to repay (see Akers 2014). This concept, predicated as it is on the availability of nearly unattainable information, seems born of a desperate attempt to justify the continued existence of the student loan program while mitigating its most visibly negative effects. That is, there are too many ways in which the student loan program fails (for individuals and society), so we try to patch solutions together, when the reality is that only reducing the prominence of student borrowing as a part of the financial aid system will address the roots of the problem.

Rooted as they are in a collapsing paradigm, these patchwork solutions are likely to exacerbate inequality, perpetuating the survival of a program that will continue to fail whole cohorts of aspiring college students, while diverting massive resources that could be deployed toward more promising approaches and stalling the collective reckoning so urgently needed.

## Overall Debt

Because recent college graduates' annual earnings are usually much lower than they will be during their later prime earning years, most young adults with student loan debt are forced to rely on credit as a key mechanism for purchasing wealth-building items such as a home (Keister 2000; Oliver and Shapiro 2006). However, delinquent and defaulted student loan accounts may be reflected in borrowers' credit scores. For many student debtors, this reveals another way in which student loans may haunt them as they embark on financial independence. Research by Brown and Caldwell (2013) indicates that students with student loans have credit scores that are 24 points lower than students without student loans.

Contrary to the idea that student loan borrowers face credit constraints, however, research using data from 2010 or earlier finds that there was a positive correlation between having outstanding student debt and other debt (such as mortgage, vehicle, or credit card), when comparing graduates with and without debt. For instance, Fry (2014) used the 2010 Survey of Consumer Finance data and found that 43 percent of households headed by a college graduate with student debt had vehicle debt and 60 percent had credit card debt. However, using 2012 data, Brown et al. (2013) found that households with student debt had lower overall debt than households without student debt. They speculate that borrowers post–Great Recession have become less sure about the labor market, causing a drop in the demand for credit. Additionally, lenders may have become more reserved about supplying loans to high-balance student borrowers in the tighter credit markets that followed the financial collapse.

## Asset Accumulation

Student loan debt's most troubling financial effects may not be its constraints on other borrowing, however, but on asset accumulation, particularly given the emerging understanding about the significance of initial assets as catalysts for later economic mobility (Elliott and Lewis 2014). Research indicates that students who graduate with average student loan debt may be forced to invest significantly less in retirement savings or to delay purchasing other wealth-building items such as a home during the early part of their working lives. Critically, this may account for a meaningful amount of the wealth inequality seen later in life between college graduates with and without outstanding student debt. In this section, we will review research on the correlational relationship between student debt and asset accumulation.

*Net worth.* Survey data indicate that 63 percent of young adults with student debt report delaying purchasing large-ticket items such as a car. Therefore, it is no surprise that researchers are finding that young adults with student debt have less net worth (i.e., total assets minus total liabilities) than students without student debt. For example, Elliott and Nam (2013) found that families with college debt may have 63 percent less net worth than those without outstanding student debt. Similarly, over the life course, Hiltonsmith (2013) found that an average student debt load ($53,000) for a dual-headed household with bachelor's degrees from four-year universities leads to a wealth loss of nearly $208,000. Fry (2014) also found a net-worth loss among households headed by a college-educated (i.e., bachelor's degree or higher) adult younger than 40 who has outstanding student debt. Specifically, he found that a household headed by a college graduate without outstanding student debt has seven times ($64,700) the typical net worth of a household headed by a college graduate who has outstanding student debt ($8,700). Cooper and Wang (2014) also found evidence that student debt had a negative correlation with wealth for households with at least some college experience and a head or spouse who was 40 years old or younger. Furthermore, they found that the negative effect that student loan debt had on net worth was more noticeable among homeowners than among renters.

*Homeownership.* There is evidence to suggest that credit constraints as a result of student loan debt may cause young adults with outstanding student debt to either delay purchasing a house or to purchase it at a much higher interest rate in the subprime loan market. The higher interest rate may make it harder to earn equity in the house and can price indebted households out of the most desirable real estate markets. For context, Mishory, O'Sullivan, and Invincibles (2012) found that the average single student debtor would have to pay close to half of his or her monthly income toward student loans and mortgage payments. As a result, the debtor would not qualify for an FHA loan or many private loans (Mishory, O'Sullivan, and Invincibles 2012). Similarly, Stone, Van Horn, and Zukin (2012) found that 40 percent of students graduating from a four-year college with outstanding student loan debt delay a major purchase, including a home.

Quantitative analysis supports descriptive findings. Shand (2007) found that student debt had a negative effect on homeownership rates when comparing four-year college graduates with and without debt. Hiltonsmith (2013) found that households with four-year college graduates and outstanding student debt had $70,000 less in home equity than similarly situated households without outstanding student debt. Potentially explaining this gap, Cooper and Wang (2014) found that student loan debt among individuals who attended college during the 1990s lowered their chances of buying a home by age 30. Similarly, Houle and Berger (2014) found that student debt was associated with a delay in buying a home among college graduates with outstanding student debt compared with those without outstanding student debt. Though Houle and Berger's findings are significant but not very strong in the aggregate, if we push the student loan system to perform above a standard of "do no harm," any evidence of distortions in borrowers' postcollege asset acquisition still raises serious concerns.

But even though the effects are not strong overall, again, some groups of students may be disproportionately affected by these pressures. Significantly, for example, Houle and Berger (2014) found evidence that suggests these effects are much stronger among black graduates with outstanding student debt. This is important for the question of whether student loans are helping to strengthen the ability of the education path to act as an equalizer in society, given the structural barriers blacks already face in the housing market (e.g., Oliver and Shapiro 2006). Similarly, given that home equity constitutes a greater proportion of the total wealth of low-income households (Kochhar, Fry, and Taylor 2011), reductions in homeownership among these disadvantaged populations may have a lasting impact.

Raising doubts about options to maneuver quickly away from these adverse outcomes, Shand (2007) found little evidence to suggest that this wealth loss is the result of credit constraints; that is, the presence of student loans on a household's balance sheet may not render the household unable to obtain a mortgage. Instead, households with outstanding student debt may be averse to obtaining a mortgage for a home. In this manner, student loans may introduce additional levers of inequality into students' postcollege lives, artificially constraining home purchase and then preventing the development of a powerful asset base (Shapiro, Meschede, and Osoro 2013).

The reason for these differences may change over time, in relation to changes in the credit markets and macroeconomic conditions in which these decisions are made. For example, as discussed above, Brown and Caldwell (2013) found that the credit scores of student loan borrowers and nonborrowers were essentially the same in 2003, but by 2012, borrowers had lower scores. Furthermore, Brown and Caldwell (2013) show that as credit scores of borrowers declined and student debt per borrower increased, homeownership rates of 30-year-old student loan borrowers decreased by more than 5 percent compared with homeownership rates of 30-year-old nonborrowers. This is a fairly substantial drop, particularly given that the overall homeownership rate for 30-year-olds is below 24 percent. The Federal Reserve Bank of New York speculates that the drop in housing rates post–Great Recession is not only due in part to credit score declines but to tighter underwriting standards and higher delinquency rates (Brown et al. 2014).

*Retirement savings.* In the American Student Assistance (2013) survey of young adults with outstanding student debt, 73 percent of borrowers say they have put off saving for retirement or other investments. In support of this finding, Elliott, Grinstein-Weiss, and Nam (2013) found that families with outstanding student debt had 52 percent less retirement savings than families with no outstanding student debt. Hiltonsmith's (2013) results indicate that dual-headed households with a college graduate and median student debt ($53,000) have about $134,000 less in retirement savings in comparison to dual-headed households with a college graduate and no student debt. Similarly, Egoian (2013) found that four-year college graduates with median debt of $23,300 had $115,096 less in retirement savings than a four-year college graduate with no student loans by the time they reach age 73.

With so many potentially intervening factors unfolding over the next few decades, the full effect may be even worse. Egoian's (2013) estimates assumed that 7 percent of an indebted college graduate's earnings go toward yearly loan repayments. This is more conservative than the recommended cutoff for unmanageable student debt of 8–10 percent (Baum and Schwartz 2005). That is, he found negative effects that kick in even at levels of indebtedness lower than recommended levels. He also based his estimates on relatively small amounts of debt—$23,000, at least far less than that apocryphal $100,000 (and even less than current estimates of average debt loads)—yet he found these relatively large effects. Moreover, his estimates assumed that households would pay off their student debt in 10 years, while, as described below, most student debtors now hold their debt longer.

Indeed, current approaches to dealing with escalating student debt largely seek to make unsustainable debt levels more bearable by extending the period of repayment. This makes monthly payments smaller, certainly, but also lengthens the period of depressed capital accumulation. Schemes such as Income-Based Repayment and Pay As You Earn plans usually require consolidating student loans and have largely been designed to prevent debt burden (how much of the borrower's monthly income has to be devoted to paying back student loans) from becoming excessive. To reduce payments, income-driven repayment plans extend the time students typically have to pay off their loans from 10 years up to 25 years, in the case of the Income Contingent Repayment plan.

We suggest that this *adds* to the student loan problem rather than solving it. Even before the growth in use of these types of programs, the length of time borrowers took to pay off loans was increasing. For example, Akers and Chingos (2014) found that the mean term of repayment in 1992 was 7.5 years; it increased to 13.4 years by 2010, largely because of students consolidating their loans. The time it takes to pay off loans is only likely to grow as income-driven repayment plans are promoted as a way to increase affordability.

Making minor changes to the terms of student loans will ultimately fail to address the problems caused by their underlying structure and mere presence in the financial aid landscape, as utilization of these modifications is growing rapidly alongside continued increases in concerns about the consequences of student borrowing. In 2013, these programs accounted for 6 percent of borrowers in repayment and, by 2014, nearly 11 percent of borrowers were in such a repayment modification (Delisle 2014b). Furthermore, these programs account for almost 22 percent of the Direct Loan portfolio in repayment (Delisle 2014b).

While these programs are lauded by many as a great way to manage loan burdens, the fact that so many borrowers require such programs should be a warning sign that the current program is flawed. That is, if so many borrowers find their regular payment plan to be unbearable, and in fact such payments are officially deemed to be unbearable, one might reasonably conclude that the United States has a student-debt problem. This realization is even more disturbing in light of evidence that the "solution" adopted to address this problem may only intensify the long-term harmful effects of student loans, while reducing the policy momentum for more substantive reforms by easing some of the pressure exerted by overburdened borrowers. In essence, then, these approaches may serve to reduce the immediate dissonance surrounding the student loan situation, even while ultimately intensifying its harms. Indeed, as Egoian's (2013) research and others makes clear, putting off asset accumulation for 10 to 20 years has real consequences; even having to divert 7 percent of one's income to paying back loans may have a large effect on long-term wealth accumulation, let alone the 10–20 percent required by income-driven repayment plans.

## CONCLUSION

In the aggregate, these findings suggest that student loans are simultaneously both more and less alarming for the future of the United States than commonly believed. Although student debt may not incite the next financial collapse, despite the sensationalist claims in some popular media coverage (for discussion of this coverage, see Karsten 2012; Harvey 2014), the long-term and cumulative effects of these derailed asset aspirations may constrain economic mobility and threaten the financial security of student borrowers throughout their lives. In turn, these effects could transmit significant, albeit indirect, economic fallout from student loans.

Unfortunately, difficulties in adequately assessing these effects, particularly on a timeline that lends itself to policy deliberations, contribute to the overly narrow frame through which student loans are judged. Even if some of the corrosive effects of deterring homeownership, for example, may not be felt until today's indebted youth lack the asset foundation with which to leverage a secure retirement (Pew Charitable Trusts 2013), that slow-moving threat is no less deserving of our urgent policy attention.

Collectively, this body of evidence makes clear that the student loan program exacerbates uneven returns on a college degree. This conclusion is all the more convincing when we consider that it is not based on one study but an aggregation of analyses conducted by a variety of different researchers, ranging across a number of different outcomes (e.g., marriage, homeownership, financial distress, etc.), using a variety of different methods and samples. Even older studies, largely conducted using datasets that predate the more dramatic, recent increase in student borrowing, usually find evidence of adverse effects. However, the intensifying pace of research into these student loan outcomes in the past few years hints at the growing number of researchers beginning to question the assumption of the existing financial aid paradigm that the primary goal of financial aid is to help pay for college. The anomalies they are discovering are contributing to individual and collective questioning of the fundamental soundness of this approach. Evidenced by the shift in scientific inquiries, the financial aid community is implicitly, if not yet explicitly, acknowledging that financial aid should do more. It is our hope that this may represent the beginning of a much needed financial aid revolution.

According to Kuhn (1962), periods of scientific revolution are often met by resistance in an attempt to maintain the current paradigm. We have seen this in the case of student debt. We are far enough down the policy path of student indebtedness to make it difficult to see our way out, and so we have adjusted to burdensome student debt as a "natural" part of the American life cycle, normalizing a rather extraordinary phenomenon that sees many U.S. college graduates *worse off* in measures of financial well-being, health, and even overall life satisfaction (Dugan and Kafka 2014) as an apparent side effect of their use of a financial aid product that is supposed to facilitate ultimate improvements in all of these indicators. Scratching the surface of the U.S. student loan debate reveals the fact that we are allowing student debt a sort of grace unparalleled in U.S. policy, continually moving the goalposts as we seek to console ourselves that a financial aid system predicated largely on borrowing can somehow work. Instead of carefully considering the kind of policy we want to facilitate our children's access to the higher education that most Americans believe is essential for economic mobility (Newport and Busteed 2013), we look for approaches that would modify the student loan system enough to allow it to survive, even while holding low expectations for this very significant investment. Perhaps like the proverbial frog in boiling water, we have gradually come to expect that for many, if not most, U.S. college students, the only path to college and the prosperity that lies beyond is high debt.

Only a recognized crisis can impel us to another policy plane. While the straw men batted about today are poor substitutes for this catalyzing realization, it is our contention that the growing body of sound evidence of student debt's true effects is more than up to this task, if we can compellingly articulate the promise of an alternative paradigm. After presenting some additional, novel analyses our own inquiries have discovered, we next turn to the discussion of what such a different lens could reveal.

# SIX

## Delayed Dreams

Most people do not dream of going to college and becoming rich; that is, higher education is, for the most, a path to the American Dream of middle-class financial security and upward mobility, not a perceived ticket to great riches. Generally, when people dream of being rich, they think of being a professional athlete, an actor, a singer, an entrepreneur, or a lottery winner. People may dream of getting rich, but it is not this illusion of quick fortune that animates individual actions nor characterizes the American ideal. Instead, Americans expect and work toward the opportunity to become middle-class through education, and it is this promise that underscores our vision of ourselves and our presumed "contract" with the institutions that govern U.S. society.

In recognition of the role that educational attainment plays in opening the door to this archetypal middle-class ideal, U.S. policy decided some time ago that children's work would be schoolwork. Children and their parents believe that the reward for innate intellectual ability and expended academic effort will be a chance to reach, not ease and opulence, but security and upward progress. U.S. policy affirms that education is the primary path for achieving the American Dream. Therefore, quick climbs from rags to riches are presumed to be quixotic, fleeting, and not necessarily even desirable. In contrast, the denial of a fair shot to enter and stay in the middle class through education imperils the foundation on which our collective identity rests and threatens to rewrite the American narrative of success through effort and ability, mediated through attainment of education.

As the nation has developed, we have expanded support for public schools, colleges, and universities and then provided government subsidies to facilitate individual access to higher education. Seen through the lens of this equation underlying the American Dream, this educational expenditure is correctly understood as an investment in economic mobility, a significant contribution toward our collective future prosperity, and a key element of the unwritten agreement between individuals and society, dictating who can get ahead and how. Critically, this relatively grandiose role for higher education policy and, specifically, financial aid, is not just theoretical but, indeed, informs Americans' expectations for their own lives.

As the calculations on which this arrangement rests shift in the changing economy, and economic mobility appears increasingly elusive, the precariousness of this education and prosperity linkage may be at the heart of rising anxiety. Although economists and others assume that subjective calculations about how much people can expect to earn by the end of their lives play significant roles in decisions to attend college, which college to attend, and whether or not to borrow, in real life, people think in terms that are simultaneously more abstract and, yet, more immediate and even narrow. If people who complete college earn double what people who do not attend college earn over the course of their lives but are still unable to live the middle-class lifestyle they expected when they went to college, or if they cannot start to live it until well into their 30s or 40s, education may cease in their minds to be a viable path to the prosperity to which they aspire, even if the calculation is still favorable on paper, at least ultimately.

In chapters 4 and 5, we reviewed a mounting body of evidence of how the student loan program has become a roadblock on the education path to achieving the American Dream of economic mobility. At the very least, student loans may be pushing the rewards of education so far out into the future that its appeal as a path may seem far less alluring than it once did. Compounding the problem is the fact that while young adults in the 1980s (ironically when student loans were just becoming the dominant means of financing education) reached the middle of the wage distribution at age 26, by 2012, young adults in the general population needed until age 30 to reach that milestone; for Black Americans, this economic security was not achieved until age 33 (Carnevale, Hanson, and Gulish 2013). Of course, this delayed launch of a strong economic foundation will have lifelong implications for individuals (Carnevale, et al. 2013, 1). Across society, these figures are rewriting the story linking education, financial well-being, and the promise of America and reshaping the trajectories that parents imagine for their children and that children see for themselves.

In the remainder of this chapter, we present new evidence of the potential negative effects that student loans can have on young adults' asset-accumulation potential. A way that student loans do this may be by hindering young adults' ability to use their income to build assets as their income is diverted to debt repayment over their lifetimes. We suggest that at the critical period of young adulthood, one's failure to build an asset foundation may create a financial deficit from which it is difficult to recover.

## STUDENT LOAN EFFECTS ON YOUNG ADULTS' NET WORTH ACCUMULATION

The evidence presented here was first presented in a study by Elliott, Lewis, and Johnson (2014), "Unequal Outcomes: Student Loan Effects on Young Adults' Net Worth Accumulation." This study examined the effects of student debt on young adults' asset accumulation by their education level. Separate samples of respondents, associate degree or some college, bachelor's degree, and graduate degree holders, were used because prior research also indicates that college and university characteristics are important predictors of student debt (Baum and Saunders 1998; Choy and Carroll 2000; Houle 2014). Discrepancies in amount owed by degree has led some researchers to suggest that if there is a college-debt problem, it is among graduate students because they are the ones with high student debt (e.g., Delisle 2014a). Part of what this line of thought assumes is that the problem is the *amount* of debt students borrow, and because graduate students borrow more, if there is a problem, it is with them. As Delisle (2014a) says, "Despite the trends, most accounts of student debt treat loans from graduate and undergraduate studies as one and the same, distorting how we view issues of college costs, student debt, and what policymakers should do in response" (1).

As Delisle (2014a) points out, there very well might be different policy considerations as well as moral commitments to consider when it comes to financing graduate degrees as opposed to an associate or bachelor's degree. Certainly, these different levels of degree attainment play different rhetorical functions in the U.S. economy, including related to the pursuit of the American Dream. However, here our focus is on whether having outstanding student debt is associated with being more likely to report having more overall debt than assets (i.e., student debt's effects on net worth) and whether this is true at one education level and not another. So, here we separate out respondents into different groups based on the level of educational attainment they achieved. For specific details about the methods used in this study, see the appendix.

### "Some College" or Associate Degree Respondents

With a set of predictors, we use the generalized ordinal logistic model to estimate the probability that a respondent reports having negative net worth (i.e., assets < debts), even (i.e., assets = debts), or positive net worth (i.e., assets > debts) (see the appendix for a more detailed discussion of methods). These models include estimates of threshold values that act as "cut points" between outcomes, a fact that we illustrate in two figures (see "Bachelor with Loans" and "Bachelor without Loans"). One threshold separates those young adults who are predicted to have negative net worth from those who are even, while another separates young adults who have positive net worth from those who are even.

In figures 6.1 and 6.2, we see the estimated probabilities as they depend on disposable income. Disposable income is the amount of monthly income a respondent has minus his or her monthly student loan payment. The light gray "negative" area represents the probability that a respondent is below both threshold values. The dark gray area, representing the chances of being in the "even" category, exists between the two thresholds. When a respondent's estimates exceed both thresholds, then we predict that the respondent will report having positive net worth.

The boundaries between the areas are not straight lines. Instead, they are actually portions of elongated S-shaped curves. The portions of these curves that are revealed in the figure are an important part of the story. In figure 6.1, one is struck by the fact that the probability of remaining in the even category is more or less fixed for young adults with some college or an associate degree and monthly student loan payments. From left to right, it appears as though young adults are moving from negative net worth into even at about the same rate that they are moving from even into positive net worth.

In figure 6.2, we see a slightly different process taking place among young adults with some college or an associate degree but who have monthly student loan payments. Notice that the light gray and dark gray areas are both shrinking as disposable income increases, meaning that the transition from negative net worth to having positive net worth is accelerated. The end result is that there is a larger area representing respondents who report having positive net worth.

Figure 6.1    Predicted Probabilities—Some College with Loans

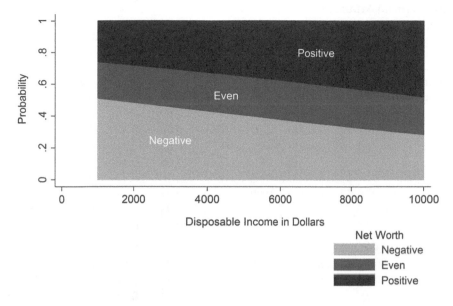

Figure 6.2    Predicted Probabilities—Some College without Loans

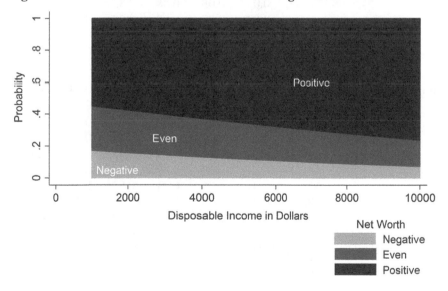

Interestingly, table 6.1 makes it clear that, unlike the other groups we examine (bachelor's degree and graduate degree), when young adults with an associate degree or some college have monthly student loan payments, it does not appear to matter whether they have more or less disposable

**Table 6.1  Predicted Probabilities for the Ordinal Logit Models by Educational Attainment**

| | Disposable Income | No Loans | | | Has Loans | | |
|---|---|---|---|---|---|---|---|
| | | Debt | Even | Ahead | Debt | Even | Ahead |
| Some College or | $1,000 | 0.17 | 0.28 | 0.55 | 0.51 | 0.23 | 0.26 |
| Associate Degree | $2,000 | 0.16 | 0.27 | 0.58 | 0.48 | 0.24 | 0.28 |
| | $3,000 | 0.14 | 0.25 | 0.60 | 0.46 | 0.24 | 0.30 |
| | $4,000 | 0.13 | 0.24 | 0.63 | 0.43 | 0.24 | 0.33 |
| | $5,000 | 0.12 | 0.23 | 0.65 | 0.41 | 0.25 | 0.35 |
| | $6,000 | 0.11 | 0.21 | 0.68 | 0.38 | 0.25 | 0.37 |
| | $7,000 | 0.10 | 0.20 | 0.70 | 0.35 | 0.25 | 0.40 |
| | $8,000 | 0.09 | 0.19 | 0.72 | 0.33 | 0.24 | 0.43 |
| | $9,000 | 0.08 | 0.18 | 0.74 | 0.31 | 0.24 | 0.45 |
| | $10,000 | 0.07 | 0.16 | 0.76 | 0.51 | 0.23 | 0.26 |
| Bachelor's Degree | $1,000 | 0.12 | 0.20 | 0.68 | 0.63 | 0.18 | 0.20 |
| | $2,000 | 0.10 | 0.17 | 0.73 | 0.57 | 0.20 | 0.24 |
| | $3,000 | 0.08 | 0.15 | 0.77 | 0.51 | 0.21 | 0.28 |
| | $4,000 | 0.06 | 0.12 | 0.81 | 0.45 | 0.22 | 0.34 |
| | $5,000 | 0.05 | 0.10 | 0.85 | 0.39 | 0.22 | 0.39 |
| | $6,000 | 0.04 | 0.08 | 0.88 | 0.33 | 0.22 | 0.45 |
| | $7,000 | 0.03 | 0.07 | 0.90 | 0.28 | 0.21 | 0.51 |
| | $8,000 | 0.02 | 0.06 | 0.92 | 0.23 | 0.19 | 0.57 |
| | $9,000 | 0.02 | 0.04 | 0.94 | 0.19 | 0.18 | 0.63 |
| | $10,000 | 0.01 | 0.04 | 0.95 | 0.16 | 0.16 | 0.69 |
| Graduate Degree | $1,000 | 0.14 | 0.14 | 0.72 | 0.70 | 0.14 | 0.15 |
| | $2,000 | 0.12 | 0.12 | 0.76 | 0.65 | 0.16 | 0.19 |
| | $3,000 | 0.10 | 0.10 | 0.80 | 0.60 | 0.18 | 0.23 |
| | $4,000 | 0.08 | 0.09 | 0.84 | 0.54 | 0.19 | 0.27 |
| | $5,000 | 0.06 | 0.07 | 0.87 | 0.48 | 0.20 | 0.32 |
| | $6,000 | 0.05 | 0.06 | 0.89 | 0.42 | 0.21 | 0.37 |
| | $7,000 | 0.04 | 0.05 | 0.91 | 0.37 | 0.21 | 0.43 |
| | $8,000 | 0.03 | 0.04 | 0.93 | 0.31 | 0.20 | 0.48 |
| | $9,000 | 0.03 | 0.03 | 0.94 | 0.27 | 0.19 | 0.54 |
| | $10,000 | 0.02 | 0.03 | 0.95 | 0.22 | 0.18 | 0.60 |

*Note*: See figures 1–6 for a picture of the predicted probabilities.
*Source*: Data from the Educational Longitudinal Study (ELS).

income. For example, these young adults have a 51 percent chance of reporting having negative net worth whether they have $1,000 of disposable income or $10,000. In contrast, if they have no monthly student loan payments, more disposable income appears to be associated with having less of a chance of reporting having negative net worth. So, for example, if they have $1,000 of disposable income, they have about a 17 percent chance of reporting having negative net worth, but this drops to only a 7 percent chance if they have $10,000 of disposable income.

This reveals graphically what other analyses suggest: for student borrowers with comparatively low levels of postsecondary education and outstanding student loan debt, college may not have been such a good bet. Therefore, finding ways to protect these students from the extra burden of student debt may be particularly important.

## Results for Bachelor's Degree Respondents

Table 6.1 indicates that the predicted probability of having negative net worth for young adults who hold a bachelor's degree and have no monthly student loan payments is 0.12 if he has $1,000 of disposable income and 0.01 if he has $10,000 of disposable income. Conversely, the predicted probability of young adults with a bachelor's degree and monthly student loan payments is higher even when the young adult with student loan payments has $10,000 of disposable income in comparison to a young adult with no student loans (0.16 versus 0.12, respectively). Moreover, if a young adult with a bachelor's degree and monthly student loan payments has $3,000 or less of disposable income, he has better than a 50 percent chance of reporting having negative net worth. Depending on whether bachelor's degree holders have $1,000 of disposable income or $10,000, the predicted probability of reporting having positive net worth ranges from 0.68 to 0.95, respectively, among those with no monthly student loan payments; in contrast, it ranges from 0.20 to 0.69 among those with monthly student loan payments.

The differences between young adults with a bachelor's degree and monthly student loan payments and those with no monthly student loan payments are graphically depicted in figures 6.3 and 6.4. These figures speak to the return on a college degree for those with and without student loans and raise questions about the ability of education to reach its full capacity as a catalyst for real economic well-being as long as student loans remain the primary instrument for financing college.

## Results for Graduate Degree Respondents

It appears from figures 6.5 and 6.6 that young adults who go on to receive a graduate degree and have monthly student loan payments also have a greater chance of reporting having negative net worth than positive

**Figure 6.3    Predicted Probabilities—Bachelor with Loans**

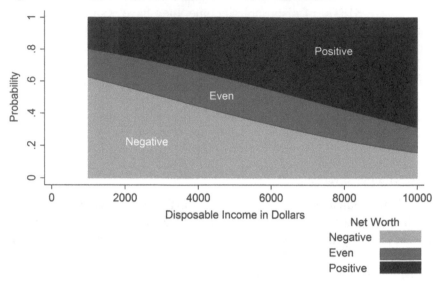

**Figure 6.4    Predicted Probabilities—Bachelor without Loans**

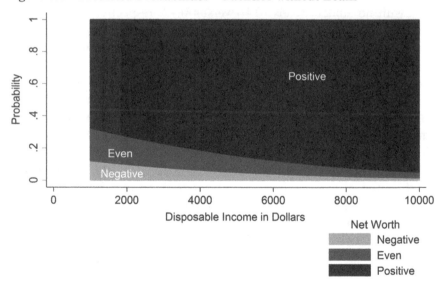

net worth in comparison to similarly situated young adults who have no monthly student loan payments. Further, table 6.1 indicates that while having more disposable income appears to buffer young adults with a graduate degree from some of the negative effects that student debt may

**Figure 6.5    Predicted Probabilities—Graduate with Loans**

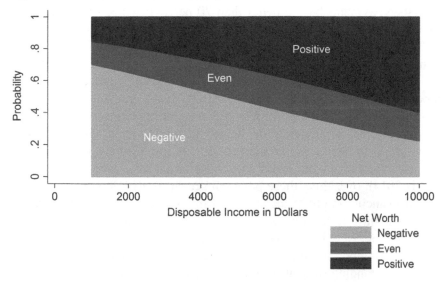

**Figure 6.6    Predicted Probabilities—Graduate without Loans**

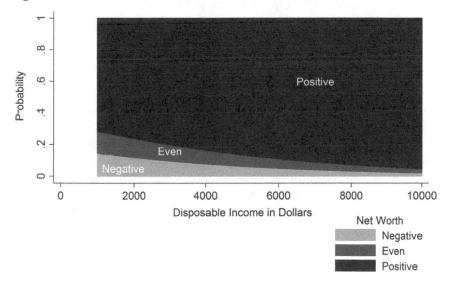

have on wealth accumulation, young adults strapped with student loan payments have a greater chance of reporting having negative net worth than positive net worth in comparison to their counterparts with no student loan payments.

For example, young adults with a graduate degree and no monthly student loan payments have a better than 70 percent chance of having positive net worth regardless of whether their disposable income is $1,000 or $10,000; it climbs to 95 percent if it is $10,000. Conversely, even if a young adult with a graduate degree and monthly student loan payments has disposable income of $10,000, he has less than a 70 percent chance of reporting positive net worth. Below $8,000, such a graduate has less than a 50 percent chance of reporting having positive net worth.

In addition to influencing the solidity of these young adults' financial foundations following higher education, with implications, then, for later economic mobility from leveraging these initial asset levels (Elliott and Lewis 2014), over time, these potential scenarios also illustrate how education financing might shape students' major and career choices, as students who have to borrow heavily have much less margin for choosing a path with relatively less immediate financial payoff.

It is also important to point out, separate from disposable income, just having outstanding student debt has a negative association with net worth for all three educational attainment levels. The fact that debt of any size may bring about financial hardship, including putting graduates in a position of negative net worth, with its associated and lasting effects, raises the question of whether making student loans the centerpiece of the U.S. financial aid system is an inherently flawed idea. Because  the ultimate purpose of higher education and, then, whatever system finances it, is not just college completion but the greater levels of financial well-being that educational attainment is supposed to secure, these findings serve to poke holes in the paradigm that holds that any financial aid approach that secures access to college is basically sound. These data also point to the potential futility of policy reforms that merely seek to tweak the student loan system to mitigate its worst effects, particularly without fully and adequately articulating the potential dimensions in which student loans' effects are felt.

As we understand student borrowing today, the factors that influence whether student debt will be harmful for a given student include not only the amount of debt but other, more complex considerations, including the kind of postsecondary institution attended, the major pursued, the kind of job students secure after graduation, what the economy will be like, and the options they have before, during and after higher education. Most of these factors are at least partially outside of the student's direct control, pointing to the need for larger, systemic reforms to create the conditions in which students' economic well-being can be secured, if not *because* of the pursuit of higher education at least *in spite* of it.

## CONCLUSION

In this chapter, we turned our attention to different measures of the extent to which student loans influence the time it takes young adults to reach the median of the income and wealth distribution, and the evidence is not just disappointing—it is alarming. These new quantitative findings align with other analyses, such as by the Pew Charitable Trusts (2014), which suggest that student debt may be a significant part of the reason why current cohorts fare poorly compared with their parents' financial positions. There is reason to believe that if we expect student loans to actually help us address our greatest collective challenges, particularly those that threaten the viability of the American Dream—rising inequality and constrained economic growth—they are not only falling short, they may be building a steeper hill for other policies to climb.

There is no more central articulation of the American Dream than the chance for one's children to do better than oneself through the exertion of ability and effort. This promise and its realization, albeit in unequal extents, is at the core of our own stories and a driving force animating the individual actions of Americans multiplied across our economy.

Here, we are faced with evidence that student loans may short-circuit those connections, delaying the American Dream to the point of derailment. The potential for depression of asset accumulation in the immediate postcollege period as a result of real financial strains of debt repayment matters when it comes to understanding the financial well-being of young adults and growing wealth inequality. Even students with outstanding debt who do well in college may struggle to understand why they are not reaping the gains of that academic achievement to the same extent as their counterparts who have no student debt. There are real opportunity costs to the student loan system, which has largely crowded out our collective capacity to imagine anything else. The policy energy consumed by tinkering with a fundamentally flawed student loan system in an effort to blunt its most negative effects could be otherwise deployed to construct new asset-empowered financial aid models that could improve student outcomes.

U.S. policy should prioritize outcomes over instruments, and we must not allow ourselves to cling to an intervention for sentimental value or because we are afraid of what would follow in its absence. Overheated debate about the "next financial crisis," on the one hand, and defensive dismissal of evidence as inconsequential, on the other, notwithstanding, evidence reveals real dangers in continuing on our current path with student loans—for individuals, for the macroeconomy, and, perhaps most importantly, for our vision of ourselves and the dream that animates us.

Just as importantly, there is evidence to suggest significant advantages from shifting course and resetting the default to saving for postsecondary education, rather than leveraging one's future for it. Taking this alternate path requires the vision to imagine better outcomes, which even with research to recommend it can demand a leap of faith, but our children deserve it. It is time for a paradigm that expects our financial aid system to deliver what education is designed to facilitate: a meaningful chance to better oneself, and a path to the same that Americans can really believe in.

# SEVEN

## Can't See the Forest for the Trees

Sometimes social reformers must labor to draw attention to the problems that concern them before they can rally allies to support their specific proposed solutions. This process of "claims making" can be lengthy (Chapin 2014, 12) and demand considerable effort as advocates seek to vault their issues onto the agenda. Not so the problems associated with student debt in the United States. The growth in the size and incidence of student debt and the repayment difficulties and related externalities that result from this previously unprecedented borrowing (Miller 2014) have created a large and vocal constituency that demands attention. Even if few policy makers or pundits publicly make the connection between the increase in student loans and growing public malaise, there is urgent demand for action from many in that public who understand that there's something wrong with how we're financing college, even if they can't precisely name it, and who want the U.S. government to protect them and their children from the erosion of the American Dream, more than anything else (Potts 2014).

Popular media coverage of repayment woes skyrocketed following the 2008 financial collapse (see Frizell 2014; Korkki 2014; Levin 2013). These high-profile examples of failure in the student loan market fuel the chatter about student borrowing and contribute to the perception that student debt is *the* issue for a generation of young adults (Wilezol 2014). Particularly as student borrowers come of age in the halls of government and the ranks of business, individuals who have been personally touched by student loans are positioned to make student loan reform an issue for legislative and regulatory action. Student loans are clearly on the table, raising the stakes for debates about precisely toward what ends to direct this momentum and how best to capitalize on this moment of political opportunity. As in so much of our political life, without clarity about the elements of the student loan landscape that are concerning and the reasons why we should care about student borrowing, we are unlikely to arrive at policy solutions that truly address the problems.

The policy attention afforded to student debt allows those seeking change to proceed directly to the *what* of reform, having clearly established that the remaining question is about the policy levers that should be used, not whether we need change. Indeed, some would argue that there is today so much appetite for student loan reform that the risk of doing the wrong thing is significant, when so much hunger exists to just do *something*. This risk is heightened within the context of a constrained national debate about student loans and their effects, where the energy is mostly centered on repayment rather than a broader view of student loan effects before, during, and after college.

Hampered by a paradigm that centers myopically on financial aid as access, even scholarly contributions are less than optimally oriented to serve as catalysts for meaningful alternatives. Without clearly connecting student debt to the constrained life chances of the Americans whose economic fortunes depend on the ladder of higher education, we may fail to recognize the hollow nature of some proposed reforms. Unless we understand what is really at stake in a conversation about student debt and pursue policy change that restores higher education's vibrant equalizing role within our society, we will struggle to realize progress.

Today, our collective vision is obscured by a rather narrow focus on one dimension of student loan effects (i.e., we cannot see the forest for the trees), which limits the range of policy options we consider to mostly tweaks at the edges of the existing student loan system rather than bold proposals to restructure and redirect financial aid policy. In the realm of student loans, the political cost of this limited scope of action is significant, representing as it does a real risk of squandering this political moment with reforms that only appear substantive but still leave American children and families exposed to the harmful educational, economic, and psychic effects of a largely failed approach to college financing. Other voices have articulated this concern as well, that incremental policy change may "neuter" the voices calling for real change, "silencing the fire" for real solutions, a consequence that would have long-term political consequences (Goldrick-Rab 2013, 6). If these proposals would have the aggregate effect of also forestalling institutional reforms (Delisle and Holt 2012) and excusing the reductions in public funding for higher education that threaten to unravel the social contract (Potts 2014), the effects could be widespread as well.

The evidence in this volume is in part our contribution to the effort to expand this debate, looking more comprehensively at the ways student loans are failing, developing more completely a set of metrics by which to evaluate loans' effects, and considering a fundamental pivot away from student borrowing as the central financial aid approach. We believe that the state of the financial aid field is poised at the precipice of a decisive crisis that could tip toward revolution, and while we have an appropriately modest expectation for our own contributions, we optimistically hope to play some role in providing this push.

Viewed in light of the growing evidence of student loans' misalignment with higher education's role as an arbiter of equity and a catalyst of economic mobility in the U.S. economy, the proposals at the forefront of the student loan debate are glaringly sparse and tragically limited. As a group, they focus almost exclusively on softening the blow dealt by student loans, rather than avoiding the damage in the first place. Most are designed to help borrowers cope with the consequences of their student borrowing, without provisions to avoid the educational, social, and financial hazards of our debt-dependent system. Most would fail to close the achievement gaps that threaten the viability of education as a path to the American Dream. Some could even exacerbate inequality by, for example, funneling low-income, largely debt-dependent students to less-expensive institutions with lower graduation rates (Goldrick-Rab and Kendall 2014) or subsidizing the advanced educations of relatively high-earning borrowers (Delisle and Holt 2012). Some might prolong the harmful effects on financial and life outcomes (e.g., Egoian 2013) by extending the repayment period or making other modifications. Others might provide some relief to student borrowers in the form of lightened repayment burdens and lower incidence of delinquency and default (Sheets and Crawford 2014) but would still fail to address the loans' deterrent effects (Baum and O'Malley 2003) or the corrosive effect of student loans on the asset accumulation of young Americans.

Any one or a combination of these approaches could serve to reinforce in the minds of young Americans the idea that individuals are ultimately responsible for their own higher education, and that mere access should be all that matters. This debate—and just as importantly what we're *not* talking about—could undermine Americans' institutional efficacy, as they rightly conclude that lowering their interest rate slightly still doesn't make student loans an institution that really works for their lives.

If policy cycles were infinite, windows of opportunity never closed, and the public's attention never waned, then some of the minor adjustments proposed to the student loan system today might be viewed as interim steps on the path to more significant financial aid reform. Policy change does not happen that way, however (Kingdon 2010), and so the political costs of these nonsolutions may be significant, along with the psychic toll exacted on struggling student borrowers who are unclear why reform has not resolved the problems they experience as a result of their student debt.

In the sections that follow, we outline some of the policy innovations that have received the most attention and some of the limitations of these approaches. Our critique is rooted in our reading of the evidence of the reasons why and how student loans are today compromising students' returns on their educational investment and hindering their upward mobility. It is grounded in our understanding that higher education matters not just for individuals' own career prospects, but as a core mechanism through which Americans have a realistic hope of realizing the gains of their expended effort and ability. It is because so much is at stake that these policies warrant careful scrutiny. With nothing less than the viability of the American Dream hanging in the balance, "a little bit better" cannot be good enough.

## GIVE STUDENTS MORE INFORMATION ABOUT DEBT

In a rare show of relative bipartisan consensus, the Empowering Students through Enhanced Financial Counseling Act passed the U.S. House of Representatives in a 405–11 vote in July 2014. The legislation was touted by supporters as "a step to help students avoid unmanageable debt" (see Shea-Porter 2014), despite not containing any provisions to actually reduce students' need to borrow. Instead of moving away from student loans as a central higher education financing mechanism—by perhaps increasing state funding for institutions (Potts 2014) or increasing need-based aid (Burd 2013)—the bill would provide more frequent and comprehensive entrance and exit counseling for student loan borrowers, informed by requirements that institutions annually project expected total student loan debt and likely repayment scenarios.

Other proposals have similarly posited that providing students with more complete information would facilitate better decisions and, by extension, better student loan outcomes, even though empirical evidence has found relatively little connection between such counseling and enrollment decisions (Bettinger, Long, Oreopoulos, and Sanbonmatsu 2009). Although students should inarguably have access to the most accurate, comprehensive, and useful information possible as they contemplate a significant step in their futures, there are two primary reasons why equipping students with information about the costs of financing and practices to manage the costs is unlikely to bring significant improvements in their total debt burden or their ability to manage their debt.

First, information about the true cost of financing is only one part of the context students need to consider in weighing their financial aid, and the substantial unknowns that surround their futures make informed decision making elusive. One's decision to borrow cannot be judged to have been good or not without considering the potential—and likely—return on the investment purchased with that debt, and here it is unreasonable to expect students to succeed where economists cannot. The subjective calculation of the return on college is not a scientific analysis, and the process of weighing even the available evidence is a highly emotional one. The data potential students collect to make this calculation are largely anecdotal, tested through life experience and colored by the hopes and dreams they carry to the point of college enrollment.

Indeed, the framing of higher education and its function in the U.S. economy is at odds with this expectation that students rationally calculate the wisdom of using debt to finance a college education. The U.S. economy is supposed to work in part by encouraging Americans to strive beyond their station, take bold risks in pursuit of their passions, and succeed where others might not. Young adults, propelled into college by a compelling vision of their futures, have mostly bought into this rhetoric, which makes the expectation that they instead coolly calculate whether college is really in their best interest infeasible and even cynical.

Even armed with information about interest rates, monthly payments, and overall debt loads, the decision to borrow is, at least in part, based on prospective students' ability to accurately predict what their particular future earnings will be. As little of the information needed for making the calculation is known (e.g., whether one will get a job after graduation, whether that job will be in the chosen field, if the field will even exist in 10 years, and how much the borrower will earn over the course of his or her life) at the time the decision is to be made, it is a qualitatively different type of calculation than the economist makes, for example, when calculating lifetime earnings.

Even in the best of economic times, there is no guarantee that past returns will come to pass in the future. This is further complicated by the fact that graduating with a four-year degree is almost a 50/50 proposition in America (NCES 2012), so initiating pursuit of a degree does not at all guarantee that one will complete it. This context of uncertainty stands in sharp contrast to the protections afforded lenders, who have been comforted by policy protections that allow debt collectors to garnish wages, including huge penalties that balloon what is owed, polices that make discharging student loans within bankruptcy nearly impossible, and government assistance in collecting unpaid debts.

But the greatest limitation in this "information as power" proposal may be the rather obvious fact that, absent meaningful alternatives, students convinced by the information shared in one of these counseling sessions that possibly they cannot really afford the student loans offered may be forced to then forego higher education altogether. Most of the information provided to students in the interest of informing their student borrowing choices centers on repayment options (see http://studentloanhelp.org) and may be expected only to reduce delinquency and default, which is just one type of indicator of student-debt distress. Information alone cannot reduce loans' adverse effects on graduates' asset accumulation, and it is unlikely to make loans more facilitative of college persistence, either.

The potential that helping students to more fully understand the true costs of student borrowing could actually deter them from college is obviously more than just an unfortunate, unintended consequence of this student credit counseling approach; it exposes the inadequacy and inherent unfairness of our current, debt-dependent financial aid system. Loan aversion is real (Perna 2000), and there is little evidence to suggest that more accurately and completely informing students of the true costs of student borrowing will soften these effects. Without meaningful options from which students can construct sound choices, providing students with additional information about college costs and, certainly, the true costs of student-debt financing earlier in their academic careers could be decidedly counterproductive. In addition, the particular tactic of information provision outlined in this intervention requires that students make it to the point of college enrollment, a tragically rare feat for many disadvantaged students (see NCES 2013).

U.S. financial aid policy should not tolerate reform that rests on an unspoken conclusion that some students are simply not exercising good judgment in deciding to borrow to attend postsecondary education—at least, deciding to borrow to attend the institution of their choice or to pursue their chosen course of study. Further, the possibility of aid should not first become known only at the moment of readiness, when so many factors inequitably contribute to this outcome. Financial aid policy should not contribute to students' sense that they are, somehow, culpable for the problems they experience as a result of their student loans and that they could have somehow avoided this fate if they had only known more, particularly when paralleled by consistent messages coaching young people to perceive higher education as their only reliable path to upward mobility. U.S. policy should not pin our hopes for restoring higher education's purpose on those who have been systematically disadvantaged by its failings nor publicly chide them for being insufficiently savvy to avoid the inherent risks of this flawed system.

Although providing more accurate information about the outcomes delivered by a given institution can facilitate better decision making by students and, indeed, better outcomes through the mutually reinforcing processes of competition and accountability (Inside Higher Ed 2014), we cannot reasonably expect to solve the student-debt problem by simply better informing students of how problematic their student debt is likely to be. Instead, policy reforms to require entrance and exit counseling, improve loan disclosures, and better train advisers to help students navigate financial aid options should be woven into reforms of the options themselves. Students need better choices—real and meaningful ones—if they are to be expected to make better decisions. Critical to the success of such a system, of course, is the existence of nondebt alternatives, such that students can be informed about true options, rather than counseled as to how to cope with the fallout or, worse, frightened away from the very human capital investment that we promise can deliver them from disadvantage.

## INCOME-BASED REPAYMENT

Income-based repayment (IBR) schemes, which set repayment expectations at a fixed percentage of the student borrower's postcollege income, are a logical policy response to a narrow view of the student-debt problem in the United States. If one views as problematic only the extent to which student borrowers struggle to keep up with payments, then setting those payments at a more affordable level would seem to resolve the issue, although considerable disagreement persists about the definition of "affordable" and how best to manipulate the repayment experience. In essence, if the problem is disruption in repayments to the *holder* of the debt, rather than the consequences—particularly related to equity, capital accumulation (Hiltonsmith 2013; Stone, Van Horn, and Zukin 2012), and overall financial strain (Fry 2014)—to the *debtor*, then income-based repayment is a far more satisfactory response. Again, this speaks to the importance of correctly understanding the dynamics of the student-debt problem and of not squandering the political momentum around student debt with policy changes that will likely fail to significantly improve these more significant indicators.

Income-based repayment (IBR) has long been an option for student borrowers in the United States, but changes enacted recently, particularly expanded eligibility through Pay As You Earn in June 2014, have significantly increased participation in IBR. Unfortunately, most analysts view that IBR was not improved with these changes. The costs of the program have increased considerably, but IBR still does not represent a stronger safety net for the borrowers who most need one. Instead, IBR may serve only to make us feel that student loans are better or safer without addressing their real effects.

This idea of IBR as blinding people to the real problem is seen in critiques of IBR proposals by groups pushing for student-debt reform that focus on expanding eligibility and increasing the types of loans included in IBR, rather than highlighting the limited effect of any IBR approach (Devarics 2011). But IBR is more than just an incomplete solution. When we more fully and accurately understand the costs of student borrowing, we can see in IBR approaches not just a lost opportunity but an actual move in the wrong direction, as extending the period of repayment can expose student borrowers to more protracted interference with wealth-building objectives. Borrowers may actually pay more because they are paying more slowly, resulting in higher overall interest costs and even negative amortization. Students may be comforted by the prospect of protection against wildly disproportionate monthly payment burdens and may then fail to see the danger in their proposed loan amount, even as their debt obligations persistently deny them equitable opportunities to build an asset foundation. In effect, student borrowers using IBR are repaying on terms that the financial literacy classes to which they may have been exposed as students would have explicitly discouraged, an illogical approach from the government lender.

Even if interest rates are adjusted so that borrowers do not pay a higher net cost for their financing in an income-based repayment scheme than they would under traditional terms, which is currently not the case, there are real risks that these individuals will miss critical opportunities to invest in their asset foundation, with lifelong effects on their overall financial status. As discussed in earlier chapters, missed opportunities to invest in one's asset foundations likely have lasting—even permanent—implications. Even with assumptions more conservative than the recommended cutoff for unmanageable student debt of 8–10 percent (Baum and Schwartz 2005) and lower than many students would pay in an income-based repayment plan (Delisle and Holt 2013), analysis still finds negative effects (Egoian 2013; Brown, Haughwout, Lee, Scally, and van der Klaauw 2015).

When debt is correctly understood as a threat to net worth accumulation, extending the period over which debtors discharge their liabilities may actually add to the student loan problem rather than solve it. Student debtors whose income is diverted over a period of many years to finance their debt obligations may struggle to ever catch up in asset accumulation, given the power of compounding and the importance of cultivating early habits of saving. As emphasized in the new studies described earlier, there is evidence that student loan debt may already be contributing to the prolonged period of transition to adulthood, with student debtors reporting delayed marriage (Gicheva 2011), childbearing (American Student Assistance 2013), and homeownership (Stone, Van Horn, and Zukin 2012), as well as a delay in reaching the median in income and wealth distributions. Using extended repayment periods and adjustments to monthly payment expectations to, in many ways, mask the true impact of student debt, may only intensify these effects.

The outcomes reported for current IBR and related modification programs are themselves evidence of the failure of these approaches to address the underlying problems associated with student loans. Among these data points is analysis that has found that forgiveness of remaining debt after allowed repayment periods accounts for as much as half of the costs of current income-based repayment programs (Akers and Chingos 2014). This policy reality suggests that debt forgiveness, not actual repayment, is the final outcome for many student borrowers, a finding that should call into question the wisdom and, indeed, the honesty of relying on student loans for financial aid in the first place. That forgiveness is not triggered for at least 10 years is disturbing in light of debt effects on asset accumulation.

Utilization of these modifications is growing rapidly alongside continued increases in concerns about the consequences of student borrowing. In 2013, these programs accounted for 6 percent of borrowers in repayment, and by 2014, nearly 11 percent of borrowers were in such a repayment modification (Delisle 2014b). Furthermore, these programs account for almost 22 percent of the Direct Loan portfolio in repayment (Delisle 2014b). This growth, along with incentive structures that allow for significant loan forgiveness, makes IBR potentially unsustainable; some analysts judge that only its relative obscurity makes it viable today (Delisle and Holt 2013), a situation likely to change as concerns about defaults increase.

Significantly, this student loan "reform" is not inexpensive, with budget estimates upward of $7.6 billion in 2015 (Delisle 2014c). This is money that could, of course, be used to finance meaningful, asset-based alternatives to student borrowing, including progressive benefits for the disadvantaged students most harmed by debt dependence today (Campaigne and Hossler 1998; Fenske, Porter, and Dubrock 2000; Paulsen and St. John 2002). For example, financing universal accounts at birth, seeded with $500 per child as called for in the ASPIRE Act, would cost an estimated $40 billion over 10 years (Newville and Cramer 2009). The lost opportunities from IBR, then, are not inconsequential.

Income-based repayment can be characterized as a self-soothing device—a way to make loans feel better to the American people, who do not want to see young adults defaulting in significant numbers on the investments made in their human capital acquisition; to student borrowers, who want some reassurance that they will be able to both pay off their student loans and feed themselves; and to policy makers, who want to see themselves doing *something* on the issue of student loans. By merely spreading out the negative effects of student debt, however, IBR approaches largely miss the mark.

Therefore, we suggest that the federal government should not invest in IBR plans with the expectation that they are a "cure." Admittedly, they are an important stopgap measure that makes the immediate harm caused by student loans more tolerable. However, they are necessary only because of a growing recognition that student debt places a destructive burden on some young adults that is counter to the American view of education as the "great equalizer." In the end, our financial aid system should work to *strengthen* the return on a postsecondary degree not weaken it.

## PAY IT FORWARD

If income-based repayment schemes masquerade as meaningful student loan reform but primarily just move the proverbial deck chairs on the Titanic, then Pay It Forward proposals are distinguished by purporting to be other than student loans, when they really operate on a credit and repayment basis. Pay It Forward proposals have gained some cachet in recent years, garnering significant policy attention in Michigan, Oregon, Ohio, and other states (Jesse 2014). They are like student loans in that students pay no upfront costs to finance their education, promising instead to pay a predetermined percentage of their incomes following college exit to repay the costs incurred while in college.

Some of the discussion in favor of Pay It Forward reflects growing understanding of the extent to which today's student loans fail students. For example, some argue that Pay It Forward could reduce sticker shock, give families more time to save, and provide an incentive for students to pursue less-lucrative fields because states could manipulate repayment terms for certain industries (Goldrick-Rab 2013). Additionally, these agreements would not have the negative effects on students' credit scores that traditional student loans do (Weissman 2013), although it is not inconceivable that the credit rating companies could find a way to quantify the exposure students incur. But the other ways they differ from current student loans do little to recommend this policy innovation, including the considerably less portability of these benefits, which are mostly proposed by specific states to provide education only at public institutions within that state (Sheffield 2014).

As envisioned in some proposals, graduates would not repay a specific dollar amount, likely because of the difficulty of managing that complex accounting, but a specific number of payments instead. This makes Pay It Forward like a graduate tax. Analysis suggests that some students may find themselves paying even more in this system than in a traditional loan. While providing a potentially valuable subsidy to low-income graduates who may be liable for relatively small monthly payments, this could lead to adverse selection problems, with those expecting higher incomes opting for more traditional student loans (Dynarski 2014) or leaving the state for education altogether. This likely bias makes Pay It Forward both politically and fiscally unsustainable, despite the potential advantages to be gleaned from encouraging thriftier spending at institutions by eliminating the release valve of tuition increases (Weissman 2013).

Additionally, Pay It Forward might reduce state funding for higher education, with predictable effects on equity and adequacy, because some proponents have specifically touted Pay It Forward as a way to encourage today's students to finance the education of tomorrow's students (see Goldrick-Rab 2013). And these approaches are not inexpensive, particularly initially; Oregon's proposal is expected to require a $9 billion upfront investment, which could come from need-based or other institutional aid (Goldrick-Rab 2013). Pay It Forward could also accelerate the trend toward stratification among institutions of higher education, leaving the public institutions the refuge of only those with few other financing options.

In a reflection of their unsuitability for the low-income students whose loan woes should be our greatest concern, Pay It Forward plans fail to cover the costs of higher education beyond the tuition itself and would leave many students still heavily dependent on borrowing in both the traditional and novel senses to finance their living costs and other expenses (Goldrick-Rab 2013). They also fail to address any of the student-debt problems in private institutions, omissions that could leave low-income students in these schools exposed and higher education out of reach. The income diversion effects that corrode asset accumulation and contribute to the unequal payoff on educational investment seen with student loans would still be real risks. Oregon's proposal would require graduates to pay 3 percent of their income per year over 24 years, resulting in higher costs than in most upfront financing options, and potentially reducing their savings capacity well into middle age. Graduates could potentially seek to reduce or shelter some of their income to limit their repayment exposure, but this, too, may decrease equity, if more sophisticated borrowers used these self-protections more than those relatively less advantaged.

Certainly U.S. financial aid policy could be improved, as could the outcomes of the higher education it aims to finance, by sending signals to prospective students that they can start their education without having to sign a large promissory note. Communicating a state interest in increasing higher education is also valuable. However, Pay It Forward approaches ultimately fail to address the underlying problem: expecting students to bear most of the costs of their own college education—whenever that bill comes due—still compromises college as an equitable path to upward mobility. Failing to attend to the particular needs of disadvantaged students before, during, and after college likely means that they will fare comparatively poorly in the resulting system. In the end, Pay It Forward is not much of an innovation. Certainly, it does not require too much imagination to connect these proposals to requirements to accurately disclose the true cost of financing, referenced above, and conclude that, after all, we expect that our higher education system produces young Americans capable of recognizing a debt when they see one.

## FREE TUITION AT TWO-YEAR COLLEGES

Some states have proposed to move more decisively away from student loans, replacing them not with borrowing-by-another-name, but with truly free higher education, in a noteworthy return to more robust public funding of postsecondary educational attainment. Expanding our understanding of what should constitute a basic education for an American in today's economy to include the first two years past what is now a high school degree may better align our educational system with labor market realities, particularly if students were guaranteed two free years of education in *any* school (Goldrick-Rab and Kendall 2014).

There is a move toward viewing U.S. education policy through the lens of a K–14 system, and ensuring that all children can transition seamlessly— and without cost—to two years of a postsecondary institution may be a wise investment. However, most of the concrete policy proposals stemming from this recognition of the changing educational landscape have fallen far short of this ideal, resulting in a policy shift that is unlikely to solve our student-debt problem or even represent a net advancement toward a vision of education as a conduit for greater economic mobility. Constrained by political and fiscal limitations, these proposals do not envision an equitable provision of opportunity, but instead would change the calculus of low-income and otherwise disadvantaged students in profound ways while likely making little difference in the lives of those with other available educational avenues.

Billed as a way to reduce student debt while increasing educational attainment and outfitting a 21st-century workforce (Perez-Pena 2014), proposals to make community college free in Tennessee, Oregon, and elsewhere have attracted considerable attention from educators, policy makers, and student groups (Fain 2014), particularly after they were incorporated into President Obama's State of the Union address and his agenda for "middle-class economics" (Stratford 2015). Certainly there is an intuitive appeal to the concept of free college. Indeed, making college more affordable for students by reducing tuition prices, subsidized by increased public support for institutions, could make significant inroads in reducing college debt (Potts 2014). Much of the increase in tuition prices, itself implicated in the run-up of student borrowing, stems from shifting costs from collective to individual responsibility (Hiltonsmith 2013; Mitchell, Palacios, and Leachman 2014); reversing this tide could restore higher education as an equalizing force in U.S. society and place college back within reach.

Eliminating college tuition altogether, however, while a fervent rallying cry of some U.S. student groups and many more radicalized student organizations in other countries (Long 2014; Smith 2014), is a highly inefficient way to address the current college affordability gap because it would mostly serve to subsidize the enrollment of privileged children (Yglesias 2013)—disproportionately disposed to attend anyway—and would do little to address the growing achievement gap or the thwarted mobility of the masses.

As would be expected, eliminating tuition is not an inexpensive proposition; estimates of the costs of Oregon's proposal for free community college run as much as $250 million per year (Hammond 2014), although other states' proposals are far lower, largely because they would require students to first leverage other available financial aid—which, of course, means that they are not really proposals for free college (Fain 2014). Like Pay It Forward, these proposals would address only tuition prices, not the living costs and other expenses associated with attending higher education. These costs are significant for many low-income students, comprising more than half of the total cost associated with attending many public community colleges (Huelsman 2014), an accounting which could mean that even "free college" does not preclude substantial borrowing, with all of its attendant risks, by many low-income students. There is a particular danger that the costs of providing free community college might crowd out other financial aid investments, including those more narrowly focused on students with unmet need, leaving them without resources with which to confront uncovered expenses.

Perhaps even more problematically, eliminating tuition only at certain institutions—particularly those with poorer track records in completion rates and postcollege outcomes (NCES 2011)—could serve to intensify the class divides in institutional selection and, then, related postcollege outcomes. There are long-term policy implications of funneling students to two-year institutions without considering whether those institutions are the best match for their interests and needs. There is significant injustice in relegating students without viable alternatives to certain institutions while students with access to independent means are still be able to choose their path to higher education unfettered by these considerations.

These implications are shaped in large part by the comparatively poor performance of two-year institutions and how they fail to provide an equitable chance at real upward mobility—again, the core function of the U.S. higher education system. Among the evidence of these gaps are labor market returns; those completing their educations with less than a bachelor's degree are most likely to work in the lowest-paid occupations and three times more likely to receive low salaries than be among the highest-compensated (Elliott and Lewis 2014). Completion rates lag behind four-year institutions, particularly for low-income and students of color, who are among those who would disproportionately take advantage of a free tuition offer. Only 20 percent of those who enroll at a public two-year institution complete an associate degree within three years (Bundy 2014).

Most students beginning at two-year schools hope to complete bachelor's degrees (Noel-Levitz 2014), but these students have relatively poor rates of successful transfer to four-year institutions. Some state proposals to make community college free have also included investments in improving quality and providing support services for students (Fain 2014), but still, the wisdom and fairness of encouraging aspiring college students to start down a two-year path as the only way to dodge debt must be questioned. Even some advocates of the free two-year college approach have concerns about students' different experiences if they start at a four-year school and about some proposals' high thresholds for GPA or credit requirements that could serve to disqualify some low-income students who lack the academic investments of their more advantaged peers (see Fain 2014). Although this reframing of educational opportunities could be expected to affect expectations over time, thereby influencing preparation, the strength of these effects likely hinges considerably on the specific parameters imposed.

As a result of increasing college costs and growing strains associated with student debt, financial considerations already figure far too prominently in the educational trajectories of low-income students, affecting even educators' recommendations for their paths (Elliott 2013a). These proposals for free community college might reduce the specter of student debt as a determinant of *whether* students attend postsecondary education, but they would only increase the salience of financial factors for determining *where* and *what* students study. As such, this policy change would do little to restore equity to higher education and could even further entrench the idea that only some students can afford to approach higher education from a place of possibility, rather than cold pragmatism. There is something seemingly un-American about disproportionately funneling students to one type of institution, based primarily on their financial situations (Weissman 2013).

Indeed, two free years of community college, while perhaps a separately useful investment, is not a substitute for or alternative to student loans at all; borrowing is, after all, designed to facilitate students' access to and completion of higher education in the context of their choice, in a manner that aligns with their abilities and orientations, as well as the labor market needs of the broader society. Receiving two free years of community college decreases the risks students incur but does not necessarily improve outcomes for those disadvantaged. This is a critical failing. If higher education is to be a conduit of economic mobility, U.S. policy must not only strengthen the connection between credential attainment and later labor market outcomes, but also simultaneously disrupt the relationship between prior socioeconomic standing and postsecondary educational prospects. This aim requires the construction of and support for financial aid tools that compensate for the disadvantage poor students bring to higher education, such that they are equitably equipped to succeed in and after college. Even if well intentioned, sending low-income children the message that only certain types of institutions with predictably inferior outcomes are within their reach fails against this measure.

This critique is not to suggest that proposals to reduce the cost of college—by eliminating tuition at two-year institutions or other approaches—are incompatible with more equitable reforms, including those that would shift U.S. financial aid to an asset-empowered system. To the extent to which eliminating tuition at some institutions could be aligned with asset-building investments that, together, then, change the calculus with which all students consider their long-term academic trajectories, they may have a role to play in reexamining the limits of free public education. They should not be mistaken, however, for the urgently needed solutions to the growing inequities in educational attainment and to the persistent correlation between one's initial position and one's ultimate educational outcomes.

## THESE POLICY PROPOSALS FAIL TO RESTORE HIGHER EDUCATION AS A CATALYST OF MOBILITY AND ARBITER OF EQUITY

Some of the policy proposals currently advanced to reform the student loan system represent real—albeit modest—improvements in this market-place. Interest rates should be set so that the government does not profit from students' hardship (Dynarski and Kreisman 2013). The private loan market should be better regulated, and repayment should be less complicated. Federal financial aid should be used as a tool to induce institutions to provide better information about their promised outcomes. Reducing the interest and payment burden when borrowers are young, least able to absorb these costs, and most in need of money to seed an asset foundation could reduce the erosion of net worth. Better targeting of subsidies to those in greatest need could more efficiently reduce harm, and ensuring that student loans do not survive bankruptcy could allow borrowers to recover from ruin. Our policy-making apparatus should function well enough to quickly dispatch these improvements.

But none of these reforms would avoid student debt—or the problems it provokes—entirely. None would ensure that higher education could serve its intended—and much needed—function in U.S. society: equally supporting the exerted effort and ability of every American child. As such, some of the student-debt reform proposals circulating today are only explicable in the context of somewhat desperate attempts to salvage the existence of the student loan system, whether from an ignorance of the true stakes in the financial aid debate or from vested interests in maintaining the status quo. They are understandably—but, at this point, inexcusably—restricted to the range of puzzles contained within the current paradigm (Kuhn 1962), when what is needed is a radical departure that positions financial aid as a fundamentally different instrument, held to a dramatically different standard.

## CONCLUSION: IMAGINING AND REACHING FOR THE FINANCIAL AID SYSTEM WE DESERVE

Some of the proposals critiqued here might lessen the repayment burden that has caused so much angst for some student borrowers. Some might send a more encouraging signal to students contemplating whether they can afford to enroll, and some might allow a student to pursue a degree or choose an institution or take a chance where they might otherwise hesitate. Those things are good. In the context of a unique window of political opportunity, however, those small measures of progress should not distract from the widespread consensus that the United States *does* have a student loan problem, and further, that that problem strikes at the core of Americans' most pressing anxiety: the sense that the American Dream is slipping beyond their grasp. The evidence contained in this book is intended to foster consensus on the precise dimensions on which this problem is felt and the best indicators by which to judge its severity so that the solutions subsequently adopted represent real, meaningful, and sustained progress.

The measure of how far we are from this today can be seen in some of the reforms currently gaining traction that could even exacerbate some of the ill effects of student borrowing. Policies that would extend the repayment period over many more years essentially trade financial security—in the form of predictable payments that cannot exceed a set percentage of the borrower's income—for economic mobility, by lengthening the period of compromised wealth building. Others could preclude students' achievement of excellent educational outcomes, the type needed for vaulting into the highest levels of the economy, by channeling them to inferior-quality institutions less prepared to support their progress. As a consequence for failing to hold financial aid policies to a standard commensurate with their significance in the U.S. economy, some of these reforms could squander precious political and fiscal capital, while primarily benefitting those who fare best in the status quo.

This is why, again, completely and honestly understanding the full parameters of the U.S. student loan problem must precede policy changes to solve it. The policy task facing today's generation of young adults is not to merely increase their ability to comply with established loan expectations, but to demand that the government make real the promise that institutions will facilitate their success. Schemes to improve debt collection, including plans to garnish even Social Security payments to meet past student loan obligations (Kitroeff 2014), focus narrowly on the government—and private lenders'—interests in repayment, while glossing over the obvious human costs. And proposals to introduce a more traditional underwriting approach to student loans would most likely reduce the default rate (Akers 2014) but would also undercut a core mission of student loans, to facilitate access to higher education for those without collateral.

Ours is not the task to find a path to some higher education that can reasonably be put within the reach of all American children—and then to convince ourselves that something is necessarily better than nothing, and therefore good enough. We are beyond the point at which normal science can meet our demands. Our challenge is, instead, to envision and then to enact a 21st-century financial aid system. This system must be up to the task of helping all children believe in and prepare for their future of higher education, supporting their academic progress to and through college, and positioning them for a lifetime of upward economic mobility, as was their motivation to attend postsecondary education in the first place. The evidence presented here exposes the ways in which student loans are incapable of being that system, and we contend that the reforms currently touted, including those here, as well as reductions in interest rates and various consumer protection regulations, do not change that fundamental assessment.

The United States needs a different, asset-empowered approach to financial aid. We need to concern ourselves with more than mere access because education is the core U.S. policy intervention aimed at future welfare. Helping children and families build assets from birth would upend our just-in-time, debt-dependent financial aid approach, with potentially transformative effects, particularly for those disadvantaged today. Financial aid should provide real opportunities for children to see their effort and ability equitably rewarded and effectively multiplied. For the well-being of individuals and the collective future of the country—in concrete economic terms and in the less tangible sense of preserving our collective identity— we need to know when to cut our student debt losses and move on.

In part II of this volume, we provide the rationale and evidence for an asset approach to financial aid, offering what we believe to be a viable and compelling alternative paradigm better aligned with U.S. values and more consistent with our reading of the best available evidence on student debt.

# PART TWO

## From Debt Dependence to Asset Empowerment

# EIGHT

## Assets Provide a Launching Pad for Economic Mobility

About 50 years ago, President Lyndon B. Johnson declared war on poverty. The program investments and policy changes instituted as part of that campaign, of which education policies were a part, have undoubtedly reduced the depth and incidence of deprivation among Americans. Just as certain, however, is the growing realization that, even in the aggregate, the policy legacies of the War on Poverty are insufficient for stopping the erosion of the American Dream. While most Americans still cling tightly to the conviction that sincere effort and talent will result in economic prosperity, evidence reveals the increasing divergence between productivity and financial reward, reflected in the declining significance of labor income in maintaining a middle class and promoting economic mobility. This recognition contributes to increasing frustration, alienation, and hopelessness among hard-working Americans plagued with a sense, even if somewhat diffuse, that the U.S. economy just doesn't work for them the way it should.

The evidence presented here helps to explain why economic mobility and a solid chance at middle-class security are slipping beyond the grasp of so many American households and why assets will be increasingly important for maintaining the American Dream moving forward. This analysis, in turn, highlights the dangers of growing student indebtedness as a threat to this asset foundation and a deterrent to the educational achievement that, in turn, could position Americans for the economic opportunities that would facilitate greater wealth. It also serves as the backdrop for the articulation of a new financial aid paradigm, one that views financial aid as an intricate part of America's economic mobility system. From this perspective, financial aid is about more than consumption (i.e., providing students with money to pay for college). It is also about building students' assets, which in turn can be used to enhance their return on a college degree. Toward this end, Children's Savings Accounts (CSAs), discussed in detail in chapter 9, are an exemplar of this new paradigm, a potential tool in the financial aid quiver for helping build students' assets.

While the rhetoric about combating poverty continues to focus almost exclusively on job creation and retention, we distinguish between standard of living, which is limited to the income available for rather immediate consumption, and economic mobility and well-being, both of which require explicit interventions beyond the labor market, in the form of support for asset building or investment in higher education as a catalyst for upward progress. By tracing the long-term drivers of the declining wage position of working Americans and highlighting the significance of assets for vaulting into higher standards of living, this analysis emphasizes the importance of building policy structures capable of helping households generate assets, not just increase income. In today's economy, this will require enhancement of transfer and capital income, as complements to labor income, as well as increased access to and improved outcomes from postsecondary education, still the primary conduit for economic mobility for most U.S. households.

While President Johnson's War on Poverty sought to bring more Americans out of abject poverty, today's battle is to salvage middle-class security as a realistically attainable goal for hard-working Americans in an economy where wages alone are inadequate tools with which to climb into middle-class life. Just as the task that ushered in the Great Society was a heightened awareness of the scourge of poverty, today, redeeming the American Dream requires exposing its flawed calculus and, then, recommitting ourselves to dedicating the resources to create real paths to prosperity.

## WHAT DOES THE ECONOMIC LADDER LOOK LIKE? WHAT DO WE MEAN BY "STANDARD OF LIVING"?

This chapter discusses the economic ladder and the constraints that may make it difficult for most Americans to ascend it, contrary to the myth of steady upward mobility advanced in the American Dream narrative. We believe that these questions about the extent to which current U.S. policy creates meaningful opportunities for American households to realize their aspirations of greater prosperity represent fundamental crises facing our nation today and significantly raise the stakes around student loan policy. Collectively, they may be sufficient to provoke a shift in the dominant paradigm of financial aid, calling into question policy interventions that, while facilitating *access* to higher education, also serve to deliver unequal *returns* on that same educational investment.

The intent of the findings and analysis in this chapter is to advance the debate about the economic and social policies and structures needed to realize not only the promise of the American Dream but also this return on a college degree as a vehicle for achieving it, given the assaults on the value of college within the high-debt context that characterizes higher education today. This requires acknowledging the rhetorical chasm that separates today's policy conversations about transfer income for those in and near poverty, which is highly stigmatized and largely dominated by critique that fails to offer compelling alternatives, and about capital income, which are mostly centered on its potential to contribute to economic growth but largely silent on questions of redistribution and equity.

Finally, while we know some might contend that discussions of financial aid and poverty are separate conversations, viewing financial aid as an economic mobility tool suggests that the two are inextricably intertwined. Through the lens of this new paradigm, having an understanding of poverty and how people climb out of poverty is essential to developing a financial aid instrument calibrated to deliver on this economic mobility front.

## Distinguishing between Standard of Living and Well-Being

Standard of living and well-being are distinct but related concepts. With the assistance of a ladder metaphor, each step on the economic ladder represents a different standard of living (i.e., the level of material goods and services associated with living in specific socioeconomic class). While there is obviously some subjectivity in the thresholds used to delineate these levels, for clarity, Gilbert's (2008) six social classes are used to label the rungs of the economic mobility ladder (bottom to top): (1) underclass (e.g., unemployed, part-time employment, public assistance); (2) working-poor class (e.g., full-time employment in the lowest-paid manual, retail, and service jobs); (3) working class (e.g., low-skill, clerical, retails sales); (4) middle class (e.g., lower managers, semiprofessional, craftsman); (5) upper middle class (e.g., upper manager, professionals, medium-sized business owner); and (6) capitalist class (e.g., investors, heirs, executives). Here, for brevity, we sometimes use the term *wage earners* when referring to the underclass through the middle class; we use the term *investor* when referring to both the upper middle class and the capitalist, as they are distinguished in large part by their greater reliance on capital as an income source to supplement labor earnings.

So, then, the amount of income a person has indicates on which rung on the ladder a person sits because income is used for consumption. Given this, when we see an individual or family move from one rung of the ladder to a higher rung, we see a change in his or her personal income and level of consumption along with it. However, this observed change in income does not explain *how* economic mobility occurs, only that it has occurred.

Income, then, is inadequate as an explanation for how a given American can expect to ascend. Further underscoring the significance of the difference between the concepts of standard of living and well-being are the significant gaps between absolute and relative mobility in the U.S. economy. The U.S. still displays high *absolute mobility* in terms of the likelihood that an individual child will attain a higher standard of living than his or her parents (Bengali and Daly 2013). Specifically, 83 percent of those in the lowest income quintile at birth had larger adult incomes than their parents had (Bengali and Daly 2013). While this analysis does not reveal the extent of this increase, and whether it is enough to be truly meaningful for one's quality of life, it is certainly evidence that standards of living consistently increase as the U.S. economy grows and advances.

Today's children can expect to be able to purchase more goods and services than their parents, as reflected in the growing ubiquity, for example, of items that were luxuries or only ideas just a few generations ago, such as cellular phones and personal computers. However, this does not mean that the American dream of relative mobility—improving one's overall position in society, as compared to peers—is within reach for most poor children. Indeed, there is evidence that this kind of mobility, while central to the rags-to-riches story that we tell ourselves as Americans, is actually less likely in the United States than in other developed economies (Corak 2009). Additionally, the growing disconnect between income and its wealth generation potential also means that some young adults today, despite surpassing their parents' earnings, have not achieved the level of overall financial well-being of previous generations (Pew Charitable Trusts 2014).

With regard to the typical citizen in today's economic climate, we posit that for economic mobility to occur, the citizen may need to (a) obtain the skills required to move into a higher class on the ladder and get a job that pays at that skill level, which most often requires an accumulation of savings to pay for college or willingness to assume debt; (b) find ways to use some of his or her wages to accumulate assets that can then pay dividends to supplement wage income; or (c) receive transfers that place him or her at a higher level on the economic ladder. Whereas standard of living is the amount of goods and services one can consume, well-being is a state where one has the capacity to achieve economic mobility. That is, well-being has more to do with what people *can do* with goods and services, the real opportunity they have to move up the economic ladder, than *how many* goods and services they can consume (see e.g., Sen 1999; Sherraden 1991). Standard of living is an important part of well-being but insufficient for creating the conditions necessary for people to have the real opportunity to advance economically. This points to serious limitations in the power of income to drive households' true prosperity.

We posit that wages are set by the market for a particular class of workers. If it was possible for wages of the working poor alone to move them into the working class, then such classifications would make little sense and add little to the discussion. Instead, because it is known that service jobs at fast-food restaurants, for instance, can only pay a set price for making a burger, constrained as they are by market demand for that burger, social class researchers such as Gilbert (2008) can state that the working-poor—relegated mostly to specific industries—have incomes below $20,000 and the middle class earn about $40,000, with a fair amount of certainty.

This does not mean that there may not be differences in the standard of living within a particular class. Some working poor, for example, have a lower standard of living than others, and wages can contribute to these types of measured changes in standard of living among individuals and families within a particular social class. The consumption-based safety net can also contribute to these differences in standard of living; all other things being equal, for example, a working-poor household with medical care provided through a means-tested state insurance program will likely have a greater ability to direct its expenditures and a somewhat greater sense of economic security than one with the same level of transfer and wage income but without those complementary supports. Importantly, though, those essential safety nets cannot be said to facilitate the true economic mobility of these households; indeed, because many of these programs come with strict limits on asset accumulation, they may explicitly serve to constrain mobility, as described below.

Further, in the modern economy where there is a growing productivity and wage gap, the problem is that wages for a certain middle-class job, for example, might drop below middle-class levels. This introduces greater risks of downward economic mobility, both within and among generations, as individuals find that their human capital accumulation and productivity no longer secure wages capable of purchasing their expected standard of living. In some cases, these jobs have been eliminated altogether, requiring individuals to compete for a scarcer pool of labor market opportunities or risk dropping out of the middle class entirely, as has happened for millions of Americans over the past decade. For example, research suggests that during the Great Recession, the United States lost about 3.5 million middle-class jobs, and since the recession, only about 2 percent of the new jobs created are middle-class jobs (Condon and Wiseman 2013).

It is with this in mind that we posit that wages alone are insufficient for generating economic mobility. When members of the underclass, for example, are forced to take a job classified as working-poor, there is little reason to believe they will move securely out of poverty by work alone unless their well-being is also considered. These limitations make asset accumulation an essential mechanism for creating economic mobility.

To a significant extent, U.S. policy recognizes the growing importance of assets in families' overall economic picture. Through the asset-based arm of the welfare system, U.S. policy confirms the goal of asset development and provides considerable subsidies to support asset building in programs such as the home mortgage interest deduction, preferential treatment of capital gains, and exclusion of employer-provided retirement benefits from taxable liability (Cramer, Black, and King 2012). However, the distribution heavily favors households who have wealth (Cramer et al. 2012) and, then, serves to exacerbate economic divides, rather than compensate for the income constraints that plague those in and near poverty. The effects—on well-being, mobility, and on the viability of the American Dream—are profound. Because assets are a stock of wealth capable of generating income, they allow people to consume at a higher class level than their wages alone will allow. In addition, accumulation of assets can be used to acquire additional skills (i.e., invest in human capital) that provide people with another opportunity to move up the economic ladder, even in today's context of reduced mobility.

U.S. policy explicitly facilitates this leveraging, as when advantaged households convert their housing wealth to educational access for their children or use their accumulated savings to finance an entrepreneurial venture or purchase other productive assets. Assets likely also create opportunity for economic mobility by empowering people to participate in, negotiate with, influence, control, and hold accountable institutions (World Bank 2002). Further, assets may provide the conditions for economic stability (e.g., when people experience income shocks due to such things as a loss of job or health problem) and economic risk taking (Sherraden 1991), both important preconditions that influence behavior in ways that tend to contribute to economic mobility. Finally, Sherraden (1991) suggests that assets provide people with social, psychological, and political effects. These effects might also assist in creating economic mobility, as they change how people relate to each other and to institutions charged with delivering opportunities for advancement. All of this is to suggest that policy mechanisms up to the task of facilitating well-being may also need to include asset development, rather than focusing too narrowly on increasing income alone. Today, such mechanisms are disproportionately unavailable to those who need them most.

Unlike the asset-based arm that supports the advancement of those already privileged, the consumption-based transfers that comprise the system typically thought of as *welfare* not only fail to facilitate asset accumulation, but can explicitly work against it. That recognition is not to negate the importance of consumption subsidies. Particularly given the growing inadequacy of wages of many Americans laboring in essential industries, policy should intervene to allow people to consume at a level they would not be able to simply by working. Again, there are obviously significant economic and moral arguments to be made for ensuring that no American's standard of living falls below a given floor. Here, then, we do not imply that transfers are not valuable contributions to the U.S. policy landscape, only that they are both inadequate—in scope and purpose—and inequitable, and that a unified system of economic mobility opportunities would better serve the American public, particularly those working at low incomes.

## THE PRODUCTIVITY AND WAGE GAP

Productivity measures the amount of goods and services workers produce per hour worked. Productivity is believed to be the basis for how people are able to maintain their living standard or, erroneously, thought to be a mechanism helping people move up or down the economic ladder. At points in our history, this flawed attribution seemed to align with economic realities; from 1948 to 1973, wages and productivity grew in concert (Mishel 2012). That is, the more productive people were, the higher their wages. However, during the last decade, there has been a growing disconnect between the use of effort and ability in the work place (i.e., productivity) and wages (e.g., Bureau of Labor Statistics 2014).

While wage earners fared particularly poorly during the recent recession, the erosion of wage earners' ability to leverage employment for real economic mobility may be understood as a long-term trend demanding significant policy change, not a temporary downturn that will naturally self-correct (Harrison and Bluestone 1988). There is a growing body of research that documents the productivity and wage gap even among college degree holders (Gomme and Rupert 2004; Mishel, Bivens, Gould, and Shierholz 2013; Rodriguez and Jayadev 2010).

While workers with a college degree fared slightly better than workers with only a high school degree during the recent recession, they also have experienced declining wage growth over the past several years. For example, between 2000 and 2011, their wages grew a modest 0.2 percent; between 2002 and 2011, they declined by -2.2 percent; and between 2003 and 2011, they declined by -1.9 percent, on average (Mishel, Bivens, Gould, and Shierholz 2013). These trends are not only significant once individuals are in the labor market; they may also serve to erode confidence in higher education's mobility potential and to reduce the effective return on degree.

Earning a college degree is perceived as a path to the American Dream, primarily through the conduit of improved productivity. That equation aligns with our understanding of how effort and ability are supposed to translate into superior economic outcomes. However, to a large extent, in today's economy, a college education may function like an insurance policy—albeit one with a rising premium, where attending college is simultaneously more essential and yet less relatively valuable (Chopra 2013), rather than a surefire investment in one's future upward mobility. Therefore, it makes it all the more important to ensure that attaining a college degree supports a person's ability to accumulate assets, a likely key component in the growth of personal income in the modern economy.

## STAGNANT OR DECLINING WAGES

Today, it is hard for wage earners to significantly increase what they earn through work, in part because stagnant or declining wages have become a fixture in the modern economy. Research indicates that, between 2002 and 2012, wages have been stagnant or on the decline for the bottom 70 percent of U.S. families (Mishel and Shierholz 2013). While these wage losses have been somewhat countered by increases in transfers such as Supplemental Nutrition Assistance Program and Earned Income Tax Credit benefits, as well as by the increased work effort exerted, in particular, by women, understanding the declining real value of workers' wages requires also taking into account the rising costs of basic goods and services—particularly energy and health care—and economic mobility levers such as higher education, both of which have increased more dramatically than overall inflation.

Stagnant or declining wages mean that wage earners are unlikely to get ahead working the jobs they are working now. However, it may be difficult for these individuals to find another, higher-paying job. Research shows that between 1979 and 2010, the share of "good" jobs (i.e., pay of at least $18.50 per hour and offered health insurance and a retirement plan) available dropped 2.8 percentage points, leaving only 25 percent of jobs that qualified as good jobs. This is despite the workforce, on average, becoming older and more educated, thus indicating a relative mismatch between worker qualifications and available job opportunities (Mishel, Bivens, Gould, and Shierholz 2013) and a belying of the axiom that greater educational attainment will translate to a stronger financial foundation.

Further tightening the screws on many in the wage-earner classes, the amount of education required to access these good jobs has increased, too, along with the cost, of course, to secure this education. It is worth pointing out, again, that these are not recent or temporal developments but, instead, trends that have evolved over the last 30 years. From this, it would seem that positive shifts in the economy have become the exceptions instead of the norm in the case of wage earners, just as episodic as the rare case of the individual who does manage to ascend the economic ladder through some chance of fate.

## WE MUST THINK ABOUT WAGE INCOME DIFFERENTLY THAN IN THE PAST

Again, personal income consists of three major components: (a) wages, (b) assets, and (c) transfers. Wage income continues to make up the largest share of personal income, but it shrank between 1992 and 2012, from 67.4 percent to 63.9 percent. There is little reason to believe that there will be large increases anytime soon (see table 8.1). While wage income has shrunk as a share of total personal income, asset and capital income has remained relatively stable, and transfer income has been on the rise (see table 8.1). However, as is so often the case in our divided society, the aggregate data do not tell the whole story.

**Table 8.1    Personal Income Sources (in billions of dollars)**

|  | 1992 | 2002 | 2012 |
|---|---|---|---|
| **Labor Income** | | | |
| Wages and salaries | $2,973.6 | $4,997.3 | $6,880.7 |
| Other labor income | $673.7 | $1,113.5 | $1,685.1 |
| Subtotal | $3,647.3 | $6,110.8 | $8,565.8 |
| Percent of total | (68.2%) | (67.4%) | (63.9%) |
| **Asset income** | | | |
| Proprietors' income | $414.9 | $890.3 | $1,202.3 |
| Rental income | $84.6 | $218.8 | $462.6 |
| Interest income | $722.2 | $911.9 | $992.6 |
| Dividend income | $187.6 | $397.7 | $757.0 |
| Subtotal | $1,409.3 | $2,418.7 | $3,414.5 |
| Percent of total | (26.4%) | (26.7%) | (25.5%) |
| **Transfer income** | | | |
| Personal transfer receipts | $745.8 | $1,282.2 | $2,375.1 |
| Less contributions for social insurance | –$457.1 | –$755.2 | –$952.9 |
| Subtotal | $288.7 | $527.0 | $1,422.2 |
| Percent of total | (5.4%) | (5.9%) | (10.6%) |
| Total personal income | $5347.3 | $9,060.1 | $13,407.2 |
|  | (100.0%) | (100.0%) | (100.0%) |

*Source*: "Personal Income." U.S. Bureau of Labor Statistics. U.S. Bureau of Labor Statistics, n.d. Web. December 31, 2013.

Among the top 1 percent of households, only 39 percent of personal income is derived from wage income (Rosenberg 2014), while 53 percent of their income is capital income (e.g., business profits, dividends, net capital gains, taxable interest, and tax-exempt interest). Having most of their personal income come from long-term investments also means they receive a discount on their taxes, as long-term capital gains tax rates top out at about 23.8 percent while standard income taxes go all the way up to 39.5 percent (IRS 2013).

Despite media attention to the volatility of the investment markets, over the long term, that instability may be far less consequential than the insecurity faced by those whose fortunes hinge on the labor market. During the Great Recession, overall incomes dropped by 17.4 percent, with 49 percent of this loss falling on the top 1 percent, a concentration of loss owed to the investments these households had in the stock market (Saez 2012). These households suffered even bigger losses during the recession of 2001, also largely the result of capital income losses (Saez 2012).

However, drops in personal income are anomalies for the top 1 percent. The top 1 percent has consistently experienced large income gains over the last 30 years, incommensurate with growths in their productivity. Between 1979 and 2007, income for the top 1 percent of households grew by 240.5 percent (Mishel, Biven, Gould, and Shierholz 2013). For our purposes, what is most important about this discussion on personal income is that assets and transfers are important ways that households can generate income outside of wages, as well as establish a foundation for accumulating assets. Economic trends toward a growing productivity and wage gap may make finding ways for poor and middle-class families to build income outside of wages increasingly important for stimulating economic mobility in America.

If personal income consists of three components and one of the components, wage income, is diminishing in its capacity to maintain a middle class, then one may conclude that policies are needed that increase the share that comprises the other two components. It is important to emphasize that this does not mean a wholesale retreat from efforts to enhance labor income, particularly in the instances where its erosion reflects an unjust, illogical devaluing of individuals' contributions to U.S. society and economy.

We do not suggest that policy efforts to create employment opportunities are not valuable or that people should not work. There is clearly an abundance of evidence of the financial, social, and psychological benefits of employment, and we believe that the U.S. society and economy would be strengthened through the pursuit of a robust full employment system (Bernstein and Baker 2003; Thomas, Boguslaw, Mann, and Shapiro 2013).

Furthermore, while our understanding of the importance of employment does not view work income as a sufficient tool for economic mobility, the other benefits secured through good jobs, particularly nonwage benefits and job security, may be important supports for the risk taking and future planning that, in turn, help to promote economic security (Thomas, et al. 2013). Children can benefit from their families' connection to these good jobs and the social capital and social norms that they transmit in ways that could be significant influences on later educational attainment.

Nonetheless, the evidence suggests that work by itself, particularly in the types of jobs available to many Americans, even many of those that require a college degree, will likely not be able to maintain a middle class. The continued survival of a relatively few exceptions do not undermine the veracity of this conclusion. Maintaining the illusion that Americans can work their way up only perpetuates the economic arrangements and mental maps that, together, conspire to keep most Americans from meaningful opportunities for real advancement. Instead, if we desire to maintain one of the core things that has made America unique, the ability for the majority of people to maintain realistic hope that they too can improve their lot in life, we must have the foresight to craft policies that align with the reality of today's economy as well as with the technological advances that will shape the economy of the future. In all aspects of U.S. policy—economic and, we contend, educational—this requires explicitly attending to assets and their unique and potent effects.

## AMERICA'S BIFURCATED WELFARE SYSTEM

By a bifurcated system of welfare, we mean that there is both a consumption-based arm and an asset-based arm of the welfare system, each serving different segments of the population and each resulting in disparate outcomes within their respective spheres. America's bifurcated welfare system consists of both a consumption-based arm (means-tested income supports and in-kind benefits, such as Temporary Assistance for Needy Families and Supplemental Nutrition Assistance Program) that is largely designed for wage earners and an asset-based arm (tax-side subsidies for higher education, homeownership, and retirement savings) that is largely designed for investors or more economically privileged households. In sum, investments in this bifurcated welfare system may exacerbate rather than mitigate inequality (Devine and Canak 1986), which is not to say that the asset-based arm is inherently or entirely superior, nor that the consumption-based arm does not make real contributions to efforts to improve Americans' lives. However, essentially denying households in the wage-earner class meaningful access to both arms of the welfare system denies them the substantial benefits that accrue to participation in the asset arm, with attendant consequences for limited earning potential beyond labor income.

Indeed, Maslow's (1948) hierarchy of need emphasizes the importance of securing the essentials for one's standard of living as a necessary prerequisite for building toward higher-level needs. As described by Xiao and Anderson (1997), Maslow contends that people will attempt to fulfill higher-level needs (e.g., by saving for college education) only after lower-level needs (e.g., purchasing groceries and paying utility bills) have been met. From this perspective, needs are categorized into two types: deficit (e.g., lower level) and growth (e.g., higher level) needs. People seek to fulfill their deficit needs first, after which they begin to direct their behavior toward fulfilling growth needs. Building on Maslow's theory, Xiao and Anderson (1997) identify three categories of financial need based on people's tolerance for risk taking (paradoxically, tolerance for risk is largely determined by initial asset holdings; see Sherraden 1991): survival needs, security needs, and growth needs. The categories are based on research conducted by Xiao and Noring (1994), who find that low-income consumers are more likely to report saving for daily expenses (survival needs), middle-income consumers are more likely to report saving for emergencies (security needs), and high-income consumers are more likely to report saving for growth.

Paralleling the differences in how similar institutions facilitate the financial well-being of different populations, the same behavior—saving—yields very different economic mobility returns, based on one's initial conditions. Again, these responses should be understood largely as learned behaviors, rather than innate differences. As such, they are amenable to modification through policy reform, such that structuring different opportunities and incentives would trigger different behavioral responses. According to this understanding of individuals' development, then, integration of the two arms of U.S. welfare policy—toward a vision of economic mobility policy—could enhance the efficacy of each approach by reducing the degree to which their aims conflict (in, for example, today's existence of asset limits in means-tested programs and in financial aid systems) and by positioning households to build from a platform of basic security, even as labor income declines in its potency.

## Bifurcated Financial Aid System

The idea that the American welfare system, of which education is a part, is bifurcated, is not new (Devine and Canak, 1986; Howard 1997; O'Connor 1973). Understanding higher education as a welfare intervention and, then, financial aid as an economic mobility tool helps to make the connection between the two divergent approaches to welfare and the need to adopt asset approaches to financial aid to maintain the value of a college degree. Instead, today, we see a similar split in financial aid policy with, we assert, similarly inequitable outcomes.

The consumption-based welfare system has become a way to set a floor below which no American should fall. It was never designed to (a) promote equality, (b) significantly redistribute income or wealth, or (c) create the chance for economic mobility among the poor. Another way of thinking about the role that the consumption-based welfare system (or transfers) has come to fulfill is to establish at which rung on the economic ladder the poor live, but without giving them the tools to ascend. If we were to label the floor (i.e., standard of living) that the consumption-based model of welfare has established, keeping in mind Maslow's hierarchy of needs theory, it might be called the *survival step*, where the poor are given what they need to survive, usually on a short-term basis. As such, beyond not providing the financial assistance needed to generate economic mobility, we posit that it is not designed to provide the embedded thought processes the poor need to think and make decisions that have their futures in mind, nor does it provide assistance adequate to capitalize future development.

The current American welfare state, initiated under Franklin Roosevelt during the 1930s, was developed on the heels of the Great Depression, when the descent down the economic ladder appeared endless and nearly ubiquitous. It is out of these unconscionable conditions that the architects of the New Deal created a conglomeration of programs cobbled together over several years to form a (still not universal) floor. The floor was built out of income-based programs that were to allow the poor to consume a minimum amount of goods and services needed to survive. Fifty years ago, President Lyndon Johnson expanded the consumption-based welfare system. While the War on Poverty also included investments in human capital opportunities—at both ends of the formal education system—designed to help low-income households secure greater well-being, the net effect was skewed more heavily in the direction of subsistence supports.

## Financial Aid as a Consumption-Based Program

Today's consumption-based welfare and financial aid systems may act as a road block to climbing the economic mobility ladder. One mechanism for these effects is the requirement of strict means tests for subsistence-based welfare programs such as the Temporary Assistance for Needy Families (TANF), Supplemental Nutrition Assistance Program (SNAP), and Medicaid. In addition to the adoption of strict income limits, which are often accompanied by stigmatizing and time-consuming application and eligibility verification procedures, the eligibility criteria for these programs may prohibit significant asset accumulation, viewing assets as a source of potential consumption, rather than a store distinct from income flows. Low-income Americans, unsurprisingly, react to what is, in essence, a penalty for saving by adopting financial behaviors that advance their short-term consumption interests, even while undercutting their long-term mobility needs.

Asset limits require poor families to keep their financial (i.e., liquid assets) and vehicle (i.e., a type of illiquid asset) assets below limits set by federal or state governments to qualify for welfare benefits. These limits are viewed as not only morally appropriate, because aid should be reserved only for the most destitute, but also pragmatic, as poor households are assumed to be unable to save anyway because their "leftover" income is very limited after meeting subsistence requirements. Indeed, saving is often theorized to be potentially harmful to individuals in poverty, as any money they might take for building assets results in having to neglect purchasing goods and services required to meet vital subsistence needs. In this way, asset limits might be seen as both paternalistic and punitive, establishing very different expectations for how the wage-earner class will accumulate assets compared to what policy assumes—and rewards—for higher earners.

Because financial aid has largely been thought of as a solution to the problem of paying for college, particularly in the case of low-income children, we suggest it also largely falls under the consumption-based arm of the welfare system. Like most consumption-based programs in the United States, the higher education financial aid system is also affected, directly or indirectly, by means testing. Like public assistance programs, the Free Application for Federal Student Aid (FAFSA) considers both income and assets when determining the Expected Family Contribution (EFC), which is the basis for calculating aid. This can lead to the perception that savings will reduce the amount of financial assistance a student is awarded, creating a disincentive to save and to apply for assistance at all, as households may believe that even very small savings will disqualify them for aid (Reyes 2008).

There are other ways that financial aid within the consumption-based welfare system works at cross-purposes to students' educational attainment, for those particularly dependent on means-tested assistance to finance their degrees. For example, the process judges more harshly those assets held in students' own names, despite evidence suggesting that it is precisely these dedicated school assets that have the most significant effects on standardized test scores, high school graduation rates, college enrollment rates, and college graduation rates (e.g., Elliott 2013b). There has been some progress toward reducing these disparate pressures, but this progress has not resulted in true equity for disadvantaged students and their families, particularly given the effects of the recession, which pushed more economically vulnerable households to depend on these supports. For example, while, as of 2010, 17 states exempted college savings held in 529 plans from financial aid determinations, these same asset protections are not afforded in the federal financial aid system or to students whose savings are held in the vehicles low-income households are more likely to use for their savings, such as traditional deposit accounts (Clancy, Lassar, and Taake 2010). Means-tested financial aid may also contribute to the short-term and consumption-centric perspective of those who depend on it, delivered as it is just in time to be deployed to pay for higher education costs.

Simultaneous with increasing reliance on debt to pay for college by low- and moderate-income families, a parallel system focused on asset building has expanded, mostly to the benefit of higher income families. Public investments in educational assets, such as Coverdell Education Savings Accounts, Education Savings Bonds, and, especially, state 529 plans, work through the tax code to provide incentives for families to begin saving for college costs prior to students enrolling in college. Money invested in these types of college savings vehicles grows tax free, and withdrawals made from them to pay for college are also tax free. Additionally, many states offer significant tax deductions or other incentives to encourage—and, really, subsidize—education savings, but because these incentives are seldom refundable, their benefits flow disproportionately to higher earners with greater tax liabilities.

Not surprisingly, higher income families respond positively to these often-generous subsidies, with the result of a growing gap in financial preparation for postsecondary education and, then, additional contributions to overall household wealth inequities. Ensuring preferential tax treatment of college savings in 529s, for example, had encouraged more than $179 billion in college savings as of 2012 (College Savings Plan Network 2012), even though fewer than 5 percent of U.S. households have used 529s (GAO 2012).

This approach to financial aid, where most assistance for higher-income households has been carved out of the tax code, while most support for low-income families is provided through means-tested, direct methods, parallels the division in other welfare spending. With the exception of increases in the maximum Pell Grant and loan subsidies, most new federal higher education resources have been provided through the tax code. Wealthy students benefit most from these changes because they have a higher marginal tax rate than low-income families and, therefore, receive larger benefits from such programs (Maag and Fitzpatrick 2004). And there are more subtle ways, even if less talked about, in which higher-income students have advantages within these institutions, such as greater access to tax professionals who can help them navigate the benefits and greater household familiarity with financial institutions. The effects of these education assets may intensify their inequitable nature, too, particularly as asset-based financial aid supports begin earlier in a child's academic career, when there is more time for expectations to shape achievement (see Elliott 2013b), while means-tested financial aid, such as Pell Grants, is currently provided just before college enrollment.

But most low-income families are not using 529 plans or other tax-advantaged savings vehicles to prepare for college. These vehicles are not designed with low-income families' imperatives in mind (Clancy, Lasser, and Taake 2010). Instead, when they are able to save, low-income families are saving in traditional, nonrestricted products such as checking, savings, or similar accounts (Sallie Mae 2009). All of these accounts are subject in public assistance programs to asset limits, which can be as low as $1,000 (thus limiting asset accumulation or risking loss of program eligibility), and count against students in financial aid determinations. Without the benefit of the tax advantages, the marginal cost of saving is effectively higher for low-income families, who cannot claim the subsidy that higher-income families receive, through the tax code, for their asset-accumulation efforts.

Thus, differences in asset accumulation for college, while stemming in large part from differences in familial capacity to save, are enhanced by the very different institutional contexts faced by low- and high-income families. As Oliver and Shapiro (2006) suggest, the inability to pay for school is largely the result of low asset accumulation. That is to say, asset inequality in the current financial aid system does not solely stem from financial aid policies themselves. These disparities also stem from the political and economic context in which financial aid operates—one of extreme wealth inequality.

## CONCLUSION

In much the same way that a bifurcated welfare system was created, so too a bifurcated financial aid system has been created. The financial aid system for low-income students is increasingly centered on helping these students incur debt, while the system for higher-income students encourages the accumulation of assets. If education is the primary conduit of economic mobility opportunities in the United States today, and financial aid is increasingly imperative for children confronting high college costs, then financial aid's inadequacies as a fulcrum unjustly deny many Americans the launch that higher education could provide. Viewing financial aid through this lens exposes its counterproductive and ultimately destructive effects, highlighting the real threat that the current approach poses to higher education and its core function as an arbiter of greater social and economic equity in U.S. society.

# NINE

## Children's Savings Accounts: The Next Evolution in Financial Aid

Distinct from traditional savings accounts as well as from means-tested income transfers, Children's Savings Accounts (CSAs) are a policy intervention to deliver transformative assets to facilitate the educational attainment and economic mobility of all American children, particularly those disadvantaged. Children's Savings Accounts are part of the welfare system broadly defined, as we have done here, to include education policy as an investment in the upward mobility and life chances of American children. They are not *just* financial aid nor just antipoverty policy, but instead represent a powerful investment in changing the trajectory of children's development by altering the institutions that today fail to adequately facilitate their success. Understanding CSAs' effects requires a long view, because they ideally start at birth and can have lifelong implications, and a broad view, because CSAs work through both asset accumulation and account-ownership effects. They are potentially potent tools with which to put higher education within reach of disadvantaged children and viable vehicles for the transfer of initial assets.

CSAs are unique, as they work on multiple dimensions and through complex identity formation to encompass a new form of "welfare" that is wholly consistent with the American Dream calculus of effort plus ability equals outcomes. CSAs are commanding attention and garnering policy momentum on the strength of their demonstrated impact and because they push the ideological boundaries that have constrained policy making in the past, giving those of all political persuasions new tools with which to potentially redeem the American Dream. As such, they represent an exemplar of a financial aid paradigm with the potential to uproot established ways of thinking and prevail in the critical contest of ideas within the arena of education policy.

Compared with the wealth erosion and compromised educational attainment associated with student loans, Children's Savings Accounts demonstrate considerable promise to help American children build financial security, improve their educational outcomes, and construct a platform for economic mobility (Elliott 2013b). This sharp contrast to student loans is likely partly responsible for CSAs' growing policy momentum; while CSAs may not be the only alternative to student loans, they are particularly attractive to those seeking a new paradigm for financial aid as representing more than just a mechanism to pay for college.

More than just a means of access at the point of enrollment, CSAs are uniquely capable of providing financing for postsecondary education, bringing low-income households into the financial mainstream and cultivating the educational expectations that can close the achievement gap. All of these ends are policy imperatives today, a calculus that has prompted public officials, educators, and advocates in many parts of the country to look seriously at CSAs. In this rush to implementation, to avoid the pitfall of urgent but ill-advised action that characterizes student loan reform today, policy makers must attend to the theory and evidence of how and why asset-building matters for disadvantaged children. Together, we must develop metrics that recognize CSAs as a truly new approach to financing college, not just an innovation to address the puzzles (Kuhn 1962) that plague the student loan system.

## WHAT ARE CSAs? WHERE DID THEY COME FROM, HOW HAVE THEY EVOLVED, AND HOW ARE THEY DIFFERENT THAN OTHER FINANCIAL INTERVENTIONS?

Children's Savings Accounts are best understood as an extension of the field of asset-based social development, a novel approach to welfare for those in poverty that stemmed from the understanding of how and why wealth matters for those already economically advantaged. Seeking to bridge the divergent strains within the U.S. welfare system, CSAs build on the theory, research, and policy on addressing poverty through asset building that emerged with the publication of Michael Sherraden's 1991 book, *Assets and the Poor.* This seminal publication distinguished assets from income in terms of their effect on well-being, introducing the concept of asset-based social policies. The introduction of asset building into the applied social sciences initiated policy demonstrations and research over the next 20 years, leading to documentation of promising effects of assets in the lives of low-income Americans and enactment of asset-building programs. CSAs apply the promise of asset building to children's development, with the added layer of using productive assets to facilitate postsecondary education, itself a strong driver of upward mobility.

Initially, much of this theory and evidence focused on families' and households' asset building and well-being, treating children as dependents with little or no agency of their own, even when children's well-being was prioritized by many savers as the goal of their wealth accumulation. Furthermore, metrics largely centered on actual asset accumulation, as the nascent focus on children's savings had not yet fully articulated the importance of the educational expectation and identity formation effects now known to accompany saving. The American Dream Demonstration (ADD) began in 1997, initiated by the Corporation for Enterprise Development to test whether low-income families and households could build assets in matched savings accounts, referred to as Individual Development Accounts (IDAs). The five-year demonstration concluded with promising results that produced insights that have informed the design of other asset-building interventions (Richards and Thyer 2011). Chief among these findings was the evidence that, indeed, low-income individuals and families can and will save when given access to supportive institutions that encourage and facilitate that economic behavior. During that same year, the Assets for Independence (AFI) Act was passed, establishing a federal grant program to provide nonprofits and government agencies with funds to offer IDAs to low-income families and households. Simultaneous changes in regulations that imposed asset tests on applicants for means-tested public assistance reduced the savings disincentive that curtails asset building among many poor households.

Today, there are over 200 AFI-supported IDA programs nationwide (U.S. Department of Health and Human Services 2012). Shifts in thinking about poverty and asset building, catalyzed partly through the realization of positive outcomes in asset-building programs, have led to integration of asset approaches throughout U.S. social policy in areas such as subsidized housing (Emple 2013), child support enforcement (Johnson 2013), and refugee resettlement.

While the policies reflected in the AFI Act and related efforts enrolled mostly adults as savers, IDAs were originally proposed as accounts that would be automatically available to every citizen in the United States, accrue earnings, and be restricted to preapproved uses such as home ownership, education, or small businesses. Account holders whose annual incomes fell below certain thresholds would be eligible for subsidies to incentivize their saving and help them build balances. Sherraden initially proposed that IDAs be opened early in life—ideally, at birth—to promote asset building and well-being across the life span. Sherraden stated,

> Because asset-based welfare is a long-term concept, some of the best applications of IDAs would be for young people. Young people would be given specific information about their IDAs from a very early age, would be encouraged to participate in investment decisions for the accounts, and would begin planning for use of the accounts in the years ahead. (Sherraden 1991, 222)

As implemented, however, in part because of funding constraints and the need to produce demonstrable outcomes on timelines acceptable to philanthropic and government investors, IDAs have mostly been short-term programs to assist families and households in achieving home ownership, education, enterprises, or other development goals.

This gap between IDA proposals as designed and their pragmatically constrained implementation created an opening for another savings vehicle that young people could access: Children's Development Accounts (CDAs). In research and policy discussions, Child Development Account (CDA) is used synonymously with Children's Savings Account (CSA). Building on the IDA concept, CSAs have the advantages of long periods of interest accrual, the opportunity to integrate into institutions such as K–12 education, and the tremendous gains associated with supporting successful completion of higher education. Additionally, according to Loke and Sherraden (2009), an advantage of asset-based policies targeting children is that they "may have a multiplier effect by engaging the larger family in the asset-accumulation process. In addition to children saving and learning about saving, members of the extended family may learn from this process, and parental expectations for children may also be positively affected" (119).

CSAs have appeal in the social development arena as a promising strategy that promotes low-income children's savings, asset accumulation, and development of financial, social, and human capital (Boshara 2003; Goldberg 2005), and somewhat more recently, among financial aid and education reform circles, in light of evidence associating asset holding with improved educational outcomes (see Elliott, Song, and Nam 2013). Far more recently still is the growing interest in CSAs as asset-based alternatives to student loan debt, particularly as dissatisfaction with the outcomes realized from student borrowing has led to a search for reforms that could fundamentally change how Americans finance college. These applications for CSAs compel new lines of research, exploring not just how individuals respond as savers, or even how that saving changes educational expectations and behaviors, but also how institutions can be altered through the introduction of the CSA innovation into the policy stream and how reshaping expectations about college financing can restructure the intervention of education itself.

Growing interest in CSAs in the early 2000s led to the first national test through the Saving for Education, Entrepreneurship, and Downpayment (SEED) initiative. Beginning in 2003, SEED was a four-year demonstration project in which more than 1,300 low-income children and youths in 12 locations across the country received matched savings accounts and financial education. Discussed in greater detail below, the SEED for Oklahoma Kids (SEED OK) research experiment tests the effects of CSAs opened at birth in a full population. Critically, this is a far more rigorous examination of educational and financial effects than that to which student loans have been subjected, and should lead to greater clarity about the precise mechanisms through which CSA effects are realized, the limits of the intervention, and CSAs' full potential. Here, ideas around asset-based financial aid benefit from the rich discovery and fervent inquiry that characterize the "pre-paradigm" phase (Kuhn 1962) of the revolution that, we believe, may be coming.

## CSA Design and Implementation

Children's Savings Accounts are savings vehicles, most commonly designed for higher education savings, that often incorporate specific incentives and explicit structures to encourage savings by disadvantaged youths and families who otherwise may not have equitable access to financial institutions (Elliott and Lewis 2014). While they have features specifically designed for encouraging saving among disadvantaged youths and families, they are meant to be universal interventions. CSAs usually allow deposits from children, their parents, and other relatives, as well as third parties, such as scholarship programs. Ideally these investments are leveraged with an initial deposit or matching funds adding public or philanthropic funds to families' savings, usually on a ratio ranging from 1:1–5:1. These progressive features are less vulnerable to charges of being "handouts" as understood in our U.S. political parlance, however, because they require some individual stake and serve to extend the meaningful incentives for saving and support for building balances to low-income savers that are already available to higher-income households through tax benefits.

At this pivotal moment in the push to scale CSAs, the children's asset-building field is actively weighing different options for CSA delivery, with debate over the relative advantages and trade-offs of traditional banks or credit unions, investment products such as education IRAs, or larger savings plans, such as the state-sponsored 529 college savings system. Researchers studying assets and education suggest that individual instruments in the marketplace do not provide a policy structure to support scaling universal and progressive CSAs. In contrast, savings plans, such as 529s, allow for universal outreach and enrollment, progressive features, and the efficiency of a centralized accounting system (Clancy, Orszag, and Sherraden 2004), although some of the features of these particular programs, which were designed to provide tax-advantaged accounts primarily to wealthy families, are less than friendly to low-income savers. The ideal CSA delivery system would enable small-dollar and high-dollar accounts to be pooled for greater efficiency and would leverage central accounting and system linkage for universal provision (Clancy et al. 2004). It would be simultaneously integrated and universal as well as progressive and appropriately targeted.

Today, centralized accounting in state-sponsored 529 plans allows states to offer a match or incentives to low- and moderate-income participants. Many states have instituted features of CSAs into their state-sponsored 529 plans. Maine's Harold Alfond College Challenge is the nation's most expansive CSA, providing universal, automatic enrollment at birth, with an initial $500 grant for all children born in the state (Clancy and Sherraden 2014). In other states, subsidies are targeted toward low-income savers (College Savings Plan Network n.d.), in part as an effort to parallel asset-building subsidies provided through the tax code to wealthier savers (Boshara 2003). Nevada, Rhode Island, Connecticut, and North Dakota all have universal CSAs implemented or under development, with the funds for initial deposits coming from the financial institution manager, participant fees, or state general funds. States can also leverage opportunities to align children's savings initiatives with other public policies, including taxation, financial aid, and child support and public assistance, increasing the capacity to deliver asset accumulation approaches within the current policy footprint. For example, Kansas has a Child Support Savings Initiative that forgives $2 of state-owed child support arrears for every $1 deposited in a child's 529 account (Johnson 2013), and other states are exploring weaving CSA principles into their system of support for children exiting foster care.

States are not the only jurisdictions innovating CSA policy; localities such as Cuyahoga County, Ohio, and, most notably, San Francisco, California, have started savings accounts for children in their school districts, to provide both asset-development opportunities and a mechanism for improving educational engagement. Wabash County, Indiana, uses the state's 529 plan as the account architecture for a highly successful college savings initiative that recruits "champions" to contribute to children's accounts and includes financial education and postsecondary preparation alongside the asset building. As concerns mount about stagnating achievement gaps, relatively low college graduation rates, and escalating debt, more policy makers are intrigued by the evidence of CSAs' potential and eager to explore options to implement CSAs within their systems.

Withdrawals from CSAs are normally permitted for higher education expenses after children turn 18 and, after college graduation, for other asset investments or retirement savings. To facilitate the development of financial capability while supporting attainment of positive educational outcomes, some scholars suggest a tiered structure for CSAs, wherein children could access some of their savings before college for educational investments such as computers, school activities, and supplemental coursework (Lewis, Cramer, Elliott, and Sprague 2013). Many CSA programs also include financial education to build human capital alongside financial deposits, although this programming is less common with scaled CSA initiatives, some of which provide only the account architecture.

## DOCUMENTING THE CASE FOR CSAS

Making the case for Children's Savings Accounts—and attending to the measures by which we gauge their true effects—requires a complete and honest accounting of the dimensions on which CSAs work, the indicators we should expect of them, and the promise they can deliver. Further, fully appreciating these dimensions of CSAs demands adherence to a financial aid paradigm that holds these policies to a more rigorous standard than simply facilitating access, to allow the direct comparison necessary to reveal the true extent of the "crisis" around student loans. Getting this application of theory and consideration of evidence right is not only essential as a driver of our assessment of the components of CSAs that contribute to these effects; it also shapes the messages we use to explain why CSAs matter and the urgent problems they can help to solve. CSAs are not necessarily superior to other financial aid approaches for the sole purpose of paying for college. While there are many reasons why they are preferable to debt dependence, certainly need-based grants and scholarships can prove just as useful in financing the actual costs of tuition and fees.

Similarly, CSAs are not the only way to address childhood poverty. While income from labor is perhaps of declining significance in the finances of privileged American households, it is still an important component of many households' economies. Acknowledging the limitations of income to secure economic mobility and real financial well-being is not to suggest that children's futures are not also shaped by their families' access to decent housing, quality medical care, healthy and safe environments, and excellent K–12 educations. Indeed, our understanding of CSAs recognizes that these institutions' contributions can magnify the positive effects to be realized from children's savings, while the power of assets is partly seen in their utility to leverage some of these advantages.

When considered through a lens that looks broadly at the ways in which assets shape the educational and life trajectories of American children, however, to account for the role of assets in helping children prepare for, engage with, and benefit from college—not just to access enrollment—there may be no other single policy lever as well suited to these challenges as CSAs.

In line with phase 5 of Kuhn's (1962) cycle of progress, we ground the remainder of the conversation in this chapter in a review of the evidence that documents *why* CSAs may matter so much, the indicators that must be monitored to ensure that the chosen delivery systems for CSAs are living up to the promise of CSAs, and the way that we need to talk—with policy makers, financial institutions, community leaders, and, perhaps most critically, the public that could become a children's savings movement—about why every American child needs an account, and why, collectively, we need a new paradigm for financial aid.

## College Preparation

Enrolling in college is not only a question of financial preparedness; evidence suggests that the longer-term challenge of ensuring that students are academically equipped to succeed in college is just as important and perhaps even more difficult to address. Here, too, CSAs show the potential for positive outcomes. Unlike most of the research on financial aid, to include student debt, CSAs' effects on children's college preparation are being tested in a randomized control trial.

The SEED for Oklahoma Kids (SEED OK) research experiment is the first experimental research on the principles of universal CSA access and automatic account opening in the United States. The SEED OK experimental sample was drawn randomly from birth records provided by the Oklahoma State Department of Health for all infants born during certain periods in 2007. The accounts were seeded with an initial deposit ($1,000) for students randomly assigned to receive them (CSA + $1,000 versus no CSA) at birth. By combining random selection from a full population of births, random assignment, and longitudinal data collection, SEED OK is well positioned to answer key questions about effectiveness of universal and progressive CSAs for a general population (Nam, Kim, Clancy, Zager, and Sherraden 2013).

Given that in many CSA programs children enter the programs at birth or when they enter kindergarten, understanding the effects of CSAs on children's academic achievement is complicated by the long timeline needed to observe these effects. While there are no experimental data yet that examine the effects of CSAs on children's academic achievement, we can point to the link between social-emotional well-being and academic achievement, which has been rigorously tested by education researchers with strong support.

First, for example, Durlak and colleagues conducted a meta-analysis of 213 school-based universal social and emotional learning (SEL) programs involving about 270,000 kindergarten through high school students. Employing an experimental randomized design, SEL participants, compared to controls, demonstrated significantly improved social and emotional skills, attitudes, behavior, and academic performance that reflected an 11 percentile-point gain in achievement (Durlak, Weissberg, Dymnicki, Tyalor, and Schellinger 2011).

Second, SEED OK's experimental test of CSAs finds no significant differences at baseline and a significant impact on children's socioemotional skills at age four, particularly for children from relatively disadvantaged households. That is, infants from households with incomes lower than 200 percent of the poverty line who were randomly assigned to receive the CSAs demonstrated significantly higher social-emotional skills at age four than their counterparts who did not receive a CSA (Huang,

Sherraden, Kim, and Clancy 2014). So there is strong, albeit indirect, evidence that CSAs are helping to equip these young children with the social and emotional competencies that later correspond to improved educational outcomes.

Socioemotional well-being basically measures how well children self-regulate—the ability to monitor and manage emotions, thoughts, and behaviors (Barkley 2004; McClelland, Ponitz, Messersmith, and Tominey 2010). Identity-based motivation (IBM) theory, a topic we will discuss in more detail in the next section, suggests that possible-selves and identities are positive and negative images of the self (Oyserman and Markus 1990). These identities can help children sustain self-regulatory action (i.e., strategic action based on planning, monitoring, and evaluating results of action and outcomes) (Oyserman, Bybee, and Terry 2006).

## How Do CSAs Generate Small-Dollar Effects?

One of the doubts that can prevent some from making the leap to an asset-empowered financial aid paradigm concerns the amount that low-income children will be able to save for college. In our discussions about CSAs, some people understandably raise questions about whether small-dollar accounts can really create positive identities. To explain the effects of small-dollar accounts, we draw on research from identity-based motivation (Oyserman and Markus 1990), planned behavior (Ajzen 1991), and self-predictions (Koehler and Poon 2006).

Research conducted by IBM theorists has shown that possible-selves can have a strong impact on self-regulatory behaviors and academic achievement (Oyserman et al. 2006). According to IBM, three principal components explain the relationship between conceptions of the self, such as a college-bound identity (i.e., child who expects to attend college) and self-regulated behavior. The three core principles of IBM include (a) identity salience, (b) congruence with group identity, and (c) interpretation of difficulty (Oyserman and Destin 2010). Salience captures the idea that children are more likely to work toward a goal when images of their own future are at the forefront of their minds. Congruence with group identity occurs when an image of the self feels tied to ideas about relevant social groups such as friends, classmates, family, and cultural groups. When this occurs, the congruent personal identity is reinforced. Finally, IBM theorists highlight the importance of having a strategy for normalizing and overcoming difficulty. From this perspective, in order for children to sustain effort and work toward an image of themselves as being college bound, they and their environment must provide ways to address inevitable obstacles to the goal of attending college, such as being unable to finance college.

Using the principles of IBM, when a child mentally designates savings for college, it indicates that college is on the child's mind and is where the child expects to end up regardless of the savings amount. Designating money for college also indicates that the child perceives that saving is a relevant behavioral strategy for overcoming the difficulty of paying for college and that college is an important, not an impossible, goal that requires acting now. When children go through the process of mentally designating savings for school, it can be said that the outcome of this process leads to the formation of a college-saver identity. It is referred to as a "college-saver identity" instead of a "college-bound identity" because it more aptly indicates that children have identified college as an important goal in the future that requires action now and that they have identified saving as a part of their strategy for taking action (Elliott 2013c). It is by facilitating the formation of college-saver identities that we suggest CSAs enable students to engage more in school.

## The Power of Future Savings

To understand how small-dollar accounts facilitate the formation of a college-saver identity, however, you have to also understand that the college-saver identity can be based on what the child has saved or on what he or she expects to be able to save in the future. The idea that expected future savings can facilitate the development of a college saver identity as well as amount actually saved is based on a body of research that indicates that people are often overly optimistic about what they can accomplish in the future through their own use of effort and ability (see research on optimistic bias in self-predictions; e.g., Amor and Taylor 1998). People base their predictions on their "current intention" without considering such things as the ease of making deposits or the ability of their parents to move out of poverty (Koehler and Poon 2006).

We posit that CSA programs facilitate children having strong current intentions to save for college and that children are unlikely to weigh the grounds on which that intention rests, its validity, if you will. Further, we posit that having an account influences children's "readiness for translating their current intentions" (i.e., provides them with a strategy) to save for college into college-savings behavior. So while their current intention to save for college sometime in the future may be an important part of their being motivated to engage in school, it might not be a good of predictor of whether they will actually save in the future because they fail to recognize the powerful impact of "situational factors" such as the ease of making deposits on their ability to save, the target behavior (e.g., Koehler and Poon 2006). It also should be clear how the potential impacts that CSAs can have on things such as school engagement and savings are distinct from one another. That is, we could see positive effects on school engagement but not see positive effects on savings behavior.

Today, the unrealistic predictions people make may contribute to the assumption of irresponsible levels of student debt. Flipping to an asset-based approach to financial aid, this same irrationality may be a potent force for harnessing the power of children's expectations for their futures, serving to actually increase the likelihood that those seemingly unattainable goals come to pass. For example, it might help explain why some research finds that having savings is associated with higher math and reading scores (for a review this research, see Elliott 2009; Elliott, Jung, and Friedline 2011). These are, in turn, effects that may have significant implications for the critical challenge of closing the achievement gap even before college. They are, significantly, dimensions on which student loans fail to even attempt to exert an influence, illustrating another reason why constructing a new financial aid paradigm is so urgent.

## College Access

While research on self-predictions and planned behavior generally suggests the stronger the current intention the more likely people are to carry out the target behavior, current intentions typically only account for about 20 percent to 40 percent of the variance in later behavior (e.g., Ouellette and Wood 1998; Sutton 1998). This might explain why children who expect to go to college (i.e., children who have a college-bound identity) are more likely to attend college shortly after graduation than children who do not, but at the same time researchers still find that an unacceptably large number of children with a college-bound identity fail to go on to college when they reach college age. Thus, we end up with wilt, discussed in chapter 4.

At the end of chapter 4, we discussed how the old financial aid paradigm did little to combat the problem of wilt. Wilt refers to the sizable number of minority and low-income children with the will and intellectual ability to attend college but who fail to enroll shortly after high school graduation or to succeed once enrolled. Wilt reflects a financial aid system that has facilitated those with wealth being able to structure role expectations such that they constrain the actions of low-income and minority students. From this perspective, role expectations result from a struggle between individuals who are acting strategically to gain advantage over the distributional resources that institutions provide. We went on to discuss how Americans generally have been unwilling or unable to acknowledge that there is an ongoing class war over who has the opportunity to attend America's higher education institutions. This war may rage simply because the self-interest of the wealthy and the self-interest of the rest of the population are often at odds in a system set up to pit their interests against each other.

Knight (1992) shines light on how this imbalance of power can be altered when he suggests that institutions can be changed "by changes in either the distributional consequences of those rules or the relative bargaining power of the actors" (145). Thus, changing the distributional consequences of role expectations and the bargaining power of minority and low-income children may be a way to change role expectations that are in conflict with attending and completing college. Children's Savings Accounts may offer a systemic answer to disadvantageous role expectations, empowering more low-income and minority students to apply for college, and to more selective colleges, and preparing them for success once there. You might ask how. Having savings designated for college may change the way children *think*—about themselves, their futures, and the institutions that can help them realize their dreams. By doing so, they place role expectations back in line with students' best interests by ensuring that college appears financially attainable to children throughout their time in school.

In support of this, there is a growing body of evidence that suggests having a college-saver identity reduces wilt:

- Students who are currently enrolled or who have graduated from college are defined as being "on course," whereas children who are not currently enrolled and have not graduated from college are defined as being "off course." One study found that 75 percent of children with their own savings are on course compared to 45 percent of children without savings of their own (Elliott and Beverly 2011).

- While only 35 percent of low- to moderate-income (below $50,000) children are on course compared to 72 percent of high-income ($50,000 or above) children, assets can alter these trajectories. Specifically, 46 percent of low- to moderate-income children with school savings of their own are on course; conversely, only 24 percent of low- to moderate-income children without savings are on course (Elliott, Constance-Huggins, and Song 2013).

- Among black students, only 37 percent are on course compared with 62 percent of white students. Controlling for similar factors as the previous two studies, findings suggest that both black and white children who have savings are about twice as likely to be on course as their counterparts without savings of their own (Elliott and Nam 2012).

- Even very low levels of school savings can significantly increase the likelihood that a child enrolls in college. Forty-five percent of low- or moderate-income students with no account, 49 percent of students with only basic savings not designated for college, 71 percent with school savings <$1, 65 percent with school savings from $1 to $499, and 72 percent of students with school savings of $500+ enroll in college (Elliott, Song, and Nam 2013).

Reducing wilt represents one of the most promising approaches to improving the educational outcomes of disadvantaged youths—individually and in the aggregate—because it builds on their own hopes and aligns their experiences with their dreams. Here, the narrative that would have us believe that poor children have different values or priorities than more advantaged children is belied by evidence of the gap between these students' expectations and aspirations and their educational attainment.

## College Completion

In contrast to high-dollar student loans, which show some potential for negative effects on college graduation (Dwyer, McCloud, and Hodson 2012; Kim 2007), research suggests that college savings show some potential for improving a student's chances of making it all the way to graduation. This is particularly significant given our understanding of the true purpose of higher education—to facilitate upward mobility and equip children for lifelong success—which demands attention not just to *access* but to educational *outcomes* as well. As we have related, it is along these measures that student loans are found particularly wanting, and it is in this dimension that pivoting to an asset approach to college financing is particularly promising.

- In the aggregate, children who have a college-saver identity and $500 or more in school-designated savings are about two times more likely to graduate from college than children who have a college-bound identity only (Elliott 2013c).

- Children in low- and moderate-income households (i.e., those that have incomes below $50,000 per year) with college-saver identities and school-designated savings of $1 to $499 or $500 or more are about three times more likely to graduate college than children who have a college-bound identity only (Elliott, Song, and Nam 2013).
- Furthermore, black children with college-saver identities and school-designated savings of $500 or more are about two and half times more likely to graduate from college than black children with a college-bound identity only (Friedline, Elliott, and Nam 2013).

Educational achievement is worth striving for and the best-known lever for building children's capacity for upward mobility. American children and their families buy into this calculation; it motivates their assumption of record levels of debt and drives their continued pursuit of degrees with uncertain returns. However, given the growing gap in educational attainment by family income and the increasing evidence of unequal gains even from equivalent credentials, the current education system—and higher education in particular—does not provide poor children with the same opportunity for economic mobility that it does for higher-income children (Haskins 2008).

Confronting this gap has never been more important than it is today. As asset-based financial aid and an alternative to reliance on student debt, Children's Savings Accounts can enhance opportunities for students to increase their self-efficacy and expectations related to educational achievement and for their families to prepare financially for college. Because the ultimate aim of higher education is to equip children for lifelong financial and life success, the true measure of an approach to financial aid should encompass an assessment of whether our policies place college graduates in a strong position to succeed financially as young adults. Again, U.S. policy debate about student loans has largely ignored these indicators, while our fuller examination of student loan effects highlights these after-college disparities as particular evidence of the need for change.

Asset-building strategies may be a way to make progress on all of these goals and maximize the benefit of going to college. For example, if family savings correlate with better student engagement at an early age (Zhan and Sherraden 2003), CSAs may allow them to take full advantage of the primary and secondary education they receive and position them for greater college achievement. If household asset accumulation correlates to greater academic performance (Zhan 2006), students may even be better able to compete successfully for financial aid, as the landscape shifts from need- to merit-based scholarships. If CSAs can prepare students to be savvy financial consumers fully integrated into the financial mainstream, they may more skillfully navigate the student loan market, even insisting on better terms than would otherwise be offered and making informed decisions about institutional selection and career planning. Given the relationship between engagement and academic attainment, the prospect of affecting children's orientation toward and functioning within their education for relatively small initial investments deserves greater attention.

### Potential for Community and Parental Effects

In the current higher education landscape, which features rapidly rising costs and offers debt as the primary means for disadvantaged students to overcome cost barriers, responsibility for challenging disadvantageous role expectations primarily lies with low-income or minority parents, philanthropic organizations, or other benevolent actors. Low-income parents are at a disadvantage for providing the kind of financial resources needed to counteract disadvantageous role expectations. Philanthropic groups tend to focus on ad hoc solutions—providing needed material goods or services to a particular low-income child—without addressing the structural factors that led to the child's lacking such necessities in the first place. Inequity is the inevitable result; even low-income children from the same neighborhood can have very different experiences.

However, while these community-level effects have not yet been rigorously studied, Children's Savings Account interventions may also give students a sense of community support for their education (i.e., help build group congruence discussed earlier in this chapter), with the attendant potential to reshape expectations and strengthen other institutions that could support educational attainment. A way that this might happen is through community-organized, third-party contributions to CSA accounts. These kinds of contributions may ensure that each child in a community forms a college-saver identity rooted in a durable community identity around college attendance and success. Citywide, statewide, and even a national CSA commitment may create positive group congruence, a potentially potent force in shaping self-concept and associated achievement.

Congruence with group identity occurs when an image of the self feels tied to ideas about relevant social groups such as friends, classmates, family, and cultural groups (Oyserman et al. 2006). When this occurs, the congruent personal identity is reinforced. Children's CSAs are almost always connected to the family or other institutions. For example, when children open an account, they are supported by parents, the city, the state, or other family members. Further, parents are often a primary source of children's income, through gifts or allowances. When a CSA is opened for a child the meta-message asserts "we save," "we go to college," reinforcing the college-saver identity through its congruence with the actions and goals of the larger group. These new relationships and this altered context can reset the messages children may hear elsewhere about the likelihood of college in their own futures, thus supporting identities that feature high educational expectations.

While the ability of CSAs to produce community effects is mainly theoretical, there is rigorous experimental evidence from SEED OK that indicates that CSAs can have positive effects on parental outcomes in addition to children's outcomes. For example, early findings from SEED OK indicate that mothers that have CSAs (i.e., treatment group) report lower levels of depressive symptoms than mothers without CSAs (i.e., control group) (Huang, Sherraden, and Purnell 2014). Further, findings indicate that mothers in the SEED OK treatment group are more likely to maintain or increase their expectations of children's college education than mothers in the control group (Kim, Sherraden, Huang, and Clancy 2015). Because parents are central to a child's community, particularly at young ages, evidence of the spread of these effects may follow as children embedded within CSAs come of age surrounded by assets and supportive institutions.

## Postcollege

If effects on children's educational expectations and identities most distinguish CSAs from other interventions to improve children's financial statuses (welfare), it is perhaps in the *postcollege* period that they most differentiate themselves from other forms of financial aid (particularly student loans). Children's Savings Accounts can have powerful educational effects, as described above, but they can also serve as the initial asset platform leveraged for later economic mobility. Full accounting of the potential benefits of account ownership from an early age should include the later result of a more diversified asset portfolio and healthier financial engagement in adulthood. Emerging research by Terri Friedline and colleagues indicates that accruing savings as a child is associated with increased likelihood of asset accumulation as young adults. As a result, particularly compared to those who have borrowed to pay for school, students may leave college better equipped to pursue important financial goals. For example, Friedline and Elliott (2013) find that children between ages 15 to 19 who have savings are more likely to have a savings account, credit card, stocks, bonds, vehicle, and a home at age 22 to 25 than if they did not have savings of their own between ages 15 to 19.

Friedline, Johnson, and Hughes (2014) find that the overwhelming majority of young adults owned a savings account at or before the acquisition of all financial products, including checking, CD, money market, savings bond, stock, and retirement accounts.

What the evidence suggests is that CSAs may be a gateway not only to greater educational attainment, itself a conduit of economic mobility, but also a more diversified asset portfolio. As such, it might matter little if children are able to accumulate large stocks of assets in their savings accounts, but the test is whether, as a *gateway financial instrument*, CSAs may lead to greater asset accumulation in other forms, such as stocks, retirement accounts, and real estate. For example, Friedline et al. (2014) find that while owning a savings account as a young adult only contributed $50 toward liquid assets, the added contribution of combined stock and retirement accounts—themselves products of savings account ownership—was $5,283.

This asset building not only stands in sharp contrast to the bleak financial fortunes of heavily indebted recent college graduates; it also may position young adults for significantly improved economic outcomes over their lifetimes. For example, the Pew Charitable Trust (2013) finds capital income has a strong relationship with moving up the economic ladder. They find that Americans who move from the bottom of the income ladder had 6 times higher median liquid savings, 8 times higher median wealth, and 21 times higher median home equity than those who remained at the bottom.

So by building a more diversified asset portfolio, CSAs may result in increased asset accumulation, which, in turn, may lead to higher odds of moving up the economic ladder. These outcomes, of course, are in addition to the effects of improved educational outcomes, which may, in turn, improve employment prospects and lifelong earning potential. And given the potential connection between initial asset levels and the subsequent ability for income to generate more assets and additional income (Elliott and Lewis 2014), young adults who leave college with at least some asset ownership may initiate a trajectory of superior earning and asset accumulation.

This virtuous cycle is the engine of the shared understanding of the American Dream. It is a pathway to prosperity that should be open to all American children and a conduit of upward progress that, today, is largely blocked by our debt-dependent financial aid system, disincentives for asset building within income support programs, and the erosion of higher education as an arbiter of equity and mobility.

It is through this more complete accounting that the true promise of CSAs is revealed. What other form of financial aid helps children prepare for, enroll in, and complete college while acting as a springboard for achieving economic mobility? What other antipoverty tool can reshape how disadvantaged children think about their educational futures? What other single policy lever can so dramatically affect outcomes on so many dimensions critical to the well-being of disadvantaged children? What other alternative paradigm can exert a vision powerful enough to bring into focus the fissures within the student-debt system, provoking the crisis that, in turn, can catalyze a scientific revolution?

## DESIGNING CSAS TO FACILITATE EDUCATIONAL OUTCOMES

These educational effects of account ownership will not happen automatically, however, without attending to CSA design features associated with increased educational expectations. Additionally, without the potential to accumulate meaningful asset levels, CSAs cannot—for long—convince a generation of low-income children that they are potent tools with which to confront college costs. Because these processes are central to realizing the power of CSAs as a conduit to improved educational outcomes and a catalyst of economic mobility, Children's Savings Accounts must be designed with this success in mind.

Critically, at this point in the development of the CSA field, we know quite a bit about what works and what it will take to build the right children's savings opportunities. The challenge now is to find the best avenues through which to advance this design, to create space within the political dialogue and policy-making apparatus by pivoting away from student loans, and then to galvanize the political commitment to make this shift possible.

### Initial Deposits for Asset Transfer

Although CSAs are popular across the ideological spectrum in large part thanks to their emphasis on individual initiative and cultivation of savings behavior, the track record of low-income families saving in CSAs and, in particular, the rising cost of the college tuition they will confront, have exposed a clear need for significant asset transfers within the CSA instrument. Making the case for transfers requires clearly articulating the underlying purpose of Children's Savings Accounts, which are best understood as catalysts of economic mobility and transformative institutions, not just savings vehicles or financial products.

To provide redress for the significant wealth inequality that confounds our sense of justice and compromises our economic growth (Picchi 2014), CSAs must be capitalized not only with the relatively meager savings that people in poverty can contribute but also with public and perhaps philanthropic asset transfers. Encouragingly, evidence from some CSA programs around the world that have long used sizable initial asset deposits indicates that these transfers, even when not requiring household savings, can still spur individuals' contributions (Lewis and Elliott 2014), likely by captivating people's imaginations and engaging them in envisioning a brighter future for their children, even while the third-party deposits may be more significant drivers of ultimate account balance. While policy experimentation can help to ascertain the precisely right level of initial asset transfer, such a calculation rests in part on the variables of age of account initiation, the probable returns from the selected vehicle, and the context in which the CSA is to be utilized, particularly with regard to the college costs expected.

Significantly, Children's Savings Accounts—and the transfers that seed them—align more closely with American values of individual effort and returns to individual investment than do other transfers aimed to assist people in poverty, particularly if the CSA vehicle is made available to all American children. In part, this reflects the importance of directing CSAs to education, given the centrality of educational attainment in our American understanding of how "welfare" is guaranteed. Additionally, the unique structure of CSAs, which usually require some individual engagement and initiative, keeps them from being pigeonholed as liberal welfare, even though they are designed to fundamentally transform the power disparities that today constrain the futures of disadvantaged children. In CSAs, transfers are understood to ensure that savings accounts pay off for low-income children as well as for higher-income ones, a progressive approach but not one that ignores our preferences for interventions that require hard work and sacrifice. Children's Savings Accounts are thus not only evidence based but also ideologically appealing, a combination that makes them particularly attractive—and particularly relevant—as alternatives to student loans.

### Incentives to Cultivate Savings Behavior

Building on this principle of individual effort correlating to savings success, Children's Savings Accounts use incentive structures that make savings a practiced—and profitable—habit for low-income households that might otherwise have had little access to or experience with financial institutions. Most often, these incentives take the form of savings matches, such that low-income individuals see their contributions leverage greater returns. The precise structure of incentives varies, but evidence affirms that using savings goals and setting matches to reward reaching them can motivate greater deposits (Beverly et al. 2008). Importantly, the practice of using savings incentives to encourage individuals to defer consumption in favor of future asset building is not only confined to low-income individuals. The premise behind generous tax benefits for retirement and college savings for high-income Americans is similar; most human beings respond favorably to positive incentives, and relatively few save without some tangible return for doing so.

## Account Structure to Foster Ownership

Because the effects of Children's Savings Accounts stem not only from the actual assets accrued but also the educational expectations and related behavior that accompany the development of a college-saver identity, CSAs must be structured to facilitate that identity development. Although research is still exploring the precise mechanisms through which a college-saver identity develops, it is believed that accounts should be in children's names, whenever possible, so that they have confidence that their savings really belong to them and cannot be diverted by an event such as a household financial emergency (Friedline 2014). Children should also have opportunities to engage with their accounts, including making their own deposits, and ideally should be able to use some of their funds for academic enrichment opportunities and educational expenses as they age. This means that, as CSAs are taken to scale, account administrators will have to attend to the ways CSAs are different from other accounts, which have a primary purpose of asset accumulation, if their full potential to shape children's lives is to be realized.

## Automatic Account Opening to Deliver Universal Engagement

If realizing the potential of CSAs hinged exclusively on the development of sizable financial assets within the accounts, perhaps the stakes associated with getting every child an account would not feel so high because relatively few households could be expected to save that much. However, evidence of the potential for significant increases in educational attainment when children have school savings accounts, even with very little actual money in them (Elliott, Song, and Nam 2013), makes it clear: CSAs are an intervention too important to leave to chance. Every child needs an account, every child deserves an account, and ensuring that every child has an account could—in itself—foster considerable progress toward our objectives of closing the achievement gap by putting more talented but disadvantaged children on the path to college completion and redeeming the viability of higher education as a path to upward mobility.

Getting every child an account is not an easy feat, however. Evidence from Children's Savings Account pilots and demonstrations around the country—and the experiences of large-scale CSA-like interventions in other countries—has affirmed that many obstacles can prevent families, particularly those separated from financial institutions and constrained by their poverty, from opening savings accounts for their children, even when they are motivated to save (see Canada's experience with a national CSA in Lewis and Elliott 2014). Again, this is not entirely dissimilar from other savings structures in the United States, in which making saving the default has been found to correlate most strongly with savings success, as opposed to investing in trying to convince people to save (Arnold 2014).

Children's Savings Account efforts today, therefore, are mostly using automatic account opening to ensure that all children have access to this savings vehicle, particularly as those whose parents might be less likely to open accounts for them may also be the children most in need of this trans-formative intervention. There are certainly some administrative hurdles in account opening, including the need to choose a delivery system that can accommodate accounts opened without the owner's explicit authorization, but policy can address these limitations. And, of course, automatic account opening does not eliminate the need for the cultivation of identification with and ownership of the CSA, believed to be instrumental in realizing the educational effects. Still, none of the benefits of a CSA can occur with-out an account. Opening accounts automatically for children is not the end of the process of facilitating their educational attainment, but it should be the beginning.

## SAVING AS A DEBT-REDUCTION STRATEGY

Too often, the enthusiasm around Children's Savings Accounts and the concern about student debt develop in a vacuum, with policy conversations occurring in parallel and relatively little attention to how these two arenas intersect. Certainly, CSAs are valuable even in a context of inevitably high student debt. To the extent to which identifying as a college saver increases the likelihood that a given student makes it to higher education, that student will be exposed to the student loan reforms that might make debt less burdensome. He or she might be better able to compete for merit-based scholarships or selectively pursue degree paths with greater potential to pay it off, even with substantial liabilities. That student may also be more likely to complete college successfully, an outcome that positions him or her for successful loan repayment. In addition, powerful effects are likely to accrue from experiencing an institution facilitative of one's success and from the recognition that policy structures exist that, indeed, seek to place the American Dream within reach.

But student debt matters, even to the student with a Children's Savings Account. The prospect of confronting high debt burdens may erode some of the economic mobility effects of the initial asset holdings, and the countervailing effects of looming student loan debt may mute some of the expectation outcomes associated with children's savings. Certainly, two children with a CSA will still likely fare very differently, in and following college, if one has to also borrow and one does not. While our current financial aid paradigm prevents us from seeing all of the ways in which asset-based financial aid approaches would deliver outcomes superior to those resulting from student debt, widening our view to examine effects prior to and following college, in particular, makes clearer how much better a fit CSAs could be for the problems to which we need financial aid to respond.

New paradigms are accepted, though, when they appear to solve an urgent problem (Kuhn 1962), and given the relatively low levels of savings that participants in existing CSA programs have demonstrated, some have questioned whether CSAs can actually provide alternatives to student debt, rather than just novel adjuncts to our debt-dependent financial aid system. Here, data revealing the potential for household savings to reduce the incidence and degree of student indebtedness are encouraging (Elliott, Lewis, Nam, and Grinstein-Weiss 2014). The data suggest that families are able to use savings not just to subsidize more expensive degree pursuits or reduce students' work obligations while in school, but also to reduce their need for student loans. Policy investments to more robustly fund CSAs with more frequent and larger savings matches, earlier account opening (to give account balances more time to grow), and larger initial seed deposits would make CSAs an even more viable counterpoint to student loans. Importantly, bridging the parallel conversations around CSAs and student loans could move children's savings more fully into the financial aid mainstream and generate more substantial resources with which to capitalize accounts. Certainly, as discussed below, rethinking the considerable resources currently dedicated to student loans could launch CSAs onto a different plane on a scale unimagined so far.

## LOW-INCOME CHILDREN CAN ALSO BENEFIT FROM ASSET-BUILDING TRANSFERS

In chapter 8, we discussed how the American welfare system is bifurcated with both a consumption-based arm and an asset-based arm and how each serves different segments of the population and results in disparate outcomes within their respective spheres. Transfers designed as part of the asset-based arm are not designed with subsistence in mind, but with creating opportunity for substantial economic mobility to occur. These transfers accrue not just to individuals and households but to entire institutions, representing significant infusions of dollars often unrecognized as part of the "welfare" system, the corollary effects of which overwhelmingly affect the most advantaged in the U.S. economy. For example, CBS News (2008) reported that through taxpayer bailouts, banks were able to award top executives nearly $1.6 billion dollars in salaries, bonuses, and other benefits (the average paid was $2.6 million).

These transfers differ most notably not just in scope and target, though, but in function. Specifically, transfers that come out of the asset-based arm of the welfare system have most often been designed to allow people to leverage them to develop future assets. For instance, transfers from the bank bailout often came in the form of asset-building items such as stock options and professional money management or large cash bonuses (CBS News 2008). More routinely, the tax-based transfers for home mortgage interest may encourage greater property accumulation, perhaps particularly by encouraging advantaged homebuyers to purchase larger or more valuable homes than they otherwise would (Hanson 2012).

In contrast, transfers that are designed out of the consumption-based arm of the welfare system are typically of the type that the poor cannot easily leverage in a way that increases the size of the transfer (i.e., generate additional assets). This has particularly been the case when talking about transfer programs such as SNAP, which have multiplier effects in the larger economy but not within the household economies of participants. Even transfer programs such as the Earned Income Tax Credit (EITC) are designed with the mind-set of subsidizing low-income jobs, as much for the producer class' benefit as for those employed in occupations that do not pay enough on their own to lift a household out of poverty. The advantages the EITC offers to individuals are constrained by rules that phase out the subsidies at the point at which they could provide enough benefit to really vault a household into a higher economic plane.

The sometimes synonymous roles that EITC and wages play in low-income families' lives are revealed in commentary that urges continuation of the EITC instead of increases in the minimum wage (see, for example, Saltsman 2013); implicit is the analysis that either policy approach is a vehicle through which to subsidize the earnings of low-wage workers. Because these transfer programs are only designed to bring participants to subsistence levels and do not have in mind asset building, it is hard to expect low-income participants to find ways to use resources from these transfers to build substantial assets for themselves or their children, for such things as paying for college or buying a home. Significantly, however, the few times in our history where we have designed transfer programs for the poor from the asset-based arm of the welfare system, such as in the case of the Homestead Act and the GI Bill, we have seen many of the poor leverage these assets to rise out of poverty and into the middle class, sometimes on a very significant scale. In pursuit of our goal of breaking the cycle of poverty, this should be a lesson about the tremendous potential if we move away from a bifurcated system where the goal is asset building for one part of society and subsistence support for another.

Acknowledging that low-income families can and do save is not the same, however, as pinning the aspirations of poor children completely on their own savings effort, any more than the extraordinary ascent of a few should be taken as evidence that a U.S. economic mobility system is still fundamentally sound. If CSAs are to be conduits of real economic mobility and greater social equity, they must be robustly funded, and the balances that poor children can accumulate should compare favorably with those of their more advantaged peers. To make this kind of asset development possible, low-income children today will need transfers on the scale that have catalyzed similar seismic shifts in mobility in generations past. They will need the next Homestead Act or GI Bill, and getting there is much more a question of political will than fiscal capacity.

## The Next Big Asset Transfer: Early Commitment Pell Grants

In our discussions about CSAs, some people understandably raise questions about whether small-dollar accounts can really create positive identities, and even if they do, do they actually just create false hopes?

Part of this contention is based on the idea that small-dollar effects are sometimes produced through unrealistic expectations about what children perceive they can save in the future. However, this focuses narrowly on what children and their families can save themselves. In our description of CSAs as a potential economic mobility tool, we not only focus on what children and their families can save but on the potential of third parties (e.g., extended family, private philanthropies, and employers) to contribute to the accounts as well to use transfers to boost amounts in CSAs. The rationale that transfers can play an important role in people's ability to save is based in part on our discussion in chapter 8 about how personal income consists not only of wage income but also capital income and transfers.

A number of observers have proposed reimagining Pell Grants as an early commitment program in which children would learn of this financial support early enough in their academic careers to cultivate the expectations and behavior associated with educational achievement (e.g., College Board 2013). For example, the College Board (2013) recommended supplementing the Pell Grant program by opening savings accounts for children—deemed likely still eligible for Pell once they reach college age—as early as age 11 or 12 and making annual deposits of 5 percent to 10 percent of the amount of their anticipated Pell Grant award. While political considerations, including concerns that any reform could lead to the undermining of Pell funding, may have prompted some to retreat from these recommendations, asset research clearly suggests some potential advantages in repurposing Pell appropriations to leverage the transformative power of asset building and educational expectations while still assuring kids have money to pay for college.

In light of the tremendous inequities woven into American labor and capital markets and transfer systems today, this redeployment of Pell resources seems relatively modest. And there is certainly historical precedence, even for a sizable asset transfer. From our perspective, transforming Pell Grants into early-commitment, asset-building accounts could mirror the Homestead Act or GI Bill. That is, it would represent a shift from thinking about financial aid as simply a way to help pay for college to thinking about how financial aid can facilitate economic mobility for low-income families. As we have seen with those historical policies, this asset investment could then become part of how a new generation of Americans understand the deal they have struck with their government, seen as an exchange of their considerable exertion for a real opportunity to leverage assets to build future wealth.

Millions of Americans have seen their own opportunity stories shaped by the doors that the GI Bill and Homestead Acts opened for them at different points in their families' origins. In the aggregate, these policies did more than just aid individual families; they rewrote our collective narrative about the mechanisms through which Americans advance and about who is eligible to seize those opportunities. So, too, could repurposing the means-tested consumption supports of the Pell Grants into productive asset stores help to vault today's young people to higher rungs on the economic ladder and, in the process, strengthen education as a mobility tool.

This would require additional federal funding for the period when the current fifth grade class, for example, starts to receive Pell Grant funds into their CSAs while current college-age students receive Pell Grant funds. A way that these additional funds could in large part be made up is by the annual profits from the current student loan program. For example, the federal government earned $41.3 billion in 2013 (Jesse 2013). Significantly, this repurposing would not change the target population or the core mission of this means-tested program. What could change is the public perception of the Pell Grant program, its ability to influence the pre-college preparation of disadvantaged children, and its potency as an institution shaping the formative years of children's lives.

As outlined here, the reframing and reformatting of Pell Grants would represent an important policy principle for CSA development: Examining current programs such as the Pell Grant program through an asset-informed lens can reveal significant, existing opportunities to use the power of asset-building to improve children's lives. Through this lens, Pell Grants could be just the beginning.

## POLICY OPPORTUNITIES FOR NATIONAL CSA DEVELOPMENT

Adequately funding Children's Savings Accounts would be a worthwhile policy endeavor even if doing so required a tremendous net new investment, but in today's policy and fiscal climate, winning support for a large expenditure is unlikely. This is where, again, drawing tighter connections between student-debt relief and Children's Savings Accounts can reveal the opportunity cost of our current commitment to student loans. We cannot continue to make student loans the central component of our financial aid system and simultaneously develop an asset-based approach without diverting resources from another function or significantly increasing our net expenditure for higher education. We could, however, reimagine financial aid entirely and, in so doing, free most of the resources needed to finance a universal Children's Savings Account system largely within the current fiscal footprint. Generating the political will necessary to do so mostly requires clarity about the outcomes we should expect from a financial aid program and the principles—of equity, adequacy, and efficiency—that we should demand. It will mean seeing the financial aid landscape through a different paradigm (Kuhn 1962), such that this approach seems not only viable but inevitable. When we are looking together through the right lens, the failings of student loans and the gains to be realized from pivoting to assets will be apparent, and the political will to find the necessary resources will follow.

## Tax Expenditures

Current tax expenditures in the arena of higher education are widely regarded by analysts as grossly inefficient, targeted too poorly to provide strong, positive outcomes in increased college enrollment. They are the largest nonloan form of federal financial aid, costing more than $34 billion in 2012, so ensuring that we are realizing positive returns on this investment is critical to righting our financial aid system (RADD Consortium 2013). Most of those who benefit from tax deductions and credits for higher education would have attended college anyway, so these benefits mostly serve to reduce the cost of attendance for those whose educational futures did not hinge on cost. While the American Opportunity Tax Credit is partially refundable, thereby resulting in families making less than $25,000 per year receiving approximately 25 percent of the total benefit, other higher education tax credits skew far more heavily to the economically advantaged (Greer and Levin 2014). More than half of the benefits of the Tuition and Fees Deduction, for example, went to households earning more than $100,000 in 2013 (RADD Consortium 2013).

The timing of educational tax expenditures is also problematic; the benefits come after costs are incurred, so a student has to have the money to pay these costs before the tax reimbursements kick in. Coming not only after enrollment but long after educational paths are determined, tax expenditures completely fail to affect pre-college outcomes (Nelson 2011). Tax expenditures also have the disadvantage of being largely invisible, so many students may not even realize that their families receive these investments (Mettler 2011). These significant expenditures largely fail—in rhetoric and in fact—as an institution to support the educational achievement of low-income children and redeem their faith in the prospect of the American Dream. Clearly, U.S. financial aid policy could deploy these resources to far greater effect, directed at the students who need support, delivered more transparently, and timed to cultivate educational development and confront real-time college costs.

## Scholarships and Local Initiatives

Pell Grants are not, of course, the only financial aid that could perhaps be used to greater effect as a savings intervention rather than a straight transfer. While scholarships and need-based grants have been positively associated with educational outcomes in the literature (Baum, McPherson, and Steele 2008), these investments often fail to reach the students who most need them, kicking in as they do only after children have qualified academically for higher education. Financial aid that does not work to reduce disparities in educational preparation cannot fully ameliorate the gaps in attainment, the roots of which are sown long before one's senior year in high school. One of the positive externalities of advancing public policy to support Children's Savings Accounts could be diffusing these asset principles throughout other financial aid efforts, such that the entities that currently award need- or merit-based scholarships reimagine these efforts to align with CSAs.

Everyone who provides money to help children pay for college at the point of enrollment could do so earlier, often realizing the same benefits for smaller initial deposits, given the power of compounding and of educational expectations. States that provide education awards to children exiting foster care could do so at age 14 instead of 17 (Rowan 2014). Communities that provide scholarships to high school seniors could give them instead to high school sophomores. School districts and localities that want to support the educational achievement of their young children could follow the lead of San Francisco and Cuyahoga County, using the mechanism of even relatively small-dollar accounts to create a college-going culture and evoke pro-savings behavior. Here, the power of the idea of children's savings and its alignment with the U.S. ethos of rewarding individual effort and investing in people's potential offers the promise that savings efforts could permeate and inform other policy initiatives, multiplying their effect.

## CONCLUSION

Policy should encourage autonomous local investment in Children's Savings Accounts by removing regulatory barriers and sharing knowledge about design practices. Even multiplying these efforts in communities around the country would fall short, however, of the ideal of universal, progressive, lifelong, asset-building accounts (Cramer and Newville 2009), a vision only federal commitment can make possible. While repurposing programs such as Pell Grants and revoking ill-advised tax expenditures can provide many of the resources needed for such a national effort, moving away from the student loan system is still a political and fiscal imperative. The U.S. government is heavily invested in student loans today, and only renouncing this debt-centric approach would create the budget slack and political energy needed to fully embrace asset-based financial aid instead. As we have outlined here, reliance on student loans as *the* mechanism for college financing is incompatible with U.S. objectives of educational attainment, financial security, and economic mobility. It represents a failed paradigm, and anything short of revolution will fail, then, as well.

While CSAs could be valuable corollaries, reducing the need for student loans and building savings habits, the real potential of children's savings is found in replacing student borrowing—at least to a significant extent—with asset building. Given the tremendous advantages represented by an asset-empowered rather than debt-dependent approach to financial aid and the multiple benefits of following an asset-empowered rather than a debt-dependent path to higher education, the United States cannot afford to be less than "all in" to children's asset building. Walking boldly away from the student loan system makes constructing a savings system financially feasible and politically conceivable. It is possible, and it is time.

# PART THREE

## Conclusion

# TEN

## Conclusion

As in so much of the U.S. policy context—and life itself—what you see when you look at student loans depends largely on where you sit and how you have been conditioned to see the world. Today, while there is near consensus that something needs to be done about the problems associated with student debt (Weise 2014), there is nowhere near as much agreement about the precise indicators of the problem, its severity, its origins, or, of course, what should be done. As we make the case for charting a dramatically different course in American financial aid policy, we begin again with our analysis that today's debt dependent financial aid model is not only incidentally problematic but wholly inconsistent with our most cherished values (Elliott and Lewis 2013). We further assert that recognition of the threat that student borrowing poses, not only to individual students but to our shared understanding of what it takes to get ahead in the United States and what government policy should do to support those aspirations, is essential if we are to raise the stakes enough to compel change.

Today, we cannot claim ignorance of student loans' failure to catalyze greater educational achievement, increase students' engagement in school, and foster stronger economic foundations (Cofer and Somers 2000; Perna 2000; Heller 2008; Kim 2007; Dwyer, McCloud, and Hodson 2011; Fry 2014, among others). There is a growing body of evidence that reveals the extent to which student loans endanger the well-being of individual borrowers, the institutions dependent on them, and our macroeconomy (Frizell 2014; Korkki 2014). Data reveal that disadvantaged students, particularly low-income and those of color, are disproportionately affected by these forces (Fenske, Porter, and DuBrock 2000; Kim 2007). These disparate effects are particularly unacceptable given the role of higher education in fostering greater equity and upward mobility (Greenstone, Looney, Patashnik, and Yu 2013).

Still, many are quick to conclude that these effects are either rather insignificant in the context of the gains associated with college (Rose 2014) or at least unavoidable, as our policy debate leaves little room for discussion of viable alternatives. As a result, despite agitation from student activists alarmed at how their futures are slipping away from them (Ramos 2014), growing concerns from many analysts convinced by their own robust findings, and populist pronouncements from politicians seeking to capitalize on the attention to student debt in the news cycle (Dickinson 2014), true reform still seems elusive. Bridging the distance between what are currently contemplated as alternatives and what is really needed as policy solutions requires making resolution of the "student loan problem" not just a political objective or a desirable policy outcome but the existential imperative that our reading suggests it is.

We have to stop quibbling about which type of Income-Based Repayment plan would represent the greatest incremental reduction in borrowers' burdens or how high we should set the loan limits. We have to stop pretending that this debate is really about interest rates rather than the future of a generation and the maintenance of the American truism that those who work hard should be able to achieve beyond their initial station. We need to look at the evidence of student loans' effects with clear eyes and a broad view. We need to ask the right questions and expect more from this central element of our financial aid system than just minimal harm from which most eventually recover (Elliott and Lewis 2014). We have to conduct this debate as though our futures depend on it, because they just may.

In this volume, we articulated a case for abandoning our reliance on student borrowing as the primary mechanism through which students finance higher education. We rooted this position in our shared American values, paying particular attention to how the status quo is failing the current generation of young adults who could be activated to build a constituency for an asset-empowered alternative to student loans. We examined the state of the scholarly evidence about asset and debt effects in pursuit of an agreed-upon suspension of the debate about whether we have a student debt problem, how we know that we do, and what indicators we should watch to see whether our policy proposals bring improvement. We believe that it is not yet too late to recognize the failings of our student loan system, pivot to approaches with demonstrated potential to bring better outcomes, and thus redeem the American Dream. It is to the political dimension of this larger battle of ideas that we now turn.

## DEBT DEPENDENCE AS CONTRARY TO AMERICAN MYTHOLOGY

As we have discussed, at its core, the American Dream holds that chances of success should primarily depend on a person's exertion of effort and reservoir of innate ability, with perhaps some luck as well. This belief has motivated the risk taking and sacrifice of generations of Americans and is responsible for much of our collective progress, even if also implicated in the individual suffering of those for whom this equation has always seemed hollow. Our economic policies have at various points reinforced this calculus (as in the Earned Income Tax Credit, which rewards the work effort of low-income households, or Social Security, which provides greater benefits to those with more accumulated work credits) or belied it (notably, in asset limits that penalize saving among low-income households on public assistance; Vallas and Valenti 2014).

Anathema to U.S. ideology, however, is any suggestion that the economy should be oligarchic, rewarding background or social standing more than individual contributions. The nation was founded in large part on a desire to distinguish the new system of governance from that of the founders' European ancestors, and although economic mobility rates are higher today in Canada and some other Western nations than in the United States (Corak 2012), Americans still largely resist policies that would explicitly solidify this reward of initial privilege, such as education systems that track students into college-bound or vocational programs from an early age.

This long history, even more prominent in our collective narrative than in policy fact, makes our current willingness to accept the dominance of student borrowing particularly odd. There is considerable evidence that our increasing reliance on student loans as the gateway to higher education access serves to entrench patterns of privilege in educational attainment (McElwee 2014), increasing the extent to which educational outcomes *follow* individuals' social and economic positions, rather than *drive* them.

When two students who receive the same degree do not equitably profit from that educational acquisition because one had to finance college with student loans and one could rely on parental assets (Elliott and Lewis 2013), those two students cannot be thought to be participating in a particularly "American" education system. When the prospect of looming student debt deters many bright, college-qualified students from enrolling in college altogether or from pursuing the degrees at the institutions best suited to them (Elliott 2013), that financial aid system seems rather remarkably out of line with our purported priorities and foundational beliefs. And when the way we pay for college distorts the education system so as to prevent its fulfillment of its most cherished aims—to allow children's ardent hopes and natural talents to be the primary determinants of what they become— that is a financial aid system that impels reform.

We are on the edge of a scientific revolution, wrought by the accumulated anomalies that have exposed the extent to which student debt fails to satisfy its policy obligations. We believe it is time to leap to a new paradigm.

## YOUNG ADULTS AND THE AMERICAN DREAM

The threat that our current overreliance on student borrowing poses to the legitimacy and potency of higher education as an engine of economic mobility should be a concern to all Americans. For the large generation of young adults coming of age in the student-debt era, however, it is alarming. Largely lacking an asset foundation from which to confront the high and rising costs of college, student debt for them has long been an inevitability (Marks and Martin 2014). There is evidence that this college financing bind has pervasive, lasting, and sometimes severe consequences for these young adults, including delay of marriage and family formation (Gicheva 2011), prolonged dependence on their parents' financial support (Dettling and Hsu 2014), and lifelong reductions in asset holdings. Surely, then, they can be forgiven for not being much consoled by assurances that borrowing heavily to finance a college degree is better than the proposed alternative: reconciling themselves to a lifetime of low wages, with few opportunities to build an asset foundation for economic mobility outside of that higher education.

In response to this growing discontent, young adults are increasingly calling for radical changes; a recent survey found that almost one-quarter of Millennials expect their student loans to be forgiven (Junior Achievement 2014). While these young adults sometimes struggle alongside other Americans to imagine a true alternative to student debt, they are perhaps the most likely to spark a real financial aid revolution in U.S. education and economic policy, as they are the most visibly and ubiquitously affected by the status quo.

However, while Millennials are at the forefront of the student debt debate, some analysis suggests that other generations may have their own particular grievances with the student loan system and their own manifestations of the negative effects of student debt. For example, a recent Pew Charitable Trusts analysis found that for Generation X, which immediately preceded the Millennial generation, high levels of student debt have resulted in wealth holdings that largely fail to keep pace with their parents', even as incomes outpace those of previous cohorts (Pew Charitable Trusts 2014). This dynamic has been characterized as the "education paradox," with Generation Xers' achievement of advanced education the very activity that then compromises their wealth holdings.

Perhaps no finding more completely underscores the real dangers student debt poses to our social contract. If student loans prevent these young generations from advancing their economic well-being or translating their education and earnings into improved wealth standings, these entire cohorts cannot truly expect that the American Dream is viable in their own lives.

While there are undoubtedly other forces buffeting these generations, including the labor market ills of the Great Recession (Mishel, Bivens, Gould, and Shierholz 2013), analysis that parses income from net worth more clearly exposes the role of student debt in compromising the overall financial health of these young adult generations. Even if contexts such as educational quality, broad shifts in labor opportunities, and demographic trends play roles as well, the evidence that implicates student loans in imperiling the fortunes of these young adults cannot be ignored.

Clearly articulating these stakes is essential, as it exposes the inadequacy of current student loan policy debates and necessitates a broader vision of fundamental policy change. Because evidence suggests that it is the *existence* of student debt that triggers some of these negative effects, not so much the size of the loan or the terms under which it is transmitted (Akers 2014; Egoian 2013), only challenging the centrality of student debt in the current financial aid system will chart improved trends.

## TAPPING INTO DEBT FATIGUE TO BUILD A CONSTITUENCY FOR ASSET DEVELOPMENT

If there is a silver lining in this assessment of the problems posed by our debt-dependent financial aid system, perhaps it is this: In the student debt crisis, the asset-building movement has found new purpose. Today, the asset-development field has moved beyond questioning whether low-income people can save to instead articulating a clearer case for why supporting asset accumulation should be a central aim of economic support for American households, distinct from support for consumption needs. Framing asset building as a college-financing alternative to student debt (Elliott and Lewis 2013) takes asset approaches from the realm of interesting policy innovations to reform imperatives. There is ample evidence of debt fatigue in the United States, with student debt a prominent political campaign issue (Gilmour 2014) and a frequent topic on blogs and in the mainstream press, and the asset movement is finding new allies among these disenchanted debtors and their defenders.

While popular media coverage of the student-debt problem (Frizell 2014; Korkki 2014; Levin 2013) often contributes to the inaccurate understanding of its dimensions—highlighting very high-dollar debt loads, for example, and focusing rather narrowly on policy prescriptions for reductions in interest rates and repayment terms—the spotlight on student debt has the effect of galvanizing a sense of urgency. Notably, the potential to build a potent political constituency around alternatives to student debt is increased by the nature of the student-debt crisis itself, particularly its effects on an ever-larger population.

As an example of this spreading swath of damage, a Government Accountability Office (GAO) analysis found significant growth in student-debt holdings among older adults, some of whom are carrying debt from their earlier lives into retirement (Jeszeck 2014), and others who are assuming debt burdens to help their children and grandchildren finance their educations (Wagner and Riepenhoff 2012). While still affecting a comparatively small percentage of older adults, particularly in contrast to the widespread indebtedness of younger generations, the coincidence of student debt burdens and retirement needs poses considerable risk to these overexposed elders (Sheridan 2014).

## ASSETS' SUPERIORITY: ATTITUDE, BEHAVIOR, PREPARATION, AND ACTUAL CAPITAL ACCUMULATION

Much of the current policy debate about student loans can be characterized as vacillating between reluctant apologizing and defensive hairsplitting. While most of those engaged in these policy conversations want to see American children succeed educationally, their positions are constrained by their own experiences with student loans, inability to imagine viable alternatives, or too-narrow lens that obscures the most serious student loan effects (Elliott and Lewis 2014). They are trapped by the paradigm they have helped to ensconce, and only realization of the crisis that now confronts us can push them to a different plane.

Confronted with the growing intensity of calls for student-debt relief, some draw false comparisons between the fates of student borrowers and those without higher education. Sandy Baum's recent article "Borrowing for College: Is It Better than the Alternative?" is indicative of this mental prison; the "alternative" she has in mind is not another way to finance higher education, but the absence of that educational opportunity altogether (Baum 2014). Others take solace in the wrong indicators, defining "crisis" so that, regardless of the status quo, today's reality doesn't sink to that level. Some concede the real problems associated with student borrowing but conclude that there is no other way to get people into college, and still others would willingly admit the need for an alternative to student loans but for fear of what might take debt's place in this particular political and economic context. At times, this can feel like a surreal conversation, with analysts, policy makers, students, and other interested parties talking past each other. Unable or unwilling to grapple with the serious challenges we face, we instead talk around the problems or tweak the edges. Meanwhile, the proverbial city burns.

## CHANGING THE METRICS AND ASKING THE RIGHT QUESTIONS

Evidence of assets' potential for superior outcomes notwithstanding, making the case for alternatives to student debt begins with accurately assessing the real costs of continuing the status quo. Given the political system's tendency toward inertia and preference for stability, achieving a significant change of any kind is inherently more difficult than just staying the course (Samuelson and Zeckhauser 1988). As long as we set the bar for "acceptable" student loan outcomes low, we are unlikely to coalesce around a sharp departure from student borrowing. We will obscure the true nature of the crisis such that it will be insufficient to impel abandonment of the current paradigm.

If instead we use the right metrics for evaluating student borrowing through a lens analyzing debt's effects on the viability of the American Dream rather than narrow indicators of repayment distress or mere incidence of borrowing, the case for reform may virtually carry itself. If Americans will rally to defend any good, surely this good will be the most esteemed element of our common story. The task that remains for those of us concerned by student loans' implications, then, is to clearly point Americans' collective attention to the right questions. The point is not, "Are students who borrow for college better off than those who don't go to college at all?" but rather, "Does student debt erode the equalizing power of higher education?" (Elliott and Lewis 2013). We should ask not, "Can students mostly, eventually, pay off their student debt?" but rather, "Do student debt obligations compromise borrowers' overall financial health by diverting resources from asset accumulation?" We should not question whether our education system can survive within a context of debt dependence, but whether our current approach to financial aid redeems the promise of higher education as a catalyst to upward mobility. Rather than asking whether these generations of young people can survive their experiences with student debt, we should consider whether this is the future that we hope for them. Instead of expecting only that borrowers will eventually rebound from the toll of their loans, we should ask ourselves whether it's good for the country that student debt erodes the return on educational investment for those who have to borrow.

## THINKING BIG: IS A BAILOUT ALSO NEEDED?

While acknowledging that powerful interests have pushed higher education and financial aid policy in the direction of serving those most advantaged, we recognize that most if not all of the reform suggestions advanced today are well-intentioned, rooted in a concern about the effects of student loans evidenced in the lives of an entire generation of Americans. Just as clear, however, is their inadequacy, particularly given the stakes involved. The U.S. policy debate about student loans, financial aid, and the higher education system is in dire need of a truly new direction and societal and political permission to acknowledge the need to change course. Our read of the cumulative body of evidence about student loan effects today is that it justifies such license.

In this book, we have contended that moving from dependence on debt to an investment in children's assets would restore higher education's role as a driver of economic mobility and facilitator of greater equity. Although replacing student debt with a significant increase in need-based grants or in state support for higher education institutions would also represent meaningful improvements, there are reasons to prefer assets even to these approaches. It seems clear from the evidence presented here that, compared with debt, assets evidence superior outcomes before, during, and following college. Every child in the United States deserves a savings account, and redirecting some of the resources currently ill-used in the student loan system could provide them. At the same time, we recognize that for today's college debtors, the promise of children's accounts is of little immediate comfort. Children's Savings Accounts are, of course, a long-term solution, bearing the greatest fruits as children age toward and through higher education. In the interim, a dramatic pivot away from student loans could spark a backlash, with those still struggling to discharge their debts indignant about the benefits they only narrowly missed.

For young adults whose financial fortunes are imperiled by debt burdens, whose asset accumulation is thwarted by ongoing repayment obligations, and whose educational and career plans were distorted by the influence of debt financing, there is a need for restorative justice, even while we plan for a different future. Here, student groups and some other advocates have called for a bailout, on the scale of those that accompanied the Great Recession, while others have decried the moral hazards of such an action (Poulous 2012), particularly absent policy changes within the student loan system going forward.

Opposition to a student loan bailout is somewhat less than entirely intellectually honest, however, as changes to income-based repayment programs have resulted in repayment scenarios that many liken to such relief (Kadlec 2014). Creation of a policy whereby borrowers can have their loans forgiven in full after 10 or 20 years, regardless of their incomes or their loan balances, reveals the considerable appetite for a bailout in fact, if not in rhetoric. Particularly perversely, this bailout disproportionately benefits the most sophisticated and most indebted students, many of whom were already advantaged in their pursuit of higher education (Delisle and Holt 2013). Indeed, today, we may have the liability of a bailout, including the significant costs (Kadlec 2014) and potential for distortion of behavior, without the benefits, including relief for the most struggling borrowers (Kelly 2014) or the collective accounting of student loans' failures.

Even if bailing out every student debtor is politically impossible and fiscally unwise, reflexively claiming moral hazard to avoid addressing the real hardship experienced by millions who did exactly what policy and our ethos of the American Dream encouraged—borrowed to finance an education that was supposed to pay dividends, for them and for us all—is indefensible. Our governmental systems are more than capable of approaching student loan bailout with some nuance, directing relief at those who evidence suggests are struggling the most, including those who never earned a degree despite costly attempts (Kelly 2014).

Too many student borrowers have been harmed as a result of their belief in the American Dream. They deferred wages to attend higher educational institutions that were supposed to prepare them for better jobs. They vested their hopes in an education system that was supposed to deliver real opportunity, if only they were bright enough and worked hard enough. Instead, with crushing frequency, they find themselves worse off, at least in terms of wealth accumulation, trapped in that "education paradox" (Pew Charitable Trusts 2014, 3). When our policy bargains fail to this extent, we must intervene decisively.

Some of the failures are not this dramatic, of course, and so the corrective action may be more modest as well. All student debtors should be protected from abusive collection practices and supported in their efforts to build balances, even while discharging their debts, as in the provision of "economic mobility accounts" (Elliott and Lewis 2014, 59). Relatively minor changes in policy could reduce the extent to which having student debt means having fewer opportunities for asset development. Student debtors could benefit from more forgiving underwriting guidelines in mortgage markets, for example, and from repayment modifications that encourage savings, as with an escrow account or a hiatus in repayment obligations at specific points. Some of these changes could even happen within a revised income-based repayment, one that has successful repayment as its objective, not extended indebtedness ending in forgiveness. A bailout would not need to be an all-or-nothing proposition, but it should be an explicit policy choice, with clear rules for eligibility (Needham 2014) and an official statement recognizing the need for a different direction.

Constructing the right policy levers within a bailout hinges, of course, on correctly understanding the causes of greatest hardship for student borrowers. It further demands clarity on the vision of higher education as a conduit of mobility and central to Americans' expectations about how they are supposed to be able to leverage their effort and ability for a real chance of success. It requires moving past the alarmist rhetoric about high absolute balances (see http://studentdebtcrisis.org) and beyond the crushingly low expectations to which many hold student loans today (Elliott and Lewis 2014) to instead demand that the pursuit of higher education—for future generations of students and for those who have already completed their studies—should not mean a lifetime of compromised financial well-being, but instead a sound investment in their productive future.

As part of a pivot away from our largely failed experiment with student loans, a large-scale but well-targeted student loan bailout is entirely consistent with our national objectives of building a more financially capable future and part of our ongoing economic recovery. It is a policy intervention for a new day, springing from a different paradigm, and it would stand as a bold but commonsense response to the true challenges we confront. It would mark, then, a break with our recent past, but also a reconnection with our historic foundation and an affirmation of our shared future.

# APPENDIX

# Methods

## DATA

This study uses longitudinal data from the Educational Longitudinal Survey (ELS) made available to the public by the National Center for Education Statistics (NCES). The survey began in 2002, when students were in 10th grade, and follow-up waves took place in 2004, 2006, and 2012. Its purpose was to follow students as they progressed through high school and transitioned to postsecondary education or the labor market, and it is an ideal dataset to test whether early experiences or resources predict later outcomes.

The ELS aimed to present a holistic picture of student achievement by gathering information from multiple sources. Students, their parents, teachers, librarians, and principals provided information regarding students' average grades, math achievement, and educational expectations and school resources and curriculum, teacher experience, student and parent work/employment, and students' post–high school enrollment in college.

## SAMPLE

We then created three separate samples of young adults who had (a) some college or an associate degree, (b) bachelor's degree, and (c) graduate degree. These samples were restricted to include students who were in the 2002 10th grade cohort and the 2012 ELS samples (i.e., those who answered the follow-up questionnaires). Further, all three samples only include students who graduated from high school.

## Family Economic Status Variables

All covariates are downloaded from 2002 unless specified otherwise.

*Household income.* In the ELS, household income included 13 distinct levels. For this study, the levels of household income were combined into three levels: (a) low-income (below $35,000); (b) middle-income ($35,000 to $75,000); and (c) high-income ($75,000 or higher). The levels were chosen, in part, to keep relatively equal cases in each category while maintaining important distinctions between income groups.

*Parent education level.* Parent education level is equivalent to whichever parent's is higher and includes eight distinct levels. The eight levels were collapsed into four for the final analysis: (a) high school diploma or less, (b) some college or associate degree, (c) bachelor's degree, and (d) graduate degree or higher.

## Young Adult's Characteristics Variables

*Student race or ethnicity.* The variable representing race included seven categories in the ELS. American Indian or Alaska Native and more than one race were not included in this analysis due to small sample sizes, and Hispanic and Latino were combined. Five categories were included in the final analysis: (a) white, (b) black, (c) Latino/Hispanic, (d) Asian, and (e) other.

*Gender.* Student's gender is a dichotomous variable: (a) male and (b) female.

*Marital status.* Marital status was recoded into a dichotomous variable: (a) married and (b) not married.

*Region of the country.* In the ELS dataset, region is coded as Northeast, Midwest, South, and West. It is the region of the country where the respondent attended high school.

*Employment status.* The employment status variable was recoded into a three-level variable: (a) unemployed, (b) part-time employment, and (c) full-time employment.

*High school GPA.* Students' grade point average (GPA) is a categorical variable that averages grades for all coursework in 9th through 12th grades. There are seven categories: $0 = 0.00-1.00$; $1 = 1.01-1.50$; $2 = 1.51-2.00$; $3 = 2.01-2.50$; $4 = 2.51-3.00$; $5 = 3.01-3.50$; and $6 = 3.51-4.00$. We collapsed categories 0–2 into one due to small frequencies (36, 156, and 782, respectively). To convert this into letter grades, a commonly used grade scale is $0 = F$; $1 = D$; $2-3 = C$; $4-5 = B$; and $6 = A$. A dichotomous variable was created: $0 =$ below 3.0 and $1 = 3.0$ or above.

*College selectivity.* The following categories made up the college selectivity variable: 1 = public, four-year or above; 2 = private, not-for-profit, four-year; 3 = private, for-profit, four-year; 4 = public, two-year; 5 = private, not-for-profit, two-year; 6 = private, for-profit, two-year; 7 = public, less than two-year; 8 = private, not-for-profit, less than two-year; and 9 = private, for-profit, less than two-year. They were recoded as a three-level variable with the following categories: 0 = public, four-year; 1 = private, four-year; 2 = private, for-profit, four year college. Downloaded from 2006 data.

*Years after college.* This was a continuous variable created by subtracting the year 2013 from the last year respondent reported attending post-secondary school.

*Occupation classification.* The ELS occupation variable was recoded into three groups: (a) highest-paying occupations ($60,000 or above), moderate-paying occupations ($35,000 to $59,999), and lowest-paying occupations (below $35,000). The Bureau of Labor Statistics employment by major occupational group was used to classify the jobs by median annual wage.[1] How jobs were classified:

**Table A.1    Classification of Jobs by Median Annual Wage**

| | |
|---|---|
| • Highest-paying occupations ($60,000 or above) | Management occupations; business and financial operations occupations; computing and mathematical occupations; architecture and engineering occupations; life, physical, and social service occupations; health care practitioners and technical occupations; and legal occupations |
| • Moderate-paying occupations ($35,000 to $59,999) | Protective services, arts, design, entertainment, sports, and media occupations; education, training, and library occupations; community and social service occupations; installation, maintenance, and repair occupations; and construction and extraction occupations |
| • Lowest-paying occupations (below $35,000) | Transportation and material moving occupations; production occupations; farming, fishing, and forestry occupations; office and administrative support occupations; sales and related occupations; personal care and service occupations; building and grounds cleaning and maintenance occupations; food preparation and serving related occupations; and health care support occupations |

## Variables of Interest

*Parents' savings for student's college.* The variable of interest came from a survey question that asked parents whether they were financially preparing to pay for their children to attend college by starting a savings account: 1 = yes, and 0 = no. Downloaded from 2002 data.

*Student debt.* The student debt outcome variable is a dichotomous variable (i.e., has student loan debt or does not have student loan debt). Downloaded from 2012 data.

*Amount of student loan debt.* The variable of interest, amount of student loan debt, was drawn from the 2012 wave and was a continuous variable.

*Disposable income.* We also created a disposable income variable. To create the disposable income variable, we first divide total annual income by 12 to determine what each respondent's monthly income was. Then we subtracted the respondent's monthly student loan payment from his or her total monthly income. For young adults with no student loans, the disposable income and the total monthly income would be the same amount.

## Dependent Variable

*Net worth.* Respondents were asked to imagine if they and their spouse were to sell all of their major possessions to include their home, turn them into cash, and pay off all of their debts to include their mortgage, would they have something left over, break even, or be in debt?

## ANALYSIS PLAN

Prior to running the regression model, we first tested for the usual symptoms of multicollinearity by computing the variance inflation factors (VIF) for every covariate in all three samples. In each of the three samples, we found all of them to be less than two (i.e., max($VIF$) < 2), which suggests that multicollinearity is not an issue.

The standard ordinal model implicitly assumes proportional odds. To validate this assumption, we conducted a test proposed by Brant (1990). From the results of the Brant test, we found (a) some college/associate degree—covariates race, gender, and loan use; (b) bachelor's degree—covariates family income, occupation, and loan use; and (c) graduate degree—covariates region, college selectivity, and occupation violate the ordinal logit models parallel lines assumption. Hence, we consider a modification to the standard ordinal logit, a generalized threshold model that accounts for the possibility of young adults using different thresholds in reporting their responses, by relaxing the assumption that the thresholds, are identical for all respondents.

The generalized threshold ordinal logit model retains the idea that young adults realize their net worth from a common distribution, but assumes that they use systematically different thresholds while reporting their net worth. A common approach to model generalized thresholds is to make the threshold parameters linear (Maddala 1983; Peterson and Harrell 1990). We estimate the parameters of this generalized threshold model using the GOLOGIT2 routine (Williams 2006a) in STATA 13.

## MARGINAL EFFECTS

The main purpose of our model is to predict the probability that a young adult who borrows student loans reports a particular level of net worth. It is important to understand how these probabilities of a young adult reporting a certain level of net worth change with student loans and other covariates. Hence, we calculated the predicted probabilities of the effect of different covariates on net worth. While measuring the marginal probability effects of any covariate, we define a typical young adult for every covariate by fixing the rest of the covariates at their mean (or the mode for categorical covariates).

## NOTE

1. See http://www.bls.gov/emp/ep_table_101.htm.

# Bibliography

Abel, J., Deitz, R., and Su, Y. 2014. "Are Recent Graduates Finding Good Jobs?" *Current Issues* 20, no. 1. http://www.newyorkfed.org/research/current_issues/ci20-1.pdf.

Adams, J. T. 1931. *The Epic of America*. New York: Blue Ribbon Books.

Advisory Committee on Student Financial Assistance. 2001. "Access Denied: Restoring the Nation's Commitment to Equal Educational Opportunity." U.S. Department of Education (Washington, D.C.). https://www2.ed.gov/about/bdscomm/list/acsfa/access_denied.pdf.

Advisory Committee on Student Financial Assistance. 2002. "Empty Promises: The Myth of College Access in America." U.S. Department of Education (Washington, D.C.). https://www2.ed.gov/about/bdscomm/list/acsfa/emptypromises.pdf.

Advisory Committee on Student Financial Assistance. 2006. "Mortgaging Our Future: How Financial Barriers to College Undercut America's Global Competitiveness." U.S. Department of Education (Washington, D.C.).

Advisory Committee on Student Financial Assistance. 2010. "The Rising Price of Inequality: How Inadequate Grant Aid Limits College Access and Persistence." U.S. Department of Education (Washington, D.C.).

Ajzen, I. 1991. "The Theory of Planned Behavior." *Organizational Behavior and Human Decision Processes* 50: 179–211.

Akers, B. 2014. "How Much Is Too Much? Evidence on Financial Well-Being and Student Loan Debt." American Enterprise Institute (Washington, D.C.).

Akers, B., and Chingos, M. 2014. "Is a Student Loan Crisis on the Horizon?" Brookings Institution (Washington, D.C.). http://www.brookings.edu/~/media/research/files/reports/2014/06/24-student-loan-crisis-akers-chingos/is-a-student-loan-crisis-on-the-horizon.pdf.

Akers, B., and Chingos, M. 2014. "Student Loan Safety Nets: Estimating the Costs and Benefits of Income-Based Repayment." Brookings Institution (Washington, D.C.). http://c.ymcdn.com/sites/www.ncher.us/resource/collection/DCBD86D9-7685-4DCF-A143-A2BF11A0869C/IBR_online.pdf.

Alter, J. 2012. "U.S. Needs More College Graduates in Order to Improve the Economy." *Huffington Post*, April 29. http://www.huffingtonpost.com/2012/04/29/college-graduates-essential-improving-economy_n_1458639.html.

American Student Assistance. 2013. "Life Delayed: The Impact of Student Debt on the Daily Lives of Young Americans." American Student Assistance (Washington, D.C.).

Armor, D. A., and Taylor, S. E. 1998. "Situated Optimism: Specific Outcome Expectancies and Self-Regulation." In *Advances in Experimental Social Psychology*. Edited by M. P. Zanna. New York: Academic Press, 309–379.

Arnold, C. 2014. "How Do Companies Boost 401(k) Enrollment? Make It Automatic." *NPR*, April 21. http://www.npr.org/2014/04/21/303683792/how-do-companies-boost-401-k-enrollment-make-it-automatic.

Aud, S., et al. 2012. "The Condition of Education, 2012." National Center for Education Statistics (Washington, D.C.).

Bailey, M., and Dynarski, S. 2011. "Gains and Gaps: Changing Inequality in U.S. College Entry and Completion." Working paper, National Bureau of Economic Research (Washington, D.C.). http://www.nber.org/papers/w17633.

Bandura, A. 1977. "Self-Efficacy: Toward a Unifying Theory of Behavior Change." *Psychological Review* 84, no. 2: 191–215.

Bandura, A. 1984. "Exercise of Personal Agency through the Self-Efficacy Mechanism." In *Self-Efficacy: Thought Control of Action*. Edited by R. Schwarzer. Washington, D.C.: Hemisphere Publishing Corporation, 3–38.

Bandura, A. 1986. *Social Foundations of Thought and Action: A Social Cognitive Theory*. Prentice-Hall Series in Social Learning Theory. Englewood Cliffs, NJ: Prentice-Hall.

Bandura, A. 1993. "Perceived Self-Efficacy in Cognitive Development and Functioning." *Educational Psychologist* 28, no. 2: 117–48.

Bandura, A. 1994. "Self-Efficacy." *Encyclopedia of Human Behavior* 4: 71–81.

Bandura, A. 1997. *Self-Efficacy: The Exercise of Control.* New York: W. H. Freeman.

Barkley, R. A. 2004. "Attention-Deficit/Hyperactivity Disorder and Self-Regulation: Taking an Evolutionary Perspective on Executive Functioning." In *Handbook of Self-Regulation: Research, Theory, and Applications.* Edited by R. F. Baumeister and K. D. Vohs. New York: Guilford Press, 301–32.

Baum, S. 2014. "Borrowing for College: Is It Better than the Alternative?" *MetroTrends* blog, May 23. Washington, D.C.: The Urban Institute. http://blog.metrotrends.org/2014/05/borrowing-college-alternative.

Baum, S., McPherson, M., and Steele, P. (Eds.). 2008. "The Effectiveness of Student Aid Policies: What the Research Tells Us." College Board (New York).

Baum, S., and O'Malley, M. 2003. "College on Credit: How Borrowers Perceive Their Education Debt." *Journal of Student Financial Aid* 33, no. 3. http://publications.nasfaa.org/jsfa/vol33/iss3/1.

Baum, S., and Saunders, D. 1998. "Life after Debt: Summary Results of the National Student Loan Survey." In *Student Loan Debt: Problems and Prospects, Proceedings from a National Symposium.* Edited by J. Davis and J. Merisotis. Washington, D.C.: Institute for Higher Education Policy, Sallie Mae Education Institute, and the Education Resources Institute.

Baum, S., and Schwartz, S. 1988. "The Impact of Student Loans on Borrowers: Consumption Patterns and Attitudes towards Repayment: Evidence from the New England Student Loan Survey." Massachusetts Higher Education Assistance Corporation (Boston).

Baum, S., and Schwartz, S. 2005. "How Much Debt Is Too Much? Defining Benchmarks for Manageable Student Debt." Commissioned by the Project on Student Debt and the College Board (Washington, D.C.). https://www.cgsnet.org/ckfinder/userfiles/files/How_Much_Debt_is_Too_Much.pdf.

Bengali, L., and Daly, M. 2013. "U.S. Economic Mobility: The Dream and the Data." The Federal Reserve Board of San Francisco's Economic Letters (San Francisco). http://www.frbsf.org/economic-research/publications/economic-letter/2013/march/us-economic-mobility-dream-data.

Bernstein, J., and Baker, D. 2003. "The Benefits of Full Employment." Economic Policy Institute (Washington, D.C.).

Bettinger, E., Long, B., Oreopoulos, P., and Sanbonmatsu, L. 2009. "The Role of Simplification and Information in College Decisions: Results from the H&R Block FAFSA Experiment." National Bureau of Economic Research (Cambridge, MA).

Beverly, S., Sherraden, M., Zhan, M., Williams-Shanks, T., Nam, Y., and Cramer, R. 2008. "Determinants of Asset Building. A Report in the Series Poor Finances: Assets and Low Income Households." U.S. Department of Health and Human Services (Washington, D.C.).

Boguhn, A. 2014 "Paul Ryan Shuns Conservative Media's 'Makers And Takers' Rhetoric, But His Policies Still Rely On Those Myths." Media Matters for America. http://mediamatters.org/research/2014/08/17/paul-ryan-shuns-conservative-medias-makers-and/200458.

Boshara, R. 2003. "The $6,000 Solution." *The Atlantic* (January/February). http://www.theatlantic.com/past/docs/issues/2003/01/boshara.htm.

Boshara, R., and Emmons, W. 2013. "After the Fall: Rebuilding Family Balance Sheets, Rebuilding the Economy." Federal Reserve Bank of St. Louis (St. Louis). http://www.stlouisfed.org/publications/ar/2012/ pages/ar12_2a.cfm.

Bowen, W., Chingos, M., and McPherson, M. 2009. *Crossing the Finish Line: Completing College at America's Public Universities*. Princeton, NJ: Princeton University Press.

Bricker, J., Kennickell, A., Moore, K., and Sabelhaus, J. 2012. "Changes in U.S. Family Finances from 2007 to 2010: Evidence from the Survey of Consumer Finances." *Federal Reserve Bulletin* 98, no. 2: 1–80. http://www.federalreserve.gov/Pubs/Bulletin/2012/articles/scf/scf.htm.

Brown, M., and Caldwell, S. 2013. "Young Adult Student Loan Borrowers Retreat from Housing and Auto Markets." Federal Reserve Bank of New York (New York): 1–21.

Brown, M., Haughwout, A., Lee, D., Scally, J., and van der Klaauw, W. 2014. "Measuring Student Debt and Its Performance." Federal Reserve Bank of New York Staff Reports, no. 668. http://www.newyorkfed.org/research/staff_reports/sr668.pdf.

Bruenig, M. 2014. "Education Subsidies for the Rich." Demos (Washington, D.C.). http://www.demos.org/blog/2/19/14/education-subsidies-rich.

Bundy, K. 2014. "Community Colleges' Most Pressing Task: Increase Completion Rates." *Diverse Education*, January 5. http://diverse education.com/article/59873.

Burd, S. 2013. "Undermining Pell: How Colleges Compete for Wealthy Students and Leave the Low-Income Behind." New America (Washington, D.C.). http://education.newamerica.net/sites/newamerica.net/files/policydocs/Merit_Aid%20Final.pdf.

Bureau of Labor Statistics. 2014. "The Compensation-Productivity Gap."
U.S. Department of Labor, Editor's Desk (Washington, D.C.). http://
www.bls.gov/opub/ted/2011/ted_20110224.htm.

Callahan, D., and Cha, J. M. 2013. "Stacked Deck: How the Dominance of
Politics by the Affluent and Business Undermines Economic Mobility in America." Demos (Washington, D.C.). http://www.demos.org/
sites/default/files/publications/Demos-Stacked-Deck.pdf.

Callender, C. and Jackson, J. 2005. "Does the Fear of Debt Deter Students
from Higher Education?" *Journal of Social Policy* 34, no. 4: 509–540.

Campaigne, D. A., and Hossler, D. 1998. "How Do Loans Affect the Educational Decisions of Students? Access, Aspirations, College Choice,
and Persistence." In *Condemning Students to Debt: College Loans
and Public Policy*. Edited by R. Fossey and M. Bateman. New York:
Teachers College Press.

Carnevale, A. P., Hanson, A. R., and Gulish, A. 2013. "Failure to Launch:
Structural Shift and the New Lost Generation." Georgetown University Center on Education and the Workforce (Washington, D.C.).
http://cew.georgetown.edu/failuretolaunch.

Carnevale, A., Rose, S., and Cheah, B. 2011. "The College Payoff."
*Georgetown University Center on Education and the Workforce*
(Washington, D.C.). https://www2.ed.gov/policy/highered/reg/hearule
making/2011/collegepayoff.pdf.

Carnevale, A., Smith, M., and Melton, M. 2011. "STEM." Georgetown
University Center on Education and the Workforce (Washington,
D.C.). http://files.eric.ed.gov/fulltext/ED525297.pdf.

Carnevale, A. and Strohl, J. 2010. "How Increasing College Access
Is Increasing Inequality, and What to Do about It." In *Rewarding
Strivers*. Edited by R. D. Kahlenberg. Washington, D.C.: The Century Foundation. http://www.tcf.org/assets/downloads/tcf-Carne
valeStrivers.pdf.

Carnevale, A., and Strohl, J. 2013. "Separate and Unequal: How Higher
Education Reinforces the Intergenerational Reproduction of White
Racial Privilege." Georgetown University Center on Education and the
Workforce (Washington, D.C.). http://www.issuelab.org/click/down-
load2/separate_and_unequal_how_higher_education_reinforces_
the_intergenerational_reproduction_of_white_racial_privilege.

Carter, J. "Remarks on Signing the Education Amendments of 1980 into
Law." 1980. In *The American Presidency Project*. Edited by J. Woolley and G. Peters, October 3. http://www.presidency.ucsb.edu/ws/
index.php?pid=45205&st=carter&st1=higher+education.

CBS News. 2008. "$1.6B of Bank Bailout Went to Execs." December 21.
http://www.cbsnews.com/news/16b-of-bank-bailout-went-to-execs.

Chapin, R. 2014. *Social Policy for Effective Practice*. 3rd ed. New York: Routledge.

Chopra, R. 2013. "Prepared Remarks by Rohit Chopra before the Federal Reserve Bank of St. Louis." Consumer Financial Protection Bureau (Washington, D.C.). http://www.consumerfinance.gov/newsroom/student-loan-ombudsman-rohit-chopra-before-the-federal-reserve-bank-of-st-louis.

Choy, S. P. and Carroll, D. 2000. "Debt Burden Four Years after College." National Center for Education Statistics (Washington, D.C.).

Clancy, M., and Lassar, T. 2010. "College Savings Plan Accounts at Birth: Maine's Statewide Program." Washington University, Center for Social Development (St. Louis). http://collegesavingsinitiative.org/content/college-savings-plan-accounts-birth-maine%E2%80%99s-statewide-program.

Clancy, M., Lasser, T., and Taake, K. "Saving for College: A Policy Primer." St. Louis: Washington University, Center for Social Development (St. Louis).

Clancy, M., Orszag, P., and Sherraden, M. 2004. "College Savings Plans: A Platform for Inclusive Saving Policy?" Washington University, Center for Social Development (St. Louis).

Clancy, M., and Sherraden, M. 2014. "Automatic Deposits for All at Birth: Maine's Harold Alfond College Challenge." Washington University, Center for Social Development (St. Louis, MO). http://csd.wustl.edu/Publications/Documents/Maine%E2%80%99s%20Harold%20Alfond%20College%20Challenge.pdf.

Cofer, J., and Somers, P. 1999. "An Analytical Approach to Understanding Student Debtload Response." *Journal of Student Financial Aid* 29, no. 3: 25–44.

Cofer, J., and Somers, P. 2000. "A Comparison of the Influence of Debtload on the Persistence of Students at Public and Private Colleges." *Journal of Student Financial Aid* 30: 39–58.

College Board. 2010. "Education Pays 2010." College Board (New York).

College Board. 2012. "Trends in College Pricing." College Board (New York).

College Board. 2013. "Rethinking Pell Grants." College Board (Washington, D.C.).

College Savings Plan Network. 2012. "Compare 529 Plans by State." College Savings Plan Network (Washington, D.C.). http://www.collegesavings.org/planComparison.aspx.

College Savings Plan Network. n.d. "529 Comparison by Feature." College Savings Plan Network (Washington, D.C.). http://www.college savings.org/planComparison.aspx.

Condon, B., and Wiseman, P. 2013. "AP Impact: Recession, Tech Kill Middle-Class Jobs." *Yahoo! News*, January 23. http://news.yahoo .com/ap-impact-recession-tech-kill-middle-class-jobs-051306434 --finance.html.

Consumer Financial Protection Bureau. 2013. "Annual Report of the CFPB Student Loan Ombudsman." Consumer Financial Protection Bureau (Washington, D.C.). http://files.consumerfinance.gov/f/201310_cfpb_ student-loan-ombudsman-annual-report.pdf.

Cooper, D., and Wang, C. 2014. "Student Loan Debt and Economic Outcomes." Current Policy Perspectives (Washington, D.C.). http:// www.bostonfed.org/economic/current-policy-perspectives/2014/ cpp1407.htm.

Corak, M. 2009. "Chasing the Same Dream, Climbing Different Ladders: Economic Mobility in the United States and Canada." Pew Charitable Trusts (Washington, D.C.).

Corak, M. 2012. "Social Mobility Is about Twice as Great in Australia and Canada than in the U.S. and United Kingdom." *Economic for Public Policy* (London, UK), May 22. http://milescorak.com/2012/05/22/ social-mobility-is-about-twice-as-great-in-australia-and-canada -than-in-the-united-kingdom-and-the-united-states-compared.

Cramer, R., Black, R., and King, J. 2012. "The Assets Report 2012: An Assessment of the Federal 'Asset-Building' Budget." New America Foundation (Washington, D.C.).

Cramer, R., and Newville, D. 2009. "Children's Savings Accounts: The Case for Creating a Lifelong Savings Platform at Birth as a Foundation for a 'Save-and-Invest' Economy." New America Foundation (Washington, D.C.).

Cuccaro-Alamin, S., and Choy, S. P. 1998. "Postsecondary Financing Strategies: How Undergraduates Combine Work, Borrowing, and Attendance." U.S. Department of Education, National Center for Education Statistics (NCES) (Washington, D.C.). http://csd.wustl .edu/Publications/Documents/PB10- 27.pdf.

Cunningham, A. F., and Kienzl, G. S. 2011. "Delinquency: The Untold Story of Student Loan Borrowing." Institute for Higher Education Policy (Washington, D.C.). http://www.ihep.org/assets/files/publications/ a-f/delinquency-the_untold_story_final_march_2011.pdf.

Delisle, J. 2014a. "The Graduate Student Debt Review." New America Foundation (Washington, D.C.). http://newamerica.net/sites/newamerica.net/files/policydocs/gradstudentdebtreview-Delisle-Final.pdf.

Delisle, J. 2014b. "Number of Borrowers Using Income-Based Repayment Doubles in One Year." New America (Washington, D.C.). http://www.edcentral.org/borrowers-using-income-based-repayment-double-one-year.

Delisle, J. 2014c. "White House Ups Cost Estimate for Income-Based Repayment." New America (Washington, D.C.). http://www.edcentral.org/white-house-ups-cost-estimate-income-based-repayment.

Delisle, J., and Holt, A. 2012. "Safety Net or Windfall?" New America (Washington, D.C.). http://newamerica.net/publications/policy/safety_net_or_windfall.

Delisle, J., and Holt, A. 2013. "Beware Savvy Borrowers Using Income-Based Repayment." New America (Washington, D.C.). http://www.edcentral.org/beware-savvy-borrowers-using-income-based-repayment.

Dettling, L., and Hsu, J. 2014. "Returning to the Nest: Debt and Parental Co-residence among Young Adults." Federal Reserve Board (Washington, D.C.). http://www.federalreserve.gov/econresdata/feds/2014/files/201480pap.pdf.

Devarics, C. 2011. "Income-Based Repayment: A Closer Look." *Diverse* (Washington, D.C.), December 5. http://diverseeducation.com/article/16683.

Dew, J. 2008. "Debt Change and Marital Satisfaction Change in Recently Married Couples. *Family Relations* 57, no. 1: 60–71.

Dickinson, T. 2014. "The Student Loan Crusader: How Elizabeth Warren Wants to Reduce Debt." *Rolling Stone*, August 20. http://www.rollingstone.com/politics/news/the-student-loan-crusader-how-elizabeth-warren-wants-to-reduce-debt-20140820.

Dugan, A., and Kafka, S. 2014. "Student Debt Linked to Worse Health and Less Wealth." *Gallup*, August 7. http://www.gallup.com/poll/174317/student-debt-linked-worse-health-less-wealth.aspx.

Duncan, G., and Morgan, J. 1981. "Sense of Efficacy and Subsequent Changes in Income—A Replication." *Journal of Human Resources* 16:649–55.

Durlak, J. A., Weissberg, R. P., Dymnicki, A.B., Taylor, R. D., and Schellinger, K. B. 2011. "The Impact of Enhancing Students' Social and Emotional Learning: A Meta-Analysis of School-Based Universal Interventions." *Child Development* 82, no. 1: 474–501.

Dwyer, R. E., McCloud, L., and Hodson, R. 2011. "Youth Debt, Mastery, and Self-Esteem: Class-Stratified Effects of Indebtedness on Self-Concept." *Social Science Research* 40, no. 3: 727–41.

Dwyer, R. E., McCloud, L., and Hodson, R. 2012. "Debt and Graduation from American Universities." *Social Forces* 90, no. 4: 1133–55.

Dynarski, S. 2002. "Race, Income, and the Impact of Merit Aid." In *Who Should We Help? The Negative Social Consequences of Merit Scholarships*. Edited by D. E. Heller and P. Marin. Boston: Civil Rights Project at Harvard University, 73–91.

Dynarski, S. 2014. "The (Fixable) Problem with Pay It Forward." Hamilton Project (Washington, D.C.). http://www.hamiltonproject.org/blog/the_fixable_problem_with_pay_it_forward.

Dynarski, S., and Kreisman, D. 2013. "Loans for Educational Opportunity: Making Borrowing Work for Today's Students." Brookings Institution, Hamilton Project (Washington, D.C.). http://www.brookings.edu/~/media/research/files/papers/2013/10/21 percent20 student percent20loans percent20dynarski/thp_dynarskidiscpaper_final.pdf.

Edmiston, K. D., Brooks, L., and Shepelwich, S. 2012. "Student Loans: Overview and Issues." Federal Reserve Bank of Kansas City Community Affairs Department (Kansas City, KS). http://www.kansascityfed.org/publicat/reswkpap/pdf/rwp%2012-05.pdf.

Egoian, J. 2013. "73 Will Be the Retirement Norm for Millennials." *Nerdwallet*, October 23. http://www.nerdwallet.com/blog/investing/2013/73-retirement-norm-millennials.

Elliott, W. 2009. "Children's College Aspirations and Expectations: The Potential Role of College Development Accounts (CDAs)." *Children and Youth Services Review* 31, no. 2: 274–283.

Elliott, W. (Ed.). 2013a. "Evaluation of the 2011 GEAR UP Priority: Lessons Learned about Integrating CSAs within GEAR UP." Asset and Education Initiative (Lawrence, KS).

Elliott, W. 2013b. "Building Expectations, Delivering Results: Asset-Based Financial Aid and the Future of Higher Education: Biannual Report on the Assets and Education Field." Assets and Education Initiative (Lawrence, KS). http://save4ed.com/wp-content/uploads/2013/11/Full-Report.pdf.

Elliott, W. 2013c. "Small-Dollar Children's Savings Accounts and Children's College Outcomes." *Children and Youth Services Review* 35, no. 3: 572–85.

Elliott, W. 2014. "Redeeming the American Dream: Children's Savings Accounts (CSAs) Build Children's Capacity for Economic Mobility." Corporation for Enterprise Development (Washington, D.C.).

Elliott, W., and Beverly, S. 2011. "The Role of Savings and Wealth in Reducing 'Wilt' between Expectations and College Attendance." *Journal of Children and Poverty* 17, no. 2: 165–85.

Elliott, W., Constance-Huggins, M., and Song, H. 2013. "Improving College Progress among Low- to Moderate-Income (LMI) Young Adults: The Role of Assets." *Journal of Family and Economic Issues* 34: 382–99.

Elliott, W., and Friedline, T. 2013. "You Pay Your Share, We'll Pay Our Share: The College Cost Burden and the Role of Race, Income, and College Assets." *Economics of Education Review* 33, no. 1: 134–153.

Elliott, W., Grinstein-Weiss, M., and Nam, I. 2013. "Student Debt and Declining Retirement Savings." Washington University, Center for Social Development (St. Louis).

Elliott, W., Jung, H., and Friedline, T. 2011. "Raising Math Scores among Children in Low-Wealth Households: Potential Benefit of Children's School Savings." *Journal of Income Distribution* 20, no. 2: 72–91.

Elliott, W., and Lewis, M. 2013. "Are Student Loans Widening the Wealth Gap in America? It's a Question of Equity." Assets and Education Initiative (Lawrence, KS).

Elliott, W., and Lewis, M. 2014. "Child Development Accounts (CDAs)." In *The Encyclopedia of Social Work*. National Association of Social Workers Press and Oxford University Press.

Elliott, W., Lewis, M., and Johnson, P. 2014. "Unequal Outcomes: Student Loan Effects on Young Adults' Net Worth Accumulation." Assets and Education Initiative (Lawrence, KS). http://www.save2limit debt.com.

Elliott, W., Lewis, M., Nam, I., and Grinstein-Weiss, M. 2014. "Student Loan Debt: Can Parent's College Savings Help?" *Federal Reserve Bank of St. Louis Review* 96, no. 4: 331–57.

Elliott, W., and Nam, I. 2012. "Direct Effects of Assets and Savings on the College Progress of Black Young Adults." *Educational Evaluation and Policy Analysis* 34, no. 1: 89–108.

Elliott, W. and Nam, I. 2013. "Is Student Debt Jeopardizing the Long-Term Financial Health of U.S. Households?" *Review* 95, no. 5: 1–20. https://www.stlouisfed.org/household-financial-stability/events/20130205/papers/Elliott.pdf.

Elliott, W., and Sherraden, M. S. 2013. "Institutional Efficacy and CSA Effects." In *Building Expectations, Delivering Results: Asset-Based Financial Aid and the Future of Higher Education*. Edited by W. Elliott. Lawrence, KS: Assets and Education Initiative, 30–49. http://save4ed.com/wp-content/uploads/2013/07/Biannual-Report_Building-Expectations-071013.pdf.

Elliott, W., Song, H-a, and Nam, I. 2013. "Small-Dollar Children's Saving Accounts and Children's College Outcomes by Income Level." *Children and Youth Services Review* 35, no. 3: 560–571.

Emmons, W. R. 2012. "Don't Expect Consumer Spending to Be the Engine of Economic Growth It Once Was." Federal Reserve Bank of St. Louis (St. Louis). http://www.stlouisfed.org/publications/re/articles/?id=2201.

Emple, H. 2013. "Asset-Oriented Rental Assistance." New America Foundation (Washington, D.C.). http://assets.newamerica.net/publications/policy/asset_oriented_rental_assistance.

Engle, J., and Tinto, V. 2008. "Moving beyond Access: College Success for Low-Income, First-Generation Students." Pell Institute (Washington, D.C.).

Fain, P. 2014. "Is Free Better?" *Inside Higher Education* (Washington, D.C.), February 6. https://www.insidehighered.com/news/2014/02/06/reaction-three-states-proposals-tuition-free-community-college.

Fenske, R. H., Porter, J. D., and DuBrock, C. P. 2000. "Tracking Financial Aid and Persistence of Women, Minority, and Need Students in Science, Engineering, and Mathematics." *Research in Higher Education* 41: 67–94. http://link.springer.com/article/10.1023%2FA%3A1007042413040.

Ferguson, T. 1995. *The Investment Theory of Party Competition and the Logic of Money-Driven Political Systems*. Chicago: University of Chicago Press.

Field, E. 2009. "Educational Debt Burden and Career Choice: Evidence from a Financial Aid Experiment at the NYU Law School." *American Economic Journal: Applied Economics* 1, no. 1: 1–21.

Financial Crisis Inquiry Commission. 2011. "The Financial Crisis Inquiry Report." U.S. Government Printing Office (Washington, D.C.). http://www.gpo.gov/fdsys/pkg/GPO-FCIC/pdf/GPO-FCIC.pdf.

Foley, M. 2013. "Bankers: College Debt Bubble Mimics Housing Crisis." *USA Today*, May 11. http://www.usatoday.com/story/money/business/2013/05/11/college-debt-bubble-looks-like-housing-bubble/2151555.

Franzblau, S., and Moore, M. 2001. "Socializing Efficacy: A Reconstruction of Self-Efficacy Theory within the Context of Inequality." *Journal of Community and Applied Social Psychology* 11, no. 2: 83–96.

Friedline, T. 2014. "The Independent Effects of Savings Accounts in Children's Names on Their Savings Outcomes in Young Adulthood." *Journal of Financial Counseling and Planning* 25, no. 1: 69–89.

Friedline, T., and Elliott, W. 2013. "Connections with Banking Institutions and Diverse Asset Portfolios in Young Adulthood: Children as Potential Future Investors. *Children and Youth Services Review* 35, no. 6: 994–1006.

Friedline, T., Elliott, W., and Nam, I. 2013. "Small-Dollar Children's Savings Accounts and Children's College Outcomes by Race." *Children and Youth Services Review* 35, no. 3: 535–547.

Friedline, T., Johnson, P., and Hughes, R. 2014. "Toward Healthy Balance Sheets: Are Savings Accounts a Gateway to Young Adults' Asset Diversification and Accumulation?" *Federal Reserve Bank of St. Louis Review* 96, no. 4: 359–89.

Frizell, S. 2014. "Student Loans Are Ruining Your Life: Now They're Ruining the Economy, Too." *Time Magazine*, February 26. http://time.com/10577/student-loans-are-ruining-your-life-now-they re-ruining-the-economy-too.

Fry, R. 2014. "Young Adults, Student Debt and Economic Well-Being." Pew Research Center's Social and Demographic Trends Project (Washington, D.C.). http://www.pewsocialtrends.org/files/2014/05/ST_2014.05.14_student-debt_complete-report.pdf.

Gans, H. 1968. *People and Plans: Essays on Urban Problems and Solutions*. New York: Basic Books.

Geiger, R. L., and Heller, D. E. 2011. "Financial Trends in Higher Education: The United States." Center for the Study of Higher Education (Washington, D.C.). http://www.ed.psu.edu/educ/cshe/working -papers/WP%236

Gicheva, D. 2011. "Does the Student-Loan Burden Weigh into the Decision to Start a Family?" University of North Carolina at Greensboro. http://www.uncg.edu/bae/people/gicheva/Student_loans_marriage March11.pdf.

Gilbert, N. 2008. *The American Class Structure: In an Age of Growing Inequality*. 7th ed. Thousand Oaks, CA: Pine Forge Press.

Gilens, M. 1999. *Why Americans Hate Welfare: Race, Media and the Politics of Anti-Poverty Policy*. Chicago: University of Chicago Press.

Gilens, M. 2012. *Affluence and Influence.* Princeton, NJ: Princeton University Press.

Goldberg, F. 2005. "The Universal Piggy Bank: Designing and Implementing a System of Savings Accounts for Children." In *Inclusion in the American Dream: Assets, Poverty, and Public Policy.* Edited by M. Sherraden. : Oxford University Press, 303–22.

Goldrick-Rab, S. 2013. "Pay-It-Forward or Pay-It-Yourself?" Century Foundation (New York). http://www.tcf.org/assets/downloads/2013–07–23-Pay-it-forward.pdf.

Goldrick-Rab, S., and Kendall, N. 2014. "Redefining College Affordability: Securing America's Future with a Free Two Year College Option." Lumina Foundation (Indianapolis).

Gomme, P., and Rupert, P. 2004. "Measuring Labor's Share of Income." Reserve Bank of Cleveland (Cleveland). http://www.clevelandfed.org/research/policydis/no7nov04.pdf.

Gould, M. 1999. "Race and Theory: Culture, Poverty, and Adaptation Discrimination in Wilson and Ogbu." *Sociological Theory* 17, no. 2: 171–200.

Greene, K. 2012. "New Peril for Parents: Their Kids' Student Loans." *Wall Street Journal*, October 26. http://online.wsj.com/article/SB10000872396390444402420457804462264851 6106.html

Greenstone, M., Looney, A., Patashni., J., and Yu, M. 2013. "Thirteen Economic Facts about Social Mobility and the Role of Education." Brookings Institution (Washington, D.C.). http://www.brookings.edu/research/reports/2013/06/13-facts-higher-education.

Greer, J., and Levin, E. 2014. "Upside Down: Tax Incentives to Save and Build Wealth." Corporation for Enterprise Development (Washington, D.C.). http://cfed.org/assets/pdfs/Policy_Brief_-_Tax_Incentives.pdf.

Hacker, J. 2006. *The Great Risk Shift: The New Economic Insecurity and the Decline of the American Dream.* New York: Oxford University Press.

Hahn, R., and Price, D. 2008. "Promise Lost: College-Qualified Students Who Don't Enroll in College." Institute for Higher Education Policy (Washington, D.C.). http://www.ihep.org/sites/default/files/uploads/docs/pubs/promiselostcollegequalrpt.pdf.

Hammond, B. 2014. "Free Community College Could Cost Oregon Taxpayers $250 Million a Year, Yield 100,000 2-year Degrees." *Oregonian,* September 12. http://www.oregonlive.com/education/index.ssf/2014/09/free_community_college_could_c.html.

Hanson, A. 2012. "Size of Home, Homeownership, and the Mortgage Interest Deduction." *Journal of Housing Economics* 21 no. 3: 195–210.

Hanson, S. L. 1994. "Lost Talent: Unrealized Educational Aspirations and Expectations among U.S. Youths." *Sociology of Education* 67, no. 3: 159–183.

Harrison, B., and Bluestone, B. 1988. *The Great U-Turn: Corporate Restructuring and the Polarizing of America.* New York: Basic Books.

Hartman, R. R. 2013. "Who Makes Money Off Your Student Loans? You Might Be Surprised." *Yahoo News*, May 23. http://news.yahoo.com/blogs/the-lookout/makes-money-off-student-loans-might-surprised-093332073.html.

Harvey, J. T. 2014. "Student Loan Debt Crisis?" *Forbes*, April 28. http://www.forbes.com/sites/johntharvey/2014/04/28/student-loan-debt-crisis/.

Haskins, R. 2008. "Education and Economic Mobility." In Getting Ahead or Losing Ground: Economic Mobility in America. Edited by J. B. Isaacs, I. V. Sawhill, and R. Haskins. Washington, D.C.: Brookings Institution, 91–104.

Haskins, R., Isaacs, J., and Sawhill, I. 2008. "Getting Ahead or Losing Ground: Economic Mobility in America." Washington, D.C.: Brookings Institution.

Heller, D. E. 1997. "Student Price Response in Higher Education: An Update to Leslie and Brinkman." *Journal of Higher Education* 68, no. 6: 624–59.

Heller, D. E. 2002. *Condition of Access: Higher Education for Lower Income Students.* Westport, CT: American Council on Education/Praeger.

Heller, D. E. 2008. "The Impact of Student Loans on College Access." In *The Effectiveness of Student Aid Policies: What the Research Tells Us.* Edited by S. Baum, M. McPherson, and P. Steele. New York: College Board, 39–68.

Herbold, H. 1994–95. "Never a Level Playing Field: Blacks and the GI Bill." *Journal of Blacks in Higher Education* 6: 104–8.

Herr, E., and Burt, L. 2005. "Predicting Student Loan Default for the University of Texas at Austin." *Journal of Student Financial Aid* 35, no. 2: 27–49.

Hiltonsmith, R. 2013. "At What Cost: How Student Debt Reduces Lifetime Wealth." *Demos* (Washington, D.C.).

Hiltonsmith, R. 2014. "The Great Cost Shift Continues: State Higher Education Funding after the Recession." *Demos* (Washington, D.C.).

Hochschild, J. L. 1995. *Facing Up to the American Dream: Race, Class, and the Soul of the Nation.* Princeton, NJ: Princeton University Press.

Hochschild, J. L., and Scovronick, N. 2003. *The American Dream and the Public Schools.* New York: Oxford University Press.

Houle, J. N. 2014. "Disparities in Debt: Parents' Socioeconomic Resources and Young Adult Student Loan Debt." *Sociology of Education* 87, no. 1: 53–69.

Houle, J., and Berger, L. 2014. "Is Student Loan Debt Discouraging Home Buying among Young Adults?" Association for Public Policy and Management (Washington, D.C.). http://www.appam.org/assets/1/7/Is_Student_Loan_Debt_Discouraging_Home_Buying_Among_Young_Adults.pdf.

Hout, M. 1984. "Status, Autonomy, and Training in Occupational Mobility." *American Journal of Sociology* 89 (May): 1379–1409.

Hout, M. 1988. "More Universalism and Less Structural Mobility: The American Occupational Structure in the 1980s." *American Journal of Sociology* 93 (May): 1358–1400.

Howard, C. 1997. *The Hidden Welfare State: Tax Expenditures and Social Policy in the United States.* Princeton, NJ: Princeton University Press.

Hoxby, C. M., and Avery, C. 2012. "The Missing 'One-Offs': The Hidden Supply of High-Achieving, Low Income Students." Working paper, National Bureau of Economic Research (Washington, D.C.). http://www.nber.org/papers/w18586.

Huang, J., Sherraden, M., Kim, Y., and Clancy, M. 2014. "Effects of Child Development Accounts on Early Social-Emotional Development an Experimental Test." *Journal of American Medical Association Pediatrics* 168, no. 3: 265–71.

Huang, J., Sherraden, M., and Purnell, J. 2014. "Impacts of Child Development Accounts on Maternal Depressive Symptoms: Evidence from a Randomized Statewide Policy Experiment." *Social Science and Medicine* 112: 30–38.

Huelsman, M. 2014. "Germany Just Eliminated Tuition: It Wouldn't Be That Hard for Us to Do the Same—And More." *Demos* (Washington, D.C.). http://www.demos.org/blog/10/2/14/germany-just-eliminated-tuition-it-wouldn%E2%80%99t-be-hard-us-do-same%E2%80%94and-then-some.

Inside Higher Education. 2014. "Fact Sheet on Final Gainful Employment Regulations." Inside Higher Education (Washington, D.C.). https://www.insidehighered.com/sites/default/server_files/files/FINAL percent20- percent20GE percent20fact percent20sheet percent20 percent281 percent29.pdf.

Institute for Higher Education Policy (IHEP). 1999. "State of Diffusion: Defining Student Aid in an Era of Multiple Purposes." IHEP (Washington, D.C.). http://www.ihep.org/assets/files/publications/s-z/State Diffusion.pdf.

Institute for Higher Education Policy (IHEP) and the Education Resources Institute (TERI). 1995. "College Debt and the American Family." Institute for Higher Education Policy and the Education Resources Institute (Washington, D.C.). http://www.ihep.org/assets/files/publications/a-f/ CollegeDebt.pdf.

Internal Revenue Service. 2013. "Reporting Gains and Losses." *IRS* (Washington, D.C.). http://www.irs.gov/publications/p17/ch16 .html.

Ishitani, T. T. 2006. "Studying Attrition and Degree Completion Behavior among First-Generation College Students in the United States." *The Journal of Higher Education* 77, no. 5: 861–65.

Janowitz, M. 1976. *Social Control of the Welfare State*. Waltham, MA: Elsevier.

Jesse, D. 2013. "Government Books $41.3 Billion in Student Loan Profits." *USA Today*, November 25. http://www.usatoday.com/story/ news/nation/2013/11/25/federal-student-loan-profit/3696009.

Jesse, D. 2014. "Pay It Forward: Plan Would Allow Michigan Students to Attend College for 'Free.'" *Detroit Free Press*, March 19. http://www .freep.com/article/20140319/NEWS06/303190038/Pay-it-forward -Plan-would-allow-Michigan-students-to-attend-college-for-free-.

Jeszeck, C. 2014. "Older Americans' Inability to Repay Student Loans May Affect Financial Security of a Small Percentage of Retirees." General Accounting Office (Washington, D.C.). http://www.gao .gov/assets/670/665709.pdf.

Johnson, L. B. 1965. "Remarks at Southwest Texas State College upon Signing the Higher Education Act of 1965." In *The American Presidency Project*. Edited by J. Woolley and G. Peters. November, 8 1965. http://www.presidency.ucsb.edu/ws/index.php?pid=27356& st=johnson&st1=higher+education.

Johnson, M. 2013. "Kansas Child Support Savings Program." Presentation on Corporation for Enterprise Development webinar, November 12.

Junior Achievement. 2014. "Nearly One-in-Four Millennials Believe Their College Loans Will Be Forgiven, According to Research from JA and PwC." Junior Achievement. https://www.juniorachievement. org/web/ja-usa/home?p_p_id=56_INSTANCE_abcdandp_p_ lifecycle=0andp_p_state=maximizedandp_p_mode=viewandp_p_ col_id=ja-column-newsandp_p_col_count=1and_56_INSTANCE_ abcd_groupId=20009and_56_INSTANCE_abcd_articleId=700788.

Kadlec, D. 2014. "The Next Massive Bailout: Student Loans." *Time*, April 24. http://time.com/72786/the-next-massive-bailout-student-loans.

Kamenetz, A. 2006. *Generation Debt*. New York: Penguin.

Karsten, T. 2012. "Will Student Debt Lead to a Financial Crisis?" CNBC, April 24. http://www.cnbc.com/id/47159110.

Keister, M. P. 2000. *Wealth in America*. Cambridge, MA: Cambridge University Press.

Kelly, A. 2014. "Who's Struggling to Pay Back their Student Loans? (Hint: It's Not Who You Think)." *Forbes*, June 30. http://www.forbes.com/ sites/akelly/2014/06/30/whos-struggling-to-pay-back-their-student -loans-hint-its-not-who-you-think.

Kiley, K. 2013. "Merit Consideration." *Inside Higher Ed*, May 8. https:// www.insidehighered.com/news/2013/05/08/merit-aid-makes -college-more-expensive-low-income-students-report-finds.

Kim, D. 2007. "The Effects of Loans on Students' Degree Attainment: Differences by Student and Institutional Characteristics." *Harvard Educational Review* 77, no. 1: 64–100.

Kim, Y., Sherraden, M., Huang, J., and Clancy, M. 2015. "Child Development Accounts and parental educational expectations for young children: Early evidence from a statewide social experiment." http:// dx.doi.org/10.1086/680014. *Social Service Review*, 89(1): 99–137.

Kingdon, J. W. 2010. *Agendas, Alternatives, and Public Policies*. 2nd ed. New York: Longman Classics in Political Science, Longman.

Kitroeff, N. 2014. "Does Student Loan Debt Make People Less Happy and Healthy?" *Bloomberg Businessweek*, August 7. http://www .businessweek.com/articles/2014–08–07/does-student-loan-debt -make-people-less-happy-and-healthy.

Knight, J. 1992. *Institutions and Social Conflict*. New York: Cambridge University Press.

Knight, W. E., and Arnold, W. 2000. "Toward a Comprehensive Predictive Model of Time to Bachelor's Degree Attainment." Paper presented at the annual forum of the Association for Institutional Research, Cincinnati, OH. Bowling Green State University (Bowling Green, OH). http://www.bgsu.edu/downloads/finance/file19270.pdf.

Kochhar, R., Fry, R., and Taylor, P. 2011. "Wealth Gaps Rise to Record Highs between Whites, Blacks, Hispanics." Pew Charitable Trusts (Washington, D.C.). http://www.pewsocialtrends.org/2011/07/26/wealth -gaps-rise-to-record-highs-between-whites-blacks-hispanics.

Koehler, D. J., and Poon, C. S. K. 2006. "Self-Predictions Overweight Strength of Current Intentions." *Journal of Experimental Social Psychology* 42: 517–24.

Korkki, P. 2014. "The Ripple Effects of Student Debt." *New York Times*, May 24. http://www.nytimes.com/2014/05/25/business/the-ripple -effects-of-rising-student-debt.html?_r=0.

Kuhn, T. S. 1962. *The Structure of Scientific Revolutions*. Chicago: University of Chicago Press.

Lam, L. T. 1999. "Assessing Financial Aid Impact on Time-to-Degree for Nontransfer Undergraduate Students at a Large Urban Public University." Paper presented at the annual forum of the Association for Institutional Research (Seattle), May. https://www.asu.edu/uoia/ pubs/papers/lam.pdf.

Leonhardt, D. 2014. "Top Colleges That Enroll Rich, Middle Class, Poor." *New York Times*, September 8. http://www.nytimes.com/2014/09/09/ upshot/top-colleges-that-enroll-rich-middle-class-and-poor .html?_r=0andabt=0002andabg=1.

Leslie, L., and Brinkman, P. 1988. "The Economic Value of Education. American Council on Education." (Ann Arbor, MI).

Levin, A. 2013. "Politicians, Ignore the Millennial Student Loan Crisis at Your Own Risk." *Huffington Post*, December 12. http://www .huffingtonpost.com/adam-levin/politicians-ignore-the-mi_b_ 4428230.html.

Levitz, J., and Thurm, S. 2012. "Shift to Merit Scholarships Stirs Debate." *Wall Street Journal*, December 19. http://www.wsj.com/articles/SB1 0001424127887324481204578175631182640920.

Lewis, M., Cramer, R., Elliott, W., and Sprague, A. 2013. "Policies to Promote Economic Stability, Asset Building, and Child Development." *Children and Youth Services Review* 36:15–21.

Lewis, M., and Elliott, W. 2014. "Examining the Canadian Education Savings Program and Its Implications for U.S. Child Savings Account (CSA) Policy." Assets and Education Initiative (Lawrence, KS).

Liu, M. C. 2011. "Do For-Profit Schools Pass the Test?" *State Legislatures* 37, no. 6: 15–17.

Lochner, L., and Monge-Naranjo, A. 2004. "Education and Default Incentives with Government Student Loan Programs." National Bureau of Economic Research (Cambridge, MA).

Loke, V., and Sherraden, M. 2009. "Building Assets from Birth: A Global Comparison of Child Development Account Policies." *International Journal of Social Welfare* 18, no. 2: 119–129.

Long, B. T. 2010. "Higher Education Finance and Accountability." In *Best in the World? Accountability and Unaccountability in American Higher Education.* Edited by Kevin Carey and Mark Schneider. Washington, D.C.: American Enterprise Institute.

Long, R. 2014. "Tuition-Free Public College Education Is Possible: Demand It." *Alternet,* January 24. http://www.alternet.org/education/tuition-free-public-college-education-possible-demand-it.

Luhby, T. 2014. "The American Dream Is Out of Reach." *CNN Money.* http://money.cnn.com/2014/06/04/news/economy/american-dream.

Maag, E., and Fitzpatrick, K. 2004. "Federal Financial Aid for Higher Education: Programs and Prospects." Urban Institute (Washington, D.C.). http://www.urbaninstitute.org/UploadedPDF/410996_federal_financial_aid.pdf.

Marin, P. 2002. "Merit Scholarships and the Outlook for Equal Opportunity in Higher Education." In *Who Should We Help? The Negative Social Consequences of Merit Scholarships.* Edited by D. E. Heller and P. Marin. Cambridge, MA: Civil Rights Project at Harvard University, 109–14.

Marks, M., and Martin, W. 2014. "Generation of Debt." *Dallas Morning News.* http://res.dallasnews.com/interactives/generation-of-debt/employment.

Martin, A. 2012. "Debt Collection Agencies Cashing in on Student Loans." *New York Times,* September 9. http://www.nytimes.com/2012/09/09/business/once-a-student-now-dogged-by-collection-agencies.html?pagewanted=all.

Mason, L. R., Nam, Y., Clancy, M., and Sherraden, M. 2014. "Saving for Education, Entrepreneurship, and Downpayment for Oklahoma Kids: Experimental Test of a Policy Innovation in a Full Population." In *SAGE Research Methods Cases.* doi:10.4135/978144627305013520671.

McCann, C. 2014. "Barking Up the Wrong Tree with the Student Debt Crisis." *The Hill,* November 26. http://thehill.com/blogs/pundits-blog/education/225360-barking-up-the-wrong-tree-with-the-student-debt-crisis.

McClelland, M. M., Ponitz, C. C., Messersmith, E. E., and Tominey, S. 2010. "Self-regulation: The Integration of Cognition and Emotion." In *Handbook of Lifespan Human Development, Vol. 4: Cognition, Biology, and Methods.* Edited by R. Lerner and W. Overton. Hoboken, NJ: Wiley, 509–33.

McElwee, S. 2014. "You Can Blame Student Debt for America's Inequality and Shrinking Middle Class. *Huffington Post*, June 16. http://www.huffingtonpost.com/sean-mcelwee/you-can-blame-student-deb_b_5469456.html.

McPherson, M., and Schapiro, M. 1998. *The Student Aid Game: Meeting Need and Rewarding Talent in American Higher Education*. Princeton, NJ: The Princeton University Press.

Mead, L. 2001. *The New Politics of Poverty: The Nonworking Poor in America*. New York: Basic Books.

Mendoza, P. 2012. "The Effect of Debt and Working while Enrolled on Baccalaureate Completion: A Counterfactual Analysis." *Journal of Student Financial Aid* 42: 25–59.

Mettler, S. 2011. *The Submerged State: How Invisible Government Policies Undermine American Democracy*. Chicago: University of Chicago Press.

Mettler, S. 2014. *Degrees of Inequality: How the Politics of Higher Education Sabotaged the American Dream*. New York: Basic Books.

Miller, B. 2014. "The Student Debt Review Analyzing the State of Undergraduate Student Borrowing." New America (Washington, D.C.). http://education.newamerica.net/sites/newamerica.net/files/policy docs/thestudentdebtreview_2_18_14.pdf.

Minicozzi, A. 2005. "The Short Term Effect of Educational Debt on Job Decisions. *Economics of Education Review* 24, no. 4: 417–30.

Mishel, L. 2012. "Understanding the Wedge between Productivity and Median Compensation Growth." Economic Policy Institute (Washington, D.C.). http://www.epi.org/blog/understanding-wedge-productivity-median-compensation.

Mishel, L., Bernstein, J., and Allegretto, S. 2006. *The State of Working America*. Ithaca, NY: Cornell University Press.

Mishel, L., Bivens, J., Gould, E., and Shierholz, H. 2013. *The State of Working America*. 12th ed. Ithaca, NY: Cornell University Press.

Mishel, L., and Shierholz, H. 2013. "A Decade of Flat Wages: The Key Barrier to Shared Prosperity and a Rising Middle Class." Economic Policy Institute (Washington, D.C.). http://www.epi.org/publication/a-decade-of-flat-wages-the-key-barrier-to-shared-prosperity-and-a-rising-middle-class.

Mishory, J., O'Sullivan, R., and Invincibles, Y. 2012. "Denied? The Impact of Student Debt on the Ability to Buy a House." Young Invincibles (Washington, D.C.). http://younginvincibles.org/wp-content/uploads/2012/08/Denied-The-Impact-of-Student-Debt-on-the-Ability-to-Buy-a-House-8.14.12.pdf.

Mitchell, M., Palacios, V., and Leachman, M. 2014. "States Are Still Funding Higher Education below Pre-Recession Levels." Center on Budget and Policy Priorities (Washington, D.C.). http://www.cbpp.org/cms/?fa=viewandid=4135.

Mullainathan, S., and Shafir, E. 2013. *Scarcity: Why Having Too Little Means So Much*. New York: Times Books.

Nam, Y., Kim, Y., Zager, R., Clancy, M., and Sherraden, M. 2013. "Do Child Development Accounts Promote Account Opening and Savings for Children's Future?: Evidence from a Statewide Randomized Experiment." *Journal of Policy Analysis and Management* 32, no. 1: 6–33.

National Association of State Student Grant and Aid Programs. 2001. "31st Annual Survey Report, 1999–2000 Academic Year." State Higher Education Services Corporation (New York).

National Center for Education Statistics. 2001. "Community College Student Outcomes: 1994–2009." U.S. Department of Education (Washington, D.C.).

National Center for Education Statistics. 2012. "The Condition of Education 2012." U.S. Department of Education (Washington, D.C.). http://nces.ed.gov/pubs2012/2012045.pdf.

National Center for Education Statistics. 2013. "The Condition of Education 2013." U.S. Department of Education (Washington, D.C.). http://nces.ed.gov/pubs2013/2013037.pdf.

Needham, V. 2014. "Lawmakers Push for Clearer Student Loan Forgiveness Rules." *The Hill*, May 16. http://thehill.com/policy/finance/206380-lawmakers-push-for-clearer-rules-on-forgiving-student-loans-for-borrowers-in.

Nelson, L. 2011. "Invisible Spending on Financial Aid." *Inside Higher Ed*, November 16. https://www.insidehighered.com/news/2011/11/16/tax-credits-tuition-growing-rapidly.

Newport, F., and Busteed, B. 2013. "Americans Still See College Education as Very Important." *Gallup USA*, December 17. http://www.gallup.com/poll/166490/americans-college-education-important.aspx.

Newville, D., and Cramer, R. 2009. "A Citizen's Guide to the ASPIRE Act." New America Foundation (Washington, D.C.). http://newamerica.net/publications/policy/citizens_guide_aspire_act.

Nielsen. 2014. *Millennials: Breaking the Myths*. http://www.nielsen.com/us/en/insights/reports/2014/millennials-breaking-the-myths.html.

Noel-Levitz. 2014. *2014 Freshmen Attitudes Report*. https://www.noellevitz.com/papers-research-higher-education/2014/2014-freshman-attitudes-report-for-2-year-colleges.

North, D. 1990. *Institutions, Institutional Change, and Economic Performance*. New York: Cambridge University Press.

O'Connor, J. 1973. *The Fiscal Crisis of the State*. New York: St. Martin's Press.

Oliff, P., Palacios, V., Johnson, I., and Leachman, M. 2013. "Recent Deep State Higher Education Cuts May Harm Students and the Economy for Years to Come." Center on Budget and Policy Priorities (Washington, D.C.).

Oliver, M., and Shapiro, T. 2006. *Black Wealth, White Wealth*. New York: Taylor and Francis.

Ouellette, J. A., and Wood, W. 1998. "Habit and Intention in Everyday Life: The Multiple Processes by Which Past Behavior Predicts Future Behavior." *Psychology Bulletin* 124: 54–74.

Owen, S., and Sawhill, I. 2013. "Should Everyone Go to College?" Center on Children and Families at Brookings (Washington, D.C.).

Oyserman, D., Bybee, D., and Terry, K. 2006. "Possible Selves and Academic Outcomes: How and When Possible Selves Impel Action." *Journal of Personality and Social Psychology* 91, no. 1: 188–204.

Oyserman, D., and Destin, M. (2010). "Identity-based motivation: Implications for intervention." *The Counseling Psychologist*, 38(7): 1001–1043.

Oyserman, D., and Markus, H. R. 1990. "Possible Selves and Delinquency." *Journal of Personality and Social Psychology* 59, no. 1: 112–25.

Page, B., Bartels, L., and Seawright, J. 2013. "Democracy and the Policy Preferences of Wealthy Americans." *Perspectives on Politics* 11, no. 1: 51–73.

Paulsen, M. B., and St. John, E. P. 2002. "Social Class and College Costs: Examining the Financial Nexus between College Choice and Persistence." *Journal of Higher Education* 73, no. 3: 189–236.

Perez-Pena, R. 2014. "Tennessee Governor Urges Two Free Years of Community College and Technical School." *New York Times*, February 4. http://www.nytimes.com/2014/02/05/education/tennessee-governor-urges-2-free-years-of-community-college-and-technical-school.html?_r=0.

Perna, L. W. 2000. "Differences in the Decision to Attend College among African Americans, Hispanics, and Whites." *Journal of Higher Education* 71, no. 2: 117–41.

Pew Charitable Trusts. 2013. "How Much Protection Does a College Degree Afford?" Pew Charitable Trusts (Washington, D.C.). http://www.pewstates.org/research/reports/how-much-protection-does-a-college-degree-afford-85899440520.

Pew Charitable Trusts. 2014. "A New Financial Reality: The Balance Sheets and Economic Mobility of Generation X." Pew Charitable Trusts

(Washington, D.C.). http://www.pewtrusts.org/~/media/Assets/2014/09/Pew_Generation_X_report.pdf.

Picchi, A. 2014. "How the Wealth Gap Is Damaging the U.S. Economy." *CBS News Money Watch*, August 5. http://www.cbsnews.com/news/how-the-wealth-gap-is-damaging-the-u-s-economy.

Potts, M. 2014. "The Student Loan Crisis That Isn't about Kids at Harvard." *Daily Beast*, November 30. http://www.thedailybeast.com/articles/2014/11/30/the-student-loan-crisis-that-isn-t-about-kids-at-harvard.html.

Poulous, J. 2012. "Smashing My Student Debt Shame: The Radical Case against Debt Relief." *Forbes*, April 27. http://www.forbes.com/sites/jamespoulos/2012/04/27/smashing-my-student-loan-shame-the-radicalcase-against-debt-relief.

Quinterno, J., and Orozco, V. 2012. "The Great Cost Shift: How Higher Education Cuts Undermine the Future Middle Class." Demos (Washington, D.C.). http://www.demos.org/publication/great-cost-shift-how-higher-education-cuts-undermine-future-middle-class.

RADD Consortium. 2013. "Reimagining Financial Aid to Improve Student Access and Outcomes." National Association of Student Financial Aid Administrators (Washington, D.C.). http://www.nasfaa.org/radd-event.

Ramos, J. 2014. "Meet the Activist Group That's Making Student Loan Debt Disappear." *Truthout*, September 24. http://www.truth-out.org/news/item/26406-meet-the-activist-group-thats-making-student-loan-debt-disappear.

Rank, M. 2004. *One Nation, Underprivileged: Why American Poverty Affects Us All*. New York: Oxford University Press.

Rank, M., and Hirschl, T. 2001. "The Occurrence of Poverty across the Life Cycle: Evidence from the PSID." *Journal of Policy Analysis and Management* 20: 737–55.

Reagan, R. 1983. "Statement on Signing the Student Loan Consolidation and Technical Amendments Act of 1983." In *The American Presidency Project*. Edited by J. Woolley and G. Peters. August 16, 1983. http://www.reagan.utexas.edu/archives/speeches/1983/81683a.htm.

Reyes, J. W. 2008. "College Financial Aid Rules and the Allocation of Savings." *Education Economics* 16, no. 2: 167–89.

Richards, K.V., and Thyer, B.A. 2011. "Does Individual Development Account Participation Help the Poor: A Review." *Research on Social Work Practice* 21: 348–62.

Rodman, H. 1963. "The Lower-Class Value Stretch." *Social Forces* 42, no. 2: 205–15.

Rodriguez, F., and Jayadev, A. 2010. "The Declining Labor Share of Income. Human Development Reports, Research Paper." United Nations Development Programme (New York).

Rose, S. 2013. "The Value of a College Degree." *Change: The Magazine of Higher Learning* (November–December).

Rosenbaum, J., Reynolds, L., and DeLuca, S. 2002. "How Do Places Matter? The Geography of Opportunity, Self-Efficacy, and a Look inside the Black Box of Residential Mobility." *Housing Studies* 17: 71–82.

Rosenberg, J. 2013. "Measuring Income for Distributional Analysis." Tax Policy Center, Urban Institute and Brookings Institution (Washington, D.C.).

Rothstein, J., and Rouse, C. E. 2011. "Constrained after College: Student Loans and Early-Career Occupational Choices." *Journal of Public Economics* 95, nos. 1–2: 149–63.

Rowan, R. 2014. "From Foster Care to College: State Programs Help At-Risk Youth." *Tuition.IO* (Washington, D.C.), January 7. https://www.tuition.io/blog/2014/01/from-foster-care-to-college-state-programs-help-at-risk-youth.

Rudolph, F. 1990. *The American College and University: A History*. Athens: GA: University of Georgia Press.

Saez, E. 2012. 2012. "Striking It Richer: The Evolution of Top Incomes in the United States (Updated with 2009 and 2010 Estimates)." University of California, Department of Economics (Berkeley, CA). http://elsa.berkeley.edu/~saez/saez-UStopincomes-2010.pdf.

Saltsman, M. 2013. "The $9 Minimum Wage That Already Exists." *Wall Street Journal*, February 13. http://online.wsj.com/news/articles/SB10001424127887324616604578302153328738108?mg=reno64-wsjandurl=http%3A%2F%2Fonline.wsj.com%2Farticle%2FSB10001424127887324616604578302153328738108.html.

Samuelson, W., and Zeckhauser, R. 1988. "Status Quo Bias in Decision Making." *Journal of Risk and Uncertainty* 1: 7–59. http://www.hks.harvard.edu/fs/rzeckhau/SQBDM.pdf.

Sanchez, M. 2012. "Student Loan Debt Isn't a Crisis." *Kansas City Star*, December 10. http://careercollegecentral.com/news/student-loan-debt-isn%E2%80%99t-crisis.

Scheier, M. F., and Carver, C. S. 1987. "Dispositional Optimism and Physical Well-Being: The Influence of Generalized Outcome Expectancies on Health." *Journal of Personality* 55: 169–210.

Schneider, M. 2013. "Does Education Pay?" *Issues in Science and Technology*. http://issues.org/30–1/does-education-pay.

Schwartz, S. 2008. "Early Commitment of Student Financial Aid: Perhaps a Modest Improvement." In *The Effectiveness of Student Aid Policies: What the Research Tells Us.* Edited by S. Baum, M. McPherson, and P. Steele. New York: College Board, 117–40.

Selingo, J. 2001. "Questioning the Merit of Merit Scholarships." *Chronicle of Higher Education* 47, no. 19: A20–A22.

Sen, A. K. 1999. *Development as Freedom.* New York: Random House.

Shand, J. M. 2007. "The Impact of Early-Life Debt on the Homeownership Rates of Young Households: An Empirical Investigation." Federal Deposit Insurance Corporation Center for Financial Research. https://www.fdic.gov/bank/analytical/cfr/2008/jan/CFR_SS_2008Shand.pdf.

Shapiro, T., Meschede, T., and Osoro, S. 2013. "The Roots of the Widening Racial Wealth Gap: Explaining the Black-White Economic Divide." Institute on Assets and Social Policy (Waltham, MA).

Shea-Porter, C. 2014. *Votes for Bipartisan Bill to Enhance Student Loan Transparency,* July 25. http://shea-porter.house.gov/media-center/press-releases/shea-porter-votes-for-bipartisan-bill-to-enhance-student loan.

Sheets, R. G., and Crawford, S. 2014. "From Income-Based Repayment Plans to an Income-Based Loan System." George Washington Institute of Public Policy (Washington, D.C.). http://www.luminafoundation.org/publications/ideas_summit/From_Income-based_Repayment_Plans_to_an_Income-based_Loan_System.pdf.

Sheffield, C. 2014. "Can 'Pay It Forward' Help Solve Student Loan Problems?" *Forbes,* March 31. http://www.forbes.com/sites/carriesheffield/2014/03/31/can-pay-it-forward-help-solve-student-loan-problems.

Sheridan, P. 2014. "Retirees' Social Security Checks Garnished for Student Loans." *CNN Money,* August 24. http://money.cnn.com/2014/08/24/news/economy/social-security-student-debt.

Sherraden, M. 1991. *Assets and the Poor: A New American Welfare Policy.* Armonk, NY: M. E. Sharpe.

Smith, D. 2014. "Germany Scraps Tuition Fees after Mass Student Protests Cause Shift in Public Opinion." *Economy Watch,* October 8. http://www.economywatch.com/features/Germany-scraps-tuition-fees-after-mass-student-protests-cause-shift-in-public-opinion.10–08–14.html.

Steiger, K. 2012. "Students, Beware: Private Loan Companies Are Not Your Friends." *The Nation,* September 4. http://www.thenation.com/article/169728/students-beware-private-student-loan-companies-are-not-your-friends.

St. John, E. P., Andrieu, S., Oescher, J., and Starkey, J. B. 1994. "The Influence of Student Aid on Within-Year Persistence by Traditional College-Age Students in Four-Year Colleges." *Research in Higher Education* 35: 455–80. http://www.jstor.org/discover/10.2307/40196136?uid=3739704&uid=2&uid=4&uid=3739256&sid=21102819913487.

Stock, L., Corlyn, J., Serrano, C., and Gieve, M. 2014. "Personal Relationships and Poverty: An Evidence and Policy Review." *Tavistock Institute of Human Relations* (London, UK). http://www.tavinstitute.org/wp-content/uploads/2014/08/Personal-Relationship-and-Poverty-Final-Report.pdf.

Stone, C., Van Horn, C., and Zukin, C. 2012. "Chasing the American Dream: Recent College Graduates and the Great Recession." Center for Workforce Development (New Brunswick, NJ). http://www.heldrich.rutgers.edu/sites/default/files/content/Chasing_American_Dream_Report.pdf.

Stratford, M. 2015. "Middle-Class Economics for Tuition." *Inside Higher Ed* (Washington, D.C.). January 21. https://www.insidehighered.com/news/2015/01/21/obama-pitches-free-community-college-higher-education-tax-credits-state-union.

Stuhldreher, A. n.d. "Yes, Poor People Do Save." New America (Washington, D.C.). http://www.newamerica.net/files/archive/Doc_File_2764_1.pdf.

Sutton, S. 1998. "Predicting and Explaining Intentions and Behavior: How Well Are We Doing." *Journal of Applied Social Psychology* 28: 1317–38.

Taylor, P. 2012. "The Lost Decade of the Middle Class." Pew Charitable Trusts (Washington, D.C.).

Thomas, H., Boguslaw, J., Mann, A., and Shapiro, T. 2013. "Leveraging Mobility: Building Wealth, Security and Opportunity for Family Well-Being." Institute on Assets and Social Policy (Waltham, MA). http://iasp.brandeis.edu/pdfs/2013/Overview.pdf.

Torche, F. 2011. "Is a College Degree Still the Great Equalizer? Intergenerational Mobility across Levels of Schooling in the US." *American Journal of Sociology* 117, no. 3: 763–807.

Trusty, J., and Harris, M. B. C. 1999. "Lost Talent: Predictors of the Stability of Educational Expectations across Adolescence." *Journal of Adolescent Research* 14: 359–82.

Urahn, S. K., Currier, E., Elliott, D., Wechsler, L., Wilson, D., and Colbert, D. 2012. "Pursuing the American Dream: Economic Mobility across

Generations." Economic Mobility Project, the Pew Charitable Trusts (Washington, D.C.).

U.S. Department of Health and Human Services. 2012. "AFI Project Location." U.S. Department of Health and Human Services and the Administration for Children and Families (Washington, D.C.).

U.S. General Accounting Office (GAO). 1995. "Restructuring Student Aid Could Reduce Low-Income Student Dropout Rate." GAO (Washington, D.C.). http://www.gao.gov/archive/1995/he9548.pdf.

Vallas, R., and Valenti, J. 2014. "Asset Limits Are a Barrier to Economic Security and Mobility." Center for American Progress (Washington, D.C.). https://www.americanprogress.org/issues/poverty/report/2014/09/10/96754/asset-limits-are-a-barrier-to-economic-security-and-mobility.

Wagner, M., and Riepenhoff, J. 2012. "More Seniors Trapped in Children's Student Debt." *Columbus Dispatch*, December 17. http://www.dispatch.com/content/stories/local/2012/12/17/more-seniors-trapped-in-childrens-student-debt.html.

Walsemann, K. M., Gee, G. C., and Gentile, D. 2014. "Sick of Our Loans: Student Borrowing and the Mental Health of Young Adults in the United States." *Social Science & Medicine* 124, no. 2015: 85–93.

Washington Post-Miller Center. 2013. "More People Express Uncertainty in Chance to Achieve the American Dream." *Washington Post* (Washington, D.C.). http://www.washingtonpost.com/local/more-people-express-uncertainty-in-chance-to-achieve-the-american-dream/2013/09/28/d8e99084-260e-11e3-ad0d-b7c8d2a594b9_story.html.

Weise, K. 2014. "The Growing Consensus on Fixing Student Loans." *Business Week*, July 17. http://www.businessweek.com/articles/2014-07-17/the-growing-consensus-on-fixing-student-loans.

Weissman, J. 2013. "Oregon's Very Radical and Very Terrible Plan to Make College 'Tuition Free.'" *Atlantic*. July 10. http://www.theatlantic.com/business/archive/2013/07/oregons-very-radical-and-very-terrible-plan-to-make-college-tuition-free/277644.

Wilezol, D. 2014. "Student Loan Reform Is Now a Major Political Issue." *Minding the Campus*, August 26. http://www.mindingthecampus.com/2014/08/student-loan-reform-is-now-a-major-political-issue.

Williams-Shanks, T. 2010. "Assets, Debt, and Their Developmental Consequences for Children and Youth." Paper presented at the Corporation for Enterprise Development's Assets Learning Conference, September 23. http://cfed.org/assets/pdfs/alc/2010/assets_debt_children-shanks.pdf.

Wilson, W. J. 1987. *The Truly Disadvantaged: The Inner City, the Under-class, and Public Policy.* Chicago: University of Chicago Press.

Woluchem, M., and George, T. 2014. "Is Student Debt Hindering Home Ownership?" Urban Institute (Washington, D.C.). http://blog.metrotrends.org/2014/07/student-debt-hindering-homeownership.

Woo, J., and Choy, S. 2011. "Merit Aid for Undergraduates: Trends from 1995–96 to 2007–8." National Center for Education Statistics (Washington, D.C.).

Woo, J. H. 2002. "Factors Affecting the Probability of Default: Student Loans in California." *Journal of Student Financial Aid* 32, no. 2: 5–25.

World Bank. 2002. "Empowerment and Poverty Reduction: A Source-book." World Bank (Washington, D.C.).

Yglesias, M. 2013. "Three Problems with Making College Free." *Slate*, November 20. http://www.slate.com/blogs/moneybox/2013/11/20/college_shouldn_t_be_free_three_big_problems_with_free_college.html.

Zhan, M. 2006. "Assets, Parental Expectations and Involvement, and Children's Educational Performance." *Children and Youth Services Review* 28, no. 8: 961–75.

Zhan, M. 2012. "The Impact of Youth Debt on College Graduation." Washington University, Center for Social Development (St. Louis). http://csd.wustl.edu/Publications/Documents/WP12–11.pdf.

Zhan, M. 2013. "Youth Debt and College Graduation: Differences by Race/Ethnicity." Washington University, Center for Social Development (St. Louis). http://csd.wustl.edu/Publications/Documents/WP13–08.pdf.

Zhan, M., and Sherraden, M. 2003. "Assets, Expectations, and Children's Educational Achievement in Female-Headed Households." *Social Service Review* 77, no. 2: 191–211.

# Index

## About the Authors

**William Elliott III** is associate professor in the School of Social Welfare at the University of Kansas and director of the Assets and Education Initiative. He is coauthor of *The Student Loan Problem in America: It Is Not Enough to Say, "Students Will Eventually Recover."* He received the distinguished Recent Contributions in Social Work Education Award, which recognizes a social work educator's achievements within the last 10 years.

**Melinda K. Lewis** is associate professor of practice in the School of Social Welfare at the University of Kansas and policy director of the Assets and Education Initiative. She is coauthor of *The Student Loan Problem in America: It Is Not Enough to Say, "Students Will Eventually Recover."*